The Resident Assistant

Working with College Students in Residence Halls

Second Edition

Gregory S. Blimling
Dean of Students
Louisiana State University

Lawrence J. Miltenberger
Dean of Residence Life
Indiana State University

KENDALL/HUNT PUBLISHING COMPANY
Dubuque, Iowa

Cover design by Dana A. Schadler

Copyright © 1981, 1984 by Kendall/Hunt Publishing Company

Library of Congress Catalog Card Number: 84–80631

ISBN 0–8403–3312–9

Printed in the United States of America

B 403312 01

Contents

Preface

The foundation of nearly every residence hall program across the country is the Resident Assistant position. These student-staff members fulfill a most difficult assignment, that of supervising and assisting an entire floor of undergraduate students. The Resident Assistant is in the vanguard of the field of student development, since comparatively speaking the RA has the opportunity for extensive interaction with a large number of students. This presents the possibility that the Resident Assistant may have a significant impact on the development of these students. The authors believe that whether or not the Resident Assistant is prepared to accept this responsibility is directly related to the quantity and quality of in-service education received.

Co-authored by individuals with extensive residence hall experience, this book is primarily designed to be used as a text in courses taught to Resident Assistants in colleges and universities. In institutions where courses for credit are not provided, the book may be used by full-time residence hall staff as a resource for development of in-service education programs for Resident Assistants. The book may also be used as a personal manual which will assist the individual Resident Assistant in doing the best possible job in a difficult assignment.

The Resident Assistant position is relatively similar across the country, but is subject to some aspects of constant alteration and is certainly variable to some degree from campus to campus. As a result, the authors have provided information that should be basic to Resident Assistant positions in almost all locales, but it is expected that residence hall staff on a particular campus will add to, alter, or otherwise enhance the information in such a way as to tailor usage to the individual campus environment.

The book is divided into six sections. The first section contains chapters dealing with the history, philosophy, and influence of residence halls on the development of students. This section also examines the unique combination of roles of the Resident Assistant position. The chapters in section two discuss aspects of college student behavior including: patterns of student development, the importance of peer counseling, and interpersonal communication. Behavior problems, conflict resolution and suicide are the topics covered in section three. Section four deals with common problems encountered by the Resident Assistant including: alcohol, drugs, human sexuality, and cults. Section five deals with two very important aspects of the RA position: the development of community in the residence hall setting and residence hall programming. The final section is directed at the personal development of the individual Resident Assistant. The chapters in this section focus on time management, stress management, and study skills.

The authors wish to avoid the use of sexist language in this book, and recognize that the consistent use of masculine personal pronouns (he, his, him, himself) is often inaccurate and may be interpreted as sexist. Because the English language does not provide us with an easy remedy to this problem, we have followed the example of other authors by using masculine pronouns throughout approximately half of the chapters and feminine pronouns throughout the remaining chapters.

SECTION 1

The History and Foundations of Residence Halls

CHAPTER 1
The Roles of the RA

You have probably heard the expression "overworked and underpaid" many times. If it ever applied, it applies to a Resident Assistant, or an RA, as this person is commonly known. If you are now at the stage where you are only contemplating becoming an RA, primarily because of the financial assistance it may offer, the job simply does not pay enough. You can earn more money and spend much less time doing any number of part-time jobs in college. Most RAs receive minimal remuneration, usually a single room and a meal contract for the year, and some receive a small stipend. This simply is not enough for all the work that you will be expected to do.

What is perhaps more important is that an RA's experience in college is uniquely different from that of other students. You need to consider this very carefully. As an RA, you will not always be a part of the group activities in the living unit. Some students in the unit will ostracize you, not because of you personally, but because of the authority figure that you may come to represent. You will be intentionally left out of some group discussions and often not invited to share in the "inside information." Many duties within the building will be asked of you, some of which will no doubt force you to reorder your personal priorities. You will be among the first students back to school in the fall of the year and among the last to leave in the spring. The same will be true of each vacation period.

Great demands by other students and by the student affairs staff will be placed on both your personal time and study time. Many activities with which you may have wanted to involve yourself will be forced to take second place to duty nights, working at the information desk, or advising students in the living unit. Even your friendship patterns will be somewhat defined by the residents that you are assigned to advise. All these demands, requirements, and expectations you assume when you accept the responsibility of a resident assistantship. It is not an easy job. Think very carefully before you accept it.

Though the responsibilities are very great and the demands that will be placed upon you throughout the academic year may be even greater, you will also benefit greatly from this experience. The RA fills a unique role as a teacher and a leader that few students are privileged to experience. No other group on campus will receive the training, assistance, and attention that you will as a resident assistant. This is a real opportunity to grow, to learn, and to experience responsibility in a working situation.

Some Expectations of the RA

From campus to campus the responsibilities of the RA vary. Below are listed some common ones shared by most resident assistants on campuses throughout the country:[1]

Administrative Details

1. Prepares necessary reports and records.
2. Assists with public relations by being able to explain residence hall programs and staff duties to faculty, guests, parents, and students.
3. Assists with room checks as required by hall operation.
4. Assists with communication among staff members, students, and residence programs.
5. Keeps residence hall director informed of major plans developed by students.
6. Maintains a good liaison relation with housekeeping personnel.
7. Regularly works the hall information desk, performing the necessary duties, and reporting on time.

Helping to Provide Control

1. Sets an example by adhering to rules and regulations of the University.
2. Knows the university and residence hall regulations.
3. Knows the rationale for given university rules and regulations.
4. Assists students in knowing what is expected of them.
5. Explains the reasons for given rules and regulations.
6. Encourages students to confront other students with violations.
7. Assists in individual growth toward accountability.
8. Knows and interprets university philosophy of discipline.
9. Reports behavioral infractions according to determined policies.
10. Supports or does not openly disagree with university regulations.

Helping to Establish a Healthy Residence Hall Environment

1. Helps students develop a respect for each others' rights and freedoms.
2. Helps students develop a respect for private and university property.
3. Encourages residents to attend residence hall and university programs.
4. Encourages faculty to visit his wing to talk informally with students.

1. Parts adapted from: Greenleaf, Elizabeth A., *et al*, [eds], *Undergraduate Students as Members of the Residence Hall Staff* [Washington, D.C.: NAWDC, 1967].

5. Knows and communicates well with the residents in his wing.
6. Is tolerant of different life-styles.
7. Encourages an atmosphere conducive to study.

Assisting Individual Student Needs
1. Is aware of individual student goals, abilities, and potential for achievement.
2. Is aware of social isolates and helps them make friends and become a part of the campus community.
3. Is aware of attitudes and behavior patterns of the residents in his/her wing.
4. Knows resources in the campus community to help students.
5. Is able to refer students for help effectively.
6. Is aware of adjustment problems for new students.
7. Is available for casual contacts and develops a pattern of available times.
8. Is a good listener and counseling helper.
9. Has good interpersonal skills.
10. Is aware of his own strengths and weaknesses (is self-aware).
11. Shows concern for people and their problems.
12. Follows up with students who have had a problem to see the results and to learn if other assistance can be given.
13. Assists students with class scheduling.
14. Assists students in developing effective study habits.

Hall Government Programs
1. Encourages students' responsibility for their own residence hall programs.
2. Helps students to get involved with university clubs and organizations.
3. Provides creative suggestions for hall programs.
4. Has activities and programs in his wing.
5. Supports hall programs by personal attendance.

The RA as a Role Model

No matter what responsibilities you are specifically assigned as an RA on whatever campus, there are four basic roles that you will assume. The first and perhaps the most influential role that you have as an RA is as a role-model. Remember, when you are placed in a living unit within a residence hall as a staff person, the very fact that you hold this position says to every student that you possess certain characteristics that the university respects and considers important. To new freshmen, you are looked to as a model for them to emulate. This, incidentally, is one of the primary arguments used for having undergraduate RAs in undergraduate residence halls. At one time, many universities used graduate student RAs, because it was thought that these graduate students would be able to assert more control over undergraduates and provide better counseling.

However, one of the key elements in determining appropriate role-models is to find role-models with which students can easily identify. If the role-model is too far removed from what the individual believes he can become, the role-model has less influence. In other words, the standards and behavior exhibited by the role-model must be perceived as attainable by the undergraduate student. Much of the behavior and many of the accomplishments of the graduate student are simply not seen as attainable by an entry-level undergraduate student. The advantage that undergraduate RAs may have is that their experience is not too far removed from the experiences of an incoming freshman. Thus, the incoming freshman can more readily identify with a younger RA than with an older one.

As an RA, you model behavior that others will come to assume as appropriate behavior for students in college. If you emulate good study skills, there is an increased chance that new students in your living unit will also begin to emulate this pattern of study. Likewise, if you spend most of your time throwing a Frisbee up and down the hallway, drinking beer with a certain group of people in your living unit, or continually find that your time is occupied by your boyfriend or girlfriend, you are setting an entirely different model of behavior and communicating your values by your actions.

As an RA you are expected, as part of the role-model responsibility, to live by the rules, regulations, and policies that the university has set. Unless you can abide by them, do not expect your residents to do so. And, if you cannot abide by these policies, you have no business being a resident assistant. When you accept responsibility as an RA, you also make a commitment to the position as it is defined. If you disagree with the institution's policies or regulations, try to change them through the appropriate supervisory channels. If you cannot change them and still cannot live with them, resign. Do not do yourself, the university, and your residents a disservice by not enforcing the rules or by pretending that the policies and regulations do not exist.

Whether you like it or not, your RA position extends outside of your residence hall and on to the campus. This does not mean that you go about campus enforcing random rules and regulations, advising students on this and that, and generally asserting your staff position in places where it is not called for or welcomed. It does mean that your role-modeling responsibility carries beyond your living unit. If you believe that you shed the cloak of resident assistant when you leave your living unit, you are mistaken. While on campus—and at some universities off campus as well—you are expected to conduct yourself as a member of the staff. It is amazing how many RAs believe that as soon as they leave the residence hall, they can become as wild and reckless as they please. Not only is this illogical, it is irresponsible.

Nor should you misuse your role as an RA. Perhaps the classic example of misusing one's position as an RA comes in writing editorials for the school newspaper. As a student, you are entitled to submit whatever opinion you wish to your newspaper. The fact that you are an RA need not enter into it. Some RAs, however, feel they must initial every item they submit as though they were making official policy statements. Thus, when they send in their editorials, they sign them with their names and their position title—resident assistant. Unless you have been elected to make an official policy statement for your residence programs office, avoid attaching your personal opinions to your position. Remember that the views you hold as a resident assistant do not necessarily reflect the views of every other resident assistant at your college or university. Not everyone reading an editorial, however, will make the same inference. A reader might instead assume that you speak from a position of authority and responsibility and, thus, that your opinion should carry more weight and stature.

Your role as a model for other students is one of the most important duties that you will assume. Handle the responsibility carefully and with the respect it deserves.

The RA as a Counselor

The second role that the RA serves is as a counselor, consultant, or advisor. The word *counselor* may be a misnomer. The RA might more appropriately be considered to hold a helping or advising role. This function is an integral and important part of being an RA. Students undergo many adjustments, many stresses, and many crises throughout the academic year. They are torn away from their families, the comfortable and familiar surroundings of their homes, and their established friends. They are asked to live among a group of peers whom they do not know and asked to study and produce more than they have ever had to before. At the same time, they are undergoing tremendous psychological adjustments in their transition to adulthood. It is in the residence hall, in the day-to-day living environment, that many of these growth experiences, emotional traumas, and crises come to light. It is in the residence hall that the students' values will be challenged by other students. Their knowledge of themselves and their ability to work with other people will be tested. For many students who are accustomed to a quiet, private environment, a group situation is very threatening and difficult. It is the RA who is expected to help students through this unique experience.

Think for a moment how many hundreds of challenges are placed before a student within just the first two weeks of college. Think back to your own experiences when you first entered college. You did not know how to register for classes, or how to get a meal pass, or what to do if you were ill, or who to go to if you were experiencing some problem with a teacher. Simple things like these can become real problems for students who want to be accepted and are afraid to ask someone for help for fear that they will be labeled as less mature, less intelligent, or not part of the group. You are the person whom they must seek out to find this information. Providing information and "advice" are very important functions of the RA position and among the primary reasons for its existence.

To do this in a counseling framework, you must begin to establish a positive, friendly relationship with every person in your living unit—not selectively with only those you like, but an open, understanding, and warm relationship with each person in the unit. You must be accessible to everyone. You must be viewed as fair, consistent, and knowledgeable about the university. Only then will people come to you with their concerns. Only after they know you as a person will they come to you with their problems. People do not talk with somebody about their feelings whom they do not know and trust.

The advising/helping role can be taken one step further. It is the RA who has the best opportunity to help students who are experiencing minor problems and to help identify students who are experiencing major problems. Identification of students who are undergoing some form of personal crisis or severe depression can literally save a student's life by preventing suicide—a critical problem in college which will be discussed later in this book.

The RA as a Teacher

The third role that the RA assumes is that of a teacher. By this we mean teaching in a formal sense, not simply the informal teaching involved in role-modeling. The RA teaches many things, specifically: (1) the RA provides general information about the university, about things that are happening on campus, and about services that the university offers; (2) when the RA, along with the members of his floor, invites a member of the counseling center or a speaker to the living unit, he is creating a situation in which formal learning takes place and, by organizing this meeting, he becomes part of the teaching process; (3) the RA teaches group-process skills, in floor meetings, in groups planning an activity, in floor elections, through student activities within the building, and through intramural activities—all situations in which the RA helps define, through modeling behavior or through formal teaching, appropriate behavior and skills; (4) the RA teaches values both through his own personal behavior and through late night discussions (bull sessions) in which such issues as sex, religion, politics, and career plans are discussed. The RA is an agent in this teaching process and at the same time becomes a learner, for not only does he challenge other students' values, but his own values are also challenged.

Of all these, however, programming is probably the most visible sign of teaching. It is the time in which the RA has the opportunity to bring a host of different ideas to the collective experience of the members of his floor.

The RA as a Student

The fourth role the RA has is that of a student. Without fail, RAs rank as their first priority their goals as students. And similarly, with few exceptions, their responsibilities as students come to take second place to the RA position. This is unfortunate. Truly the first responsibility of the RA is to his studies. However, RAs often find their studies pushed to a second priority, and the RA position becomes all-consuming. People place unreasonable demands on RAs' time, and, wishing to do a good job, many RAs find an increasing amount of their time is spent working with other people's problems while their own studies are neglected. Though some RAs find that the additional responsibilities make them better budget their time, many find that they enjoy being an RA much more than they enjoy being a student. Thus, they end up putting all their time and energy into being an excellent RA, while their grades slip below an acceptable level. Obviously it does no one any good if the RA loses the position because of poor grades or is academically dismissed from school. So when you take time to study and pursue important academic interests, you will be fulfilling one of the expectations that the student affairs staff has of you as an RA.

Do not be afraid occasionally to put a note on your door asking people not to disturb you for an hour or two unless it is an emergency. You will find that students will seek you out at the times that you are available. Some of your residents will want to occupy all of your attention and will often spend much of their time in your room procrastinating. It is easy for these people to consume monumental amounts of needed study time. This can create a difficult situation; you do not want to alienate any residents or inhibit any person from sharing a personal problem. There is, however, a balance between ordering your personal priorities—i.e. studying—with attending to the needs of some residents on your floor. If you have an exam or need to do some important studying, many of the routine everyday questions should be able to wait until you take a break or have finished your studying. If you have established a positive relationship with your residents, you will find that they will interrupt you only for the truly important things. If there is a crisis of some type, you will surely be interrupted. If there is a strong personal problem with which a resident needs to talk to you, he will need to consider it pressing enough to interrupt you during your study time.

Part of this adjustment in your availability can be explained in your first unit meeting. You should reinforce on every occasion during the unit meeting that you are available, that you are accessible, and that you want to be consulted about matters of concern to the residents. At the same time, you should make the point that you, like them, are a student who needs to study, and that you would find it helpful if they would use some mature judgment as to when they believe a problem important enough to interrupt you. Once this pattern is established, you should begin to find students less likely to interrupt you during study periods. Close your door when you are studying, or perhaps leave it opened only a crack. An open door is an invitation to be interrupted. When you are not studying and you are in your room, leave your door open so that the students will feel welcome to come in and talk with you.

Conclusion

The RA serves the most comprehensive role in the entire student affairs division. No student problem escapes his involvement. This job is beyond question one of the most difficult student positions to hold and to perform well. To be called on to do so many things, to hold so many responsibilities, to be accountable for so many other people—and all during the time when you are shaping your own education and are under academic pressures—is perhaps one of the greatest challenges you will face during early adulthood.

CHAPTER 2
*The History of Residence Halls**

The Historical Development of Residence Halls in Europe

Residence halls are not a product of the twentieth century. They reach back as far as the thirteenth century to universities in Bologna, Oxford, and Paris. The first attempt to develop these group living situations came at Bologna, where students organized in houses that were called *soccii*. Students at the University of Paris soon formed similar living arrangements in what they called *paedagogies,* and at Oxford, students grouped themselves together in common living arrangements in what they referred to as *halls* and *colleges*.

These houses were totally self-governed, and the universities did not concern themselves with where the students lived until the mid-1400's. In 1452, the chancellor of the University of Paris required all students to live in *paedagogies* and restricted their movement from one to another. These houses were democratic, autonomous units. Each was governed by an elected body of students from the house. At the University of Paris, these students were called the *regents,* and at Oxford they were referred to as *principals*.

At about this same time, Oxford University began establishing *domus pauperums* (meaning *endowed hostels*) for the purpose of providing housing for poorer students. Originally, the university exerted very little control over these special or endowed hostels; however, gradually the university began selecting the principals. At first, they chose older students but soon moved to hiring faculty members. By the time of Elizabeth I, universities in England had permanently fixed control over student hostels.

Some 150 years before the Reformation, the German universities established a system of halls that were called *Bursen*. These halls were large, barrack-style dormitories with, generally, one sleeping room that could house upward of two hundred students. They were organized and run by monks who lived in the barracks and taught at the university.

*The historical facts prior to 1934, presented in this chapter are based primarily on the historical research of Dr. W. H. Cowley who in 1934 published "The History of Student Residential Housing" in *School and Society.*

11

The Reformation, however, changed the fate of residential education in Europe. The German *Bursen* system fell but eventually gave rise to a new system of boarding houses, which have since that time come to be associated with the German form of education. European universities generally stressed scholarship, research, and instruction. When there was money available, the universities used it to support research and instruction instead of constructing student residences. When the University of Berlin was built in 1809, no provisions were made for student housing; instead, this money was spent to further research.

The French system of forty residential colleges fell with the French Revolution. When the University of Paris was reorganized in 1808, it was reorganized without residence halls. Thus, the influence of the Reformation, the research orientation of the Encyclopedists, and the impact of the French Revolution all but abolished the collegiate residential system in Europe. Only in England, at Oxford and Cambridge, did the college and residence hall concept continue.

The Foundation of the American Residence Hall System

When the English colonized North America, they brought with them the traditions and concepts of the collegiate residence system. In 1630, the Congregationalists founded Harvard University and established an educational institution modeled after what they had known as students at Oxford and Cambridge.

In the colonial era, nine colleges were established on the Oxford and Cambridge model. These institutions and their founding organizations are as follows:

1. Harvard College (1636)—Congregational Church.
2. New Jersey University (Princeton) (1746)—Presbyterian Church.
3. Yale University (1701)—Congregational Church.
4. College of William and Mary (1693)—Church of England.
5. King's College (Columbia University) (1754)—Church of England.
6. Philadelphia Academy (University of Pensylvania) (1754)—Nonsectarian/Benjamin Franklin.
7. College of Rhode Island (Brown University) (1764)—Baptist Church.
8. Queen's College (Rutgers University) (1720)—Dutch Reformed Church.
9. Dartmouth College (1770)—Congregationalist Church

With the exception of the Philadelphia Academy and the College of William and Mary, all of these institutions were founded by graduates of either

Cambridge or Oxford. The College of William and Mary was founded by James Volaire, a graduate of Edinburgh, the Philadelphia Academy by Benjamin Franklin.

The English heritage of the founders of the colonial colleges is one of the primary reasons for residence halls in the United States today. Several factors, however, had an influence on this development. Students during the 1700s who attended college were much younger than college students are today—most were in their early teens. Students at this early age were not yet ready to fend for themselves, and many came from distant villages at a time when travel was difficult. Thus, it was expected that students would board at the college they were attending. Boarding became even more important as education moved into the Midwest—the new western territory. Here the pockets of education were so isolated that it took up to a week or longer for some students to travel to a college. This made boarding at the college imperative.

Colleges and universities in the colonial period were established by religious groups; in fact, the only college that was not founded by either the Congregational, Presbyterian, Baptist, Dutch Reformed, or another church group was The Philadelphia Academy. Colleges and universities during this period functioned not only to disseminate the knowledge of past generations and to stimulate the mind but even more importantly, to train ministers and to develop students who were strong in moral character and knowledgeable in the doctrines of their particular church groups. Students attending these church-operated colleges were instructed to rise at 5 A.M., perform a number of chores, attend class, and study on a rigid schedule. Students were in bed by 9 P.M. Each student was expected to pray regularly, to know the doctrines of his church, and to obey his instructors. Violations of any type met with harsh punishment in the form of whippings. It was during this time that colleges and universities exercised the most control over students.

Though the American system of higher education in the 1700s reflected many of the English traditions, it nevertheless was distinct from the English system. Whereas the English system consisted of universities that were a collection of different colleges located in the same area, the American universities were generally single, isolated colleges located at great distances from one another. Under the English system, residence halls were looked on as a highly significant educational agent that helped shape the character and total development of the student as a scholar and as a gentleman. The American system of dormitories in the 1700s provided little more than shelter and a place for the university to exercise control.

The early 1800s were times of turmoil for higher education in America. This was the time of expansion for many religious groups in the Midwest, but it was also a time of student revolt, riot, and disciplinary problems of monumental proportions. Dormitories were looked on as places where students gathered to hatch devious crimes against the university and the community. Some faculty and staff members trembled at the thought of being asked to go into a college dormitory. Historian Frederick Rudolph (1962) writes of the problems that were associated with dormitory living:

> In the commons room of a dormitory at South Carolina College in 1833, two students at the same moment grabbed for a plate of trout. Only one of them survived the duel that ensued. Among the victims of the collegiate way were the boy that died in the duel at Dickinson, the students who were shot at Miami of Ohio, the professor who was killed at the University of Virginia, the President of Oakland College in Mississippi who was stabbed to death by a student, the student who was stabbed at Illinois College, the students who were stabbed and killed at the University of Missouri, the President and professor who were stoned at the University of Georgia, and the University of North Carolina. For this misfortune these victims of the college life could thank the dormitory, the time house of incarceration and infamy that sustained the collegiate way. (p. 97).

William H. Cowley (1934), another historian, writes of similar incidents in the following passage:

> At Yale in 1828 the food at the commons precipitated the famous "Bread and Butter Rebellion." Two years later the sophomore class, none too politely, declined to recite their mathematics as the rules required and the riots that ensued have come down in history as the "Conic Section Rebellion." George Bancroft, greatest American historian of his day, lost an eye, when as a Harvard tutor, he attempted to quell an incipient uprising. Another Harvard tutor went through the remainder of his life with a limp after an encounter with a group of student assailants. And many were the black eyes and bruised skulls nursed by students and faculty alike (p. 709–710).

It is little wonder that, in 1852, President Henry Philip Tappen of the University of Michigan converted one of the dormitories at the university into classrooms and began an onslaught of attacks against dormitories and their place in higher education. In support of this move, Tappen offered this rationale: "The dormitory system is objectionable in itself. By withdrawing young men from the influence of domestic circles and separating them from the community, they are often led to contract evil habits and are prone to fall into disorderly conduct. It is a mere remnant of the monkist cloisters of the middle ages still retained in England but vanished from the universities of Germany (Cowley 1934, p. 711)."

It was this philosophy that tore at the roots of the collegiate system of dormitory living. Tappen was joined in his objections by President Francis Wayland of Brown University and by Frederick Bernard of Columbia University. Tappen and the others were proponents of the German system of education, which looked on higher education as the development of the intellect and the intellect alone. Education in the minds of these men meant classroom instruction, research, and the pursuit of academic excellence. The personal growth and development of individual students as gentlemen was considered outside the responsibility of the universities. There was, therefore, no educational reason to board students, and the money formerly devoted to the construction and maintenance of residence halls could better be used for instruction and for research. Overall, housing during this period was very poor, and becoming worse as colleges expanded. Students were housed wherever rooms could be found. Townspeople boarded many of the students. The faculty and the president were also usually involved in housing a number of students. Other places students were housed in the early 1800s included the south wing of the basement at the town meeting house for students at Hiram College; about twenty boys lived in the attic of the first building at Oberlin College; and at Amhurst College the same rooms were used as bedrooms, classrooms, study halls, and chapel. (Leonard, 1956).

Colleges and universities founded in the late 1800s were influenced significantly by the German philosophy of education. Few if any residence halls were built, and the state institutions that were being established or were expanding during that time found that the money to build dormitories could better be spent on instruction and academic equipment. As higher education approached the twentieth century, most state institutions of higher education were without any residential facilities for students.

Residence Halls in the Late 1800s and Early 1900s

As educators viewed higher education in the mid 1800s, they saw that the collegiate way of life, the experience of college, had succumbed to academic demands consistent with the German philosophy of education. The humanistic element of comradeship and community attachment that many associate with college life today was absent.

Entering the twentieth century, most colleges had no extracurricular activities, no intramural sports, and no organized athletics. There were no football games as we know them today, no debate teams, no school colors, no "college spirit." What existed was an emphasis on research and the academic way of life. The first intercollegiate contest of any type took place in 1852, when Harvard and Yale had a boat race. Intercollegiate football started about 1869, but it was not until 1880 that it was played with eleven men to a team (previously it had been played with as many as twenty men to a side). College colors were not used until 1853. These organized athletics were begun ostensibly to curb disciplinary problems. There was some interest in them; however, most students were more interested in debating, speech contests, and similar intellectual pursuits with particular applications for such areas as law, business, and the ministry.

William Rainey Harper, as president of the University of Chicago, in 1893 constructed four dormitories, which at that time comprised 53 percent of the buildings on the campus. By 1900, he had constructed three more. Harper's influence on higher education in the Midwest and throughout the country rekindled interest in the collegiate experience and a concern for the student as a complete individual. As President Harper began ensuring the collegiate experience at the University of Chicago, he was joined by Arthur T. Hadley, then president at Yale University, and Andrew F. West, who was the dean at Princeton. (West was also responsible for constructing the first "graduate" dorm in 1901.) In 1907, Woodrow Wilson, then president of Princeton University, first proposed the quadrangle plan for dormitories, which was one of the first attempts during the twentieth century to integrate the academic and residential experiences in the United States. Though Wilson's plan was not approved originally, it later met with success.

In 1927, Lawrence Lowell, president of Harvard University, developed the "Harvard House Plan," which incorporated the academic and residential experience within individual houses—a program very similar to the English system. It met with success and is still in use at Harvard today.

The rekindling of concern for the individual student and for a need to experience a collegiate way of life was an important first step toward the revitalization of dormitory living. The second step came with the emancipation of women and the recognition of the woman's place in higher education. During the mid-1800s women's colleges such as Vasser, Smith, Mount Holyoke, and Wellesley were organized. It was the belief at these colleges, reflecting the societal belief of the time, that the young women who attended them needed to be protected. The administrators of these colleges, believed it was their *in loco parentis* (in place of parents) responsibility to ensure that morality and integrity was maintained by the young women students. Preceptresses, who were the forerunners of what later were called housemothers, enforced a Victorian morality for the young women in the sanctuary of their dormitories. Women had strict curfews. They were expected to be chaperoned at all times while in the company of a male (if they were allowed to see a male at all in a social situation), and generally they observed strict, scrupulously controlled lives under the watchful care of their preceptresses and professors. It was easy for a college to see the need for dormitories to protect young women and to ensure their chastity and morality.

As dormitories for women increased, a new organization that promoted residential education was born. In 1902, at Northwestern University, the National Association of Deans of Women (today called the National Association of Women Deans, Administrators, and Counselors) was formed. This was one of the first professional organizations to promote the importance of residential living and the education provided through that experience. Though their scope of concerns has grown over the years, this is still one of the basic philosophies that binds the organization together.

The influence on the American system of residential education before 1930 can be summarized in four categories. First is the influence of the English system of education, which stressed the development of the individual's character and intellect. Though the colonial colleges imitated many of the attributes of the English system, they were unable to develop the same integrated living and learning environment.

The second major influence was the establishment of colleges in the Midwest by religious groups. Both the moral doctrines of these groups and the isolation of the colleges made dormitories essential.

The German view of education as only intellectual was the third important influence on the residential college. This period of influence in higher education enriched the academic caliber of most colleges and universities, but it almost abolished the humanistic importance of the college experience.

The establishment of colleges for women and the emancipation of women was the fourth major influence. Until this time, most colleges were exclusively for men. Educators and society in general believed that men were capable of ensuring their own safety and were less concerned about any possible moral transgressions. The sanctity of American womanhood was, however, another matter. Women needed, it was believed, the protection of dormitories and the moral direction of a housemother.

The American system of residence halls in 1930 reflected a compromise of these influences. Though some institutions of higher education attempted to unite the in-class and the out-of-class experiences, most never realized this goal. Before 1930, dormitories in America were only living places that provided little more than shelter and varying degrees of social interaction. They were not recognized as an integral part of the extracurricular life of students at most colleges.

Residence Halls after 1930

The years between 1930 and 1940 were years of turmoil and uncertainty for higher education. The unstable economic condition of the country forced universities into retrenchment of faculty, programs, and buildings. Faculty salaries were cut, and few, if any, new teachers were hired. Student activism on campuses throughout the country focused on organizing labor unions, supporting the Communist party, and seeking solutions to the general economic ills of the country through the guidance of a mild benevolent dictatorial direction from Washington, D.C.

The end of World War II brought with it the dawn of the golden years for higher education. These were years of amazing growth for American colleges and universities. The G.I. bill made it possible for over 360,000 veterans to postpone working and enter higher education. In demonstrating the impact of this monumental surge of enrollment experienced by higher education, Frederick Rudolph (1962) writes:

> In 1870 American institutions of higher learning enrolled somewhat over 50,000 young men and women; a hundred years later the City University of New York alone would be enrolling almost four times that number. In 1870 but 1.7 of the young people aged 18 to 21 were enrolled in colleges and universities; by 1970 half of the age group 18 to 21 would be at a college. In 1960 approximately 3,500,000 young men and women attended institutions of higher learning; by 1970 that figure would be doubled. In 1876 there were 311 colleges and universities; in 1960 there were 2,026. For the first time in history, American institutions of higher learning experienced prosperity and called it a problem (p. 486).

The federal government came to the aid of colleges and universities with an estimated billion dollars in funds. By 1958, the federal government had assumed nearly 25 percent of the cost of all construction and by 1960 provided almost 20 percent of the actual operating income of most colleges and universities (Rudolf, 1962). This was the era in which most of the residence halls were built, because the great influx of students created an immediate need for student housing. Many institutions turned to temporary housing in an army-barracks arrangement. Relying on federal funds and on a new system of selling institutional bonds to raise money for construction, universities constructed residence halls at an amazing rate. No longer were these buildings an extension of the small intimate family that was created in a hall of sixty to eighty people; now they were large high-rises that housed upwards of a thousand students.

After Sputnik and with the threat of war with Russia, higher education was called upon to meet the challenge of sophisticated technology. Research money and new programs increased at a record pace.

As the first influx of the postwar baby boom was felt in higher education, the residence halls extended even further. Institutions grew from small state teachers' colleges of four thousand students to state universities of over twenty thousand. Almost all well-known universities throughout the country more than doubled their size. Admission standards and selection into the universities became more rigid as higher education was sought as a refuge by many men to avoid military service during the Vietnam conflict.

It was in this period of change and re-examination, between the late 1940s and the mid-1970s, that higher education came to examine its role in the total development of the student. Educational programming, resource centers in the residence halls, faculty-in-residence programs, living and learning centers, and many other things that today are taken for granted as part of an active residence hall educational program were developed in this era of expansion. These things were all done to integrate the large numbers of students, living together in the new multistory dormitories, into the collegiate experience. It was during this time that resident assistants were first used as they are today. The role of the RAs as student educators and role-models took on new meaning as the recognition of their impact upon other students became apparent.

The large high rise residence halls built in the '60s and early '70s brought new challenges to residence hall personnel. The close supportive environment that characterized smaller residence halls was more difficult to establish in buildings housing a thousand or more students. The importance of resident assistants, educational programming, special interest housing units, and professionally trained full-time staff was soon recognized.

This period of the late '60s and '70s brought many changes to higher education. In roughly a ten year span, policies regulating student behavior in the residence halls moved from strictly enforced curfews for men and women, sign in and sign out logs, strictly enforced dress codes, strict rules governing alcohol use, etc.; to open visitation, co-ed residence halls, abandonment of dress codes, and a more tolerant attitude toward alcohol. Add to this the rise in drug usage, student activism, and a significant increase in financial aid programs giving access to higher education to many who had previously not been given the opportunity. Within a relatively short time frame, RA's and other student affairs staff were confronted with a host of new problems.

In the late '70s and early '80s, higher education has been confronted with strained economic conditions, gradually declining enrollments, and diminishing research funds. Many institutions with large residence hall complexes and accompanying large bonded indebtedness are now being confronted with some serious economic questions as occupancies dwindle. The few institutions who are constructing residence halls are moving in the direction of smaller living units, often in apartment-type arrangements.

Today's students also have changed in comparison with the students of the '60s and early '70s. Levine (1981) describes them as being more self-centered, more narcissistic, highly career oriented, and less concerned with major social issues of our time. Levine believes that the change in attitude among today's students is the result of such events as the Vietnam war and the watergate scandal that took place while today's students were developing. Having experienced these events, Levine contends today's students have lost faith in the traditional institutions of church, family, government and education. He observes that students have turned inward to escape what they perceive to be an unstable and inhospitable world.

Even though many colleges and universities today face retrenchment and tight fiscal budgets, higher education will adjust to these changes as it has done throughout its long history. Residence halls will continue to be places for students to live and to integrate life experiences in their growth toward adulthood. The role of the RA will continue to be crucial in the facilitation of this growth and in helping to make the residence hall a positive educational experience.

CHAPTER 3
A Philosophy for Residence Halls

There have been many different philosophies for working with students. One of the first, as described in chapter 2, held that the primary purpose of residence halls was the custodial care of students. This philosophy dominated higher education until the mid-nineteen hundreds. After World War II, higher education saw a new student arrive on campus. Students were more mature, more career-oriented, and, perhaps most importantly, more were from working-class backgrounds. The influx of students after World War II created a new community of students on campus. Prior to the 1940s, higher education had been reserved for an elite social class who could afford a college education. As higher education became more accessible to people from working-class backgrounds, the previously homogeneous nature of the college population changed. Higher education became more egalitarian.

This trend of egalitarianism has continued in higher education since the 1940s. Many factors have influenced it, including the technological race with the USSR after the launching of the Sputnick, the influx of students attempting to evade the military draft during the Vietnam conflict, and the increased efforts to provide civil rights for minorities.

The Student Personnel Point of View

As the university has changed, so has the emphasis on the student-institutional relationship, as defined by what is commonly referred to as the "student personnel philosophy," of which residence halls are a part. The idea that residence halls were basically custodial, changed gradually to a belief that the purpose of the university was to act *in loco parentis* (in lieu of parents). This philosophy changed in the 1930s and 1940s to what was described as a "student personnel point of view," which recognized the following about students:

1. The individual student must be considered as a whole person.
2. Each student is a unique person and must be treated as such.

3. The total environment of the student is educational and must be used to achieve his full development.
4. The major responsibility for the student's personal and social development rests with the student and his personal resources (Miller and Prince 1976, p. 4).

The personnel point of view was translated into two different approaches. The first approach called itself the "student services approach." It defined the relationship with students as one of providing services for students. Residence halls were a service for students, just as student union activities were a service for students. The university might be described as a market basket of different activities and programs from which a student could choose. The second philosophy was a "student affairs philosophy," which defined the university as concerned with the management, administration, and general affairs of students. This approach took a more comprehensive view of dealing with students and saw that the university had a definite responsibility to control, develop, and provide services for students.

The Student Development Approach

In the past decade, a new theory has emerged in the field of student personnel work that has a direct impact on residence halls and offers another alternative for working with students. It is based in part on the "student personnel point of view." This theory is called the "student development approach." It might be described by saying that the purpose of working with students is to help identify areas in which students wish to grow, provide programs in those areas, and assess their success in meeting the goals they set. It does not make decisions for students or define for students what they should be doing. However, it does more than provide services, manage the student's affairs and activities, and control the behavior of students.

The student development approach may be said to be characterized by the following:

1. An acceptance of developmental philosophy characterized by the belief that the individual growth toward maturation is sequential, increasing in complexity, universal, and quantitatively different.
2. An acceptance of students as determinors of their own destinies.
3. A belief that the role of student personnel people (residence hall staff) as educators with definable skills is to assist students in accomplishing goals that they have identified for themselves.
4. The belief that students are able to determine what is best for themselves.

5. A recognition that the student is a total living organism and that the university must deal with both his cognitive and his affective development; that it is not possible to develop the mind and simply assume that the rest of the person's development will occur naturally.

One model used in implimenting a student development philosophy contains five basic steps. The first step is a self-assessment or goal-setting stage. In this stage, students determine what they wish to accomplish. The goal-setting may be done informally or formally, using testing instruments and exercises. However, the end result should be the same—a list of definable goals a student wishes to accomplish.

In the second stage of the student development model, students assess their strengths and weaknesses in the areas they have identified as being desirable ends for themselves. For example, suppose that a person wishes to become president of the Student Government Association. To do this, it is determined with the assistance of professional staff that a number of skills in public speaking, organizing others, parliamentary procedure, and human relations will be necessary. In these areas the student can assess his strengths and weaknesses. Once having determined areas for growth, he can determine the areas in which he needs to work.

In the third stage, the student pursues experiences that will aid in the accomplishment of skills necessary to meet the goal he has set. This stage is most often referred to as the instruction stage or the teaching stage. Programming, organizational activities, workshops, and similar forms of goal-producing experiences are the mediums the student uses to develop what he believes he needs in order to achieve his goals.

The fourth stage is the reassessment or testing stage where students determine how well they have acquired the skills they wish to develop and to what level they have developed these skills. As a result of the testing stage or the reassessment stage, students set new goals to improve further in areas where they want to improve or to meet other objectives.

In brief, the student development model can be viewed as: (1) self-assessment and goal-setting; (2) assessment; (3) teaching/instruction; (4) assessment/evaluation; (5) goal setting. At the end of the goal setting stage, the process is repeated until the student has accomplished the goals he wished to accomplish.

Now, how does this apply to you as a resident assistant? The relationship comes in understanding your specific role in working with students. Your basic role is to assist students in achieving what they wish to achieve. There is no preconception of what a student *should* achieve, other than what that student wishes to achieve. No person's goal is necessarily better than another person's goal. Everyone has a right to pursue the kind of life he wishes to lead. Some may wish to go on to vocational endeavors after college, whereas others may wish to continue their educations. Our role as educators is to help students determine what they wish to accomplish in life, as opposed to what we think they should accomplish; to help them assess the things they need to accomplish to meet their goals; to provide the experiences that will give them the skills they need to accomplish their goals; to help them evaluate and improve their skills; and to help them set new goals.

The skills involved in the theory of student development break down into four basic groups. The first group are the skills necessary to lead an enriched and fulfilling life, such skills as flexibility, creativity, inventiveness, the ability to enjoy life, self-confidence, and a willingness to experience new things. These skills lead the student to a higher level of self-actualization.

The second area we can call intellectual fitness. In this area, we place all the basic cognitive skills necessary to analyze data, understand and handle concepts, synthesize new ideas and material, apply knowledge, and perform at a level of intellectual satisfaction. This translates into finding an occupation that is meaningful, intellectually challenging and having hobbies that are intellectually stimulating. This also means that the student acquires the motivation for continued life-long learning. Too often people graduate with the feeling that once they have completed college, they have finished their educations. An educated person should have a desire to continue learning, to enjoy learning, and to continue to improve his mind.

The third group of skills involve physical fitness. Exercise and physical health are also important parts of education. If one is sick, weak, and generally leads an unhealthy life-style marked by smoking, poor nutritional habits, erratic sleeping patterns, etc., it will be difficult to live a well-balanced life and to achieve at an optimum level. Remember, the student development philosophy accepts the person as a whole: therefore, it must include all aspects of the person.

The fourth group of skills develop a sense of "spiritual fitness." Some may define this as a sense of religious commitment, although that is not necessarily the intended meaning. There is a sense of internal harmony, or perhaps religious commitment, a sense of faith in oneself or about oneself, that makes up a sense of internal wellness. For a strong Christian, it may mean a sense of unity with Christ. For a Buddhist, it may mean paying the necessary homage and leading life as Buddha described it. Whatever one's religious or philosophical orientation, these skills should help the student develop a sense of internal peace. These four component groups of skills together produce what has been called a wellness.

How does all this apply to your role as an RA? Very simply, this is the purpose for which you exist. It is an educational role defined by the division of student life on your campus, and it is why your institution spends time training you in human relation skills, crisis management, counseling techniques, and all of the other skills necessary to aid students in their personal development toward goals that they have identified. Your function is to serve as a catalyst, an identifier of services, a role-model which may help students identify goals they wish to achieve, and an informal assessor of students strengths and weaknesses through feedback that you may give them.

Institutions can no longer stand by while students graduate with only the most minimal levels of skills necessary for a productive and fulfilling life. Though many students graduate with strong cognitive skills, other aspects of their life may go begging. In residence halls and through student development programming, some institutions are assisting with the affective development of their students. Institutions have recognized that cognitive development and specific professional skills are not enough to ensure a student's success in life after graduation. People also need such qualities as honesty, integrity, trustworthiness, enthusiasm, and motivation. The college experience can be an excellent opportunity to learn or develop these skills and qualities. The residence halls and other areas outside the classroom can provide these experiences.

Goals for Residence Halls

What then are the objectives that must be set for residence halls if they are to accomplish the holistic development of the students who live there? We can identify the following:

Goal 1. A primary goal of residence halls should be to assist students with their growth and development. The student development model is a viable approach to the accomplishment of this goal.

Goal 2. Residence halls must be appealing places to live. This means that not only should the tangible physical facilities, such as heat, shelter, air-conditioning, room size, etc., be appealing, but the total environment should also be appealing. Residence halls should be as free as possible from noises from other people's rooms, from practical jokes, from general disruptions, irritations, and distractions. Residence halls must be places where students feel comfortable and at home.

Goal 3. Students should be given maximum control over their surroundings. The need to control one's environment and to mark that environment as one's territory is important. Students should be given as much freedom as possible in the decoration of their rooms and in the control of that environment. This is, after all, the only space they have that they can—for the time being—call their own.

Goal 4. Residence halls should teach group living skills and a sense of responsibility to the community. They should teach the ability to interact with peers and to contribute as a member of a group. Residence halls should help students learn the necessary human relations skills to socialize with others, work with others toward the accomplishment of projects, share values and ideas with others, and to model positive behaviors for others. Residence halls should strive to establish a central community among small groups of individuals.

Goal 5. The primary purpose of residence halls must be educational, not managerial. The residence hall staff must choose whether they are going to be monitors of student behavior, or facilitators of student growth, because it is much simpler for residence halls to function as hotels than it is for them to be an extension of the educational experience of college. For this extension to occur in a realistic and meaningful manner, the staff and the students must accept the legitimate educational role of the residence halls.

Goal 6. Residence hall staff should have basic skills in the following areas:

1. Conceptual Application Skills—This means a basic understanding of the skills and concepts necessary to help students develop in areas where they wish to develop.
2. Counseling Skills—These skills should be in listening, referring people for additional help, empathizing, and helping others resolve problems.
3. Basic Information Skills—These skills involve knowledge of the basic services and procedures on individual campuses—such things as how to register, where the health center is located, and where a person can go for assistance with various problems.
4. Administrative Skills—All RAs need some organizational skills, paperwork-management skills, time-management skills, and follow-through skills.
5. Teaching Skills—The RA needs two types of teaching skills: educational programming skills, and effective role-modeling skills.
6. Leadership Skills—For the RA, these include good objective-setting skills and the ability to motivate and influence others.
7. Crisis-Management Skills—This is the ability to view a crisis situation and handle it effectively, controlling others, remaining calm, and assisting other individuals, through crises.
8. Good Human Relations Skills—These include both an understanding of the nature of human beings in such areas as motivation, sexuality, and patterns of behavior, and the ability to interact freely with and communicate with others in a personal way that invites other people to want to know you.

CHAPTER 4

The Influence of Residence Halls on the Development of Students

Are residence halls influential in the development of students? Do they aid students in academic pursuits, help students integrate their personal values, and, in general, provide an environment that contributes to the students' overall growth toward maturity? Researchers have answered *yes*.

Comparisons between Students Who Live in Residence Halls and Students Who Do Not

One method of examining the effects of residence halls is to compare the students who live in them with students who do not. Arthur Chickering, in a book appropriately titled *Commuting Versus Residence Students* (1974), did this. He found that residence hall students did better in college, were more likely to succeed, and advanced more quickly. He summarizes some of these findings as follows:

Residents, in response to immersion in a college environment, change most during the first two years. They decelerate and may even slightly regress after that, as they move back toward the home culture as graduation approaches. They change most quickly in the nonintellectual areas where the differences between high school and college are greatest. And change in intellectual areas accelerates as college courses and patterns of study become more challenging. In contrast, commuters' change is slower. They are constrained by internal conflicts and by pressures from parents, peers, and prior community. These constraints operate with least force for intellectual development, where the college experiences of commuters and residents are most similar. Thus the commuters more quickly approximate the scores of residents in the intellectual area. But because substantial differences exist, and persist, in the range of noncourse experiences and interpersonal relationships, nonintellectual changes occur more slowly. Beginning college with fewer advantages than resident students, commuters as a group slip further and further behind residents despite these changes. And, as a consequence, college has the effect of widening the gap between the have-not students and the haves. (page 44)

Prior to Chickering's study, Alexander Astin (1973) conducted a national survey of both private and public colleges and universities for the American Council on Education. He compared students who lived in residence halls with students who did not and found at least six major differences.

1. Students who lived in residence halls were more likely to achieve a higher grade-point average than those students who did not live in residence halls.
2. Students who lived in residence halls were more likely to complete their baccalaureate degrees in four years and to apply for admission to graduate school than students who did not live in residence halls.
3. Students who lived in residence halls were more likely to major in an area of humanities (education, social science, etc.) or one of the arts, whereas commuter students were likely to major in business or engineering.
4. Students who lived in residence halls were generally reported to participate in more social activities, such as dating, going to parties, smoking, drinking, etc.
5. Living in a residence hall generally had a positive effect upon the student's self-image. The experience seemed to enhance self-confidence, public speaking ability, and similar measures of self-reliance.
6. Students who lived in residence halls reported greater satisfaction with their living environment than those students who did not live in a residence hall. Much of this satisfaction was due to the feeling of the resident students that they had greater contact with faculty and more opportunity to discuss their academic work with professors.

In a later study, Astin (1977) again compared students living in residence halls with students who did not. He concluded that "students who live in residence halls have more contact with faculty, interact more with student peers, do better academically, and are more satisfied with their undergraduate experience than are commuters" (page 22). Astin goes on to say: "Perhaps the most significant impacts of living on-campus versus commuting are on achievement and career development. Living on-campus substantially increases the student's chances of persisting in college and of aspiring to graduate or earn professional degrees. Residents are also more likely to achieve in extracurricular areas, in particular leadership and athletics" (page 220).

Smallwood and Klas (1973) compared three different forms of on-campus living with living off-campus. Students on-campus and off-campus entered the university with approximately the same academic backgrounds, grades, and other similar predictors. However, the students who lived on-campus performed better academically than those students who lived off campus. Smallwood and Klas found that the on-campus students also developed better study habits and were more involved in volunteer programs, social activities, and similar forms of university involvement. The students living in residence halls also reported a greater sense of community with the university. Studies by Albrow (1966) confirm these findings and suggest that students who live off-campus feel more isolated from the college experience. Feldman's and Newcomb's (1970) studies summarized the primary advantages for residence hall students as more social interaction and a better chance for academic success. These opportunities led to other developmental advantages, such as social and interpersonal skills, and generally provided increased academic motivation allowing students to utilize their academic abilities more fully.

Though it would be enough to say that residence halls helped students achieve academic goals, provided more opportunities for social interaction, assisted students in making career plans, and promoted a greater satisfaction with the college experience, these studies do not answer how the individual is aided, develops, and matures. In 1975, Scott compared students who lived in residence halls with students who did not. He was particularly interested in the effect that residence halls had on student leaders, such as RAs. Scott chose to use the Personal Orientation Inventory (POI) to measure the differences between residence hall students and commuter students. This inventory is a standardized testing instrument designed to measure personal development or, more accurately, characteristics of self-actualization. The POI consists of twelve scales as follows: time competence/time incompetence, inner-directed/outer-directed, self-actualizing value, existentiality, feeling reactivity, spontaneity, self-regard, self-acceptance, nature of man, synergy, acceptance of aggression, and capacity for intimate contact. A person scoring high on the POI would be a person who is more fully functioning, has a more mature outlook on life, and leads a less inhibited life with greater personal freedom than does the average person.

Scott found that students who lived in residence halls achieved higher scores on the POI than students who lived off-campus or were commuting. He also found that students in leadership positions in the residence halls or who were RAs achieved higher scores on the POI than did other resident students. Scott reached the following conclusion:

> Based on the increase in self-actualization from beginning to the end of the academic year, it was concluded that student assistants (also called resident assistants) and student leaders did differ from other students in their personal development and that these differences were related to their experiences in their position. Because an increase in self-actualization on at least twice as many scales of the POI occurred for residence hall students than for off campus students or commuting students, it was concluded that more development was fostered among students living in residence halls than among students living off campus or commuting from home. (page 218)

It is clear from these studies that residence halls have a positive influence upon the lives of students. Students who live in residence halls perform better academically, develop social and interpersonal skills more rapidly, and come closer to a level of self-actualization than students who have not had this experience. Residence halls do assist in the accomplishment of these important educational objectives. But how does living in a residence hall accomplish them? What is unique about this experience? Perhaps most importantly, how can the environment be shaped to increase, enhance, or ensure these important educational objectives?

How Residence Halls Influence Students

Family Background

One of the key reasons residence halls accomplish more has less to do with the residence hall program or the staff than with the students who chose to live in residence halls. Newcomb (1960), in some of the early work on the development of college students, found that a student's background was the most important factor in determining a student's success or failure in college. Nothing the college can do inside or outside the classroom will have as much influence on the student's ability to achieve as the experiences the student was afforded prior to college. Early childhood development, translated into opportunities to learn, prepares the individual for future learning—both affectively and cognitively.

It has generally been the case that students who attend residential colleges and live on campus come from somewhat more affluent backgrounds than commuter students. These residential students are often afforded more developmental advantages prior to college, more often have parents who attended college, and more often associated with peers who planned to attend college. These background factors contribute to the overall development of the student, her motivations, and her ability to cope with an environment of ideas. The residential experiences further enhance these developmental advantages.

Leaving Home

As important as this background experience is to the student, the break with it when the student moves away from home is an important new beginning and a critical step in the maturation process not experienced by those students who remain at home and attend college. The very act of moving into a new environment, free from parental influences and former friends, provides the student with new opportunities to learn. Meanwhile, the commuter student's environment remains relatively unchanged. She is not faced with the same challenges of adjusting to a new environment with a new pattern of social role expectations.

Peer-Group Influences

Of all the factors that influence a student's development once in college, the student's peer group is the most powerful (Newcomb 1960). Classroom instruction, course of study, and association with members of the faculty will not be as important to the student's personal development, values, career expectations, and desire to complete college or to go on to graduate school as other students with whom she associates.

In a residence hall, it is possible to predict who will make up a student's peer group—defined here as that group of students with whom the person commonly chooses to associate. A number of studies (Menne and Sinnet 1971; Ecklund 1972; Priest and Sawyer 1967; and Martin 1974) have shown that a student's friends, or what might be called her primary peer group, in a residential setting will be determined most by the opportunities that groups of students have to interact. Students who live in close proximity are generally afforded the most opportunities to interact with one another, and thus, one determinant of who a student's primary peer group will be is who lives close to that student.

Other factors obviously enter into friendship selection. Common interests, the size of the living unit, the location of a student's room in relation to the traffic pattern in the living unit, homogenity of the group, and isolation of the group all play important roles in increasing opportunities for certain individuals to interact and select their primary peer group.

Once selected, the peer group will be critical in the student's development and growth. It carries so much influence because it acts as what Whittacker (1969) describes as the intermediate social environment between the family and society. Peer groups take on almost a parental role by setting standards of expected conduct and holding the power to reward and punish. The rewards offered by peers consist mostly of emotional support and interpersonal esteem or influence within the group through acceptance. The punishments of the group are also emotional, based on actions such as ridicule, isolation, reprimand, or ostracism.

The residential experience heightens this peer-group influence. The similarity of backgrounds, the frequent and continual interaction by virtue of proximity, and similar academic and career goals contribute to the intensification of this influence in the residence halls.

The effects that peer groups have in setting attitudes, values, acceptable behavior, and in fostering maturity are many. Feldman and Newcomb (1969) summarize what the peer group provides the individual student as follows:

1. Helps the student achieve independence from home and family.
2. Supports and facilitates, or impedes, the academic intellectual goals of the institution.

3. Offers general emotional support to students and fulfills needs not met by the curriculum, classroom, or faculty.
4. Provides the student the occasion for practice in getting along with people whose backgrounds, interests, and orientations are different from her own.
5. Provides the student support for not changing.
6. Provides the student support for changing. It can challenge old values, provide intellectual stimulation, act as a sounding board for new points of view, present new information and new experiences to the student, help to clarify new self-definitions, suggest new career possibilities, and provide emotional support for change.
7. Offers an alternative source of gratification and of positive self-image and rewards a variety of nonacademic interests for students who are not satisfied academically. Can also serve to discourage voluntary withdrawal from college for other than academic reasons.
8. Can help in postcollege careers of students by providing general social training and development of personal ties that may be useful later (pages 236–37).

As an aside, fraternities and sororities serve this same peer-support function. These organizations formalize the experience through rituals and ceremonies. The rituals serve as rites of passage into the organized group; however, most importantly, they serve to increase the commonality of experiences among the group members. Pledge pranks, hazing, and similar activities are used by the organization to solidify the group and to promote group trust—though hazing usually has the opposite effect.

Students in residence halls generally do not have formal rites, but they do have informal rituals that serve the same function. The experience of preparing for midterm and final examinations, of getting intoxicated together, of participating in intramural sports together, of undergoing the same social pressures for dating, of working together on a particular program or a student government project, and of simple physical contact through proximity and interaction serve the same function. Compare for a minute the experience of a practical joke played in a residence hall by a group of students and a fraternity prank. Both groups of students share in the same secretive adventure and undergo much the same unifying experience by selective inclusion into responsibility for the act. The difference between a group of students in a residence hall having a shaving-cream fight, "pennying" someone into a room, secretly discharging fireworks, or some similar activity within the residence hall is little different in function from the "kidnapping" of an active member of a fraternity or sorority by the pledge class, the stealing of a composite picture of a particular fraternity or sorority, or the painting of the fraternity or sorority's letters in prominent places about the campus. The action of the group, at the exclusion of others, promotes trust, confidence, mutual dependence, and community, further solidifying the group.

Roommate Influence

One element of influence in a student's peer environment is the student's roommate. During the freshman year, the roommate is a particularly important influence (Upcraft and Higginson, 1975). Heath (1968) studied the influence of roommates in a male residence hall and found that roommates forced individuals to become more tolerant, more understanding, more expressive, and either increased or retarded the individual's maturity. Vreland (1970) went further, taking the position that freshman roommates who were also good friends could be identified as the primary force for attitude change while in college.

Attitudes, values, and maturity are not the only things affected by a student's roommate. Murray (1961) found that a student's grades will deviate from predicted grades, either higher or lower, in the same direction the student's roommate's grades deviate. In other words, if one roommate does well academically, the chances are better for the other roommate to do well. Conversely, if one student in the room does poorly, chances are better that the other student in the room will also do poorly. Sommer (1969) provides one rationale for this observation in similar studying habits. He found that if one roommate was studying, there was a 75 percent chance that the other roommate would also be studying. Conversely, there was only approximately a 33 percent chance that the student would be studying alone. Blai (1971) also looked at the influence of a person's roommate on academic performance when he experimentally assigned students in residence halls as roommates in an attempt to increase their academic performance. Roommate assignments were based on classification of the students as average, below-average, or above-average as indicated by their high school grades. Four experimental groups were formed. The results of the study indicated that the average students and the below-average students who were paired with high-ability students did better academically than their counterparts assigned with average or below-average students. This study confirms Murray's (1961) observation on grade influence.

The Influence of the RA

Another developmental influence in the residence hall is the RA. This was the conclusion of a study by Zirkle and Hudson (1975) at Pennsylvania State University. In this study, the researchers compared the influence of RAs who had been identified as "counselor-oriented" and RAs who had been identified as "administrator-oriented" on the development of maturity in freshman males. These students were randomly assigned to floors with either the counselor-oriented RA or the administrator-oriented RA. At the end of the academic year, the students were administered the "Perceived Self Questionnaire," which is a standardized instrument measuring "overall maturity." The researchers found some interesting things. They found a significant relationship between the RA's behavior and the development of maturity among these freshman males. Students who lived in a unit with a counselor-oriented RA had maturity scores significantly higher (.001) than those students from units with the administrator-oriented RAs. The researchers also measured the effect of not having an RA and found that those units with the RAs, whether counselor- or administrator-oriented, yielded significantly higher maturity levels than did units without an RA. Freshmen living in the units with the counselor-oriented resident assistant also had significantly (.05) higher grade-point averages than did students living in units with either the administrator-oriented RA or units without any RA. The students in the counselor-oriented units, as compared with the other groups, had generally more positive environments. Zirkle and Hudson report that students who lived in this counselor-oriented environment:

(a) had more contacts with resident assistants concerning theft prevention, personal concerns, and informal matters;
(b) had lower assessments for physical damage to the unit;
(c) made more room changes within the unit and fewer requests to move out of the unit;
(d) had considerably more unit activities;
(e) felt they knew their resident assistant better, saw him more as a counselor and friend, and preferred to have him as their resident assistant again (page 32).

The researchers conclude by saying: "the behavior of the resident assistant has a significant effect upon student development. And this carries implications which are important to the role of the residence hall staff member and, more specifically, to the resident assistant in the total university educational program" (pp. 32–33).

These five important developmental factors—the student's background, the experience of moving into a residence hall, the student's association with a group of peers, the student's roommate, and the influence of the RA—must be viewed in the context of other environmental factors. The physical condition of the building, the predominance of students within a particular academic discipline; the composition of the residence hall as male, female, or coed; the rules, policies, and regulations of the university; the geographical location of the college or university; the selectivity of the institution; the size of the institution; and a number of other factors go into the overall impact that the residence hall environment will have on an individual student at a particular college or university.

Environmental Structuring of Residence Halls

Universities have used this knowledge to design living environments that enhance opportunities for self-actualization, increase grade performance, and fulfill other developmental goals. Universities have taken several approaches to shaping the environment. One category of approaches has attempted to increase students' academic performances by assigning students to live together on the basis of their academic majors or common course schedules. Sneed and Cable (1971) assigned groups of students to live together based upon their academic majors and the results of the environmental assessment technique at the University of Missouri-Columbia. In this study, students were first divided into groups by their academic majors and then by the environmental assessment technique, which defined six groups as follows: realistic, intellectual, social, conventional, enterprising, and artistic. Two small living units were used for this experiment—one male and one female. This environmental structuring resulted in higher than predicted grade point averages for the homogeneously grouped students when compared with other students.

In a similar study by Taylor and Hanson (1971) at the University of Minnesota, freshmen engineering students were grouped into two small residence halls. When the grade-point averages were compared at the end of three consecutive quarters, the researchers found that this arrangement, too, produced higher grades for these engineering students than for engineering students who did not participate in the special program.

Not all studies have shown that such special assignment programs work. Studies by Morishma (1966), Elton and Bate (1966), and Beae and Williams (1970) examining the same relationship between academic performance and assignment of students to residence halls on the basis of academic classification or major course of study have not been able to establish any significant causal relationship between grades and assignment within the residence hall. These researchers do, however, note that students in the special assignment programs do have a more positive attitude about scholastic achievement. It stands to reason that in time this attitude will have a beneficial effect on a student's academic performance and personal growth.

Research at Southern Illinois University by Duncan and Stone (1977) on high-ability honor students assigned together shows that this particular form of assignment tends to increase the grade performance of these students when compared with other high-ability students assigned at random. DeCoster, in two studies (1966, 1968) conducted at the University of Florida, earlier found this to be true when he grouped high-ability students together to comprise 24 to 50 percent of a residential unit. When he compared the academic performance of these students with other high-ability students assigned at random, he also found that the homogeneously assigned honor students achieved grades higher than other honor students assigned at random. A two-year longitudinal study was undertaken by Blimling and Hample (1979) to determine the effect of a controlled study environment (controlled study hours enforced by the resident assistant in voluntary units during prescribed hours) on average-ability students. After examining the grade performance of over 1,500 students for the two-year period, the researchers concluded that the intervention of study-floor guidelines created an environment that facilitated academic pursuits and produced grade performances higher than those of students assigned at random.

It is evident from these studies that structuring the residential environment, either by homogeneously grouping students by academic major or academic ability, or by controlling the study environment, can positively affect the academic performance of students who live in residence halls.

Another major attempt to structure the residence hall environment has been through "living and learning" programs. The first program to draw national attention was at Michigan State University in the Case Hall program. Since that time, a number of research studies (Olson 1964; Rockey 1969; DeCoster 1969, 1970; and Ogen 1969) have shown that these special living and learning environments, in which students usually live and take classes together, have a positive effect upon:

(1.) the student's satisfaction with the residence hall and the college;
(2.) the student's cultural sophistication and aesthetic appreciation; and
(3.) the student's peer relationships.

These living and learning programs appear to be particularly beneficial to new freshmen (Pemberton 1968). Newcomb (1962) suggests that the overlap of the residence hall and the classroom experience, as found in the living and learning programs, is one of the most viable means of utilizing peer influence in academic matters.

Summary

Residence halls have a positive impact upon the educational achievement of students who live in them and upon a student's personal growth compared with students who do not live in residence halls. Much of this academic and personal growth can be attributed to the student's background, her decision to live in a residence hall, the peer group that exists within the residence hall, the student's roommate, and the influence of the resident assistant. Universities can structure residence hall environments to enhance academic achievement and personal growth through special educational intervention programs that shape interaction within the residence hall environment.

SECTION 2

Understanding and Working with College Students

CHAPTER 5

The Growth and Development
of College Students

The process of maturation and growth may be viewed as a series of developmental stages or tasks that begins with early childhood and progresses through late adulthood in the mid-sixties. Theorists such as Havinghurst (1953), Piaget (1956), Maslow (1962), Perry (1970), Coons (1974), and Miller and Prince (1976), have identified sets of behavior that occur sequentially and are called stages of development or developmental tasks. Mussen, Conger, and Kagan (1969) define a stage as "a complicated set of characteristics or segments of behavior that occur together and may, therefore, be conveniently grouped." (p. 23)

Havinghurst (1953) defines a developmental task similarly as "a task which arises at or about a certain period in the life of an individual, successful achievement of which leads to happiness, and to success with later tasks while failure leads to unhappiness in the individual, disapproval by society, and difficulty with later tasks" (p. 2). A developmental task is comprised of both the normal maturational process of growth and societal expectations of the individual at a particular age.

Developmental theorists contend that growth throughout life occurs in stages that are brought on by societal demands to alter current behavior and master new behavior consistent with the age-level expectations of society. This demand to master new behavior brings about a crisis, and the resolution of the crisis helps move the individual into the next stage of maturity.

Prince, Miller and Winston (1977), in discussing their Student Development Task Inventory, conclude that the two most important concepts in understanding stage-development are the following:

1. Growth and development are continuous. They start the day an individual is born, and change continues to take place throughout his lifetime. Normal maturation may lead to developmental changes irrespective of the environment but not independent of it. Growth tendencies can be modified by experiences the individual has in the

environment, and such experiences can determine whether change will be optimal, minimal, or somewhere in between.

2. Growth and development is cumulative. Simple behavior must be mastered before complex behavior can be, assuming that the simple behavior is a component of the complex behavior. Some developmental tasks have to be mastered at least at a minimal level before moving on to another developmental task (p. 10).

Development and maturation of students through the college years play an important role in forming peer relationships. It is these maturational adjustments, crises, and transitions to higher-level development that will define the student's relationship to the institution. It is the interplay in this relationship that must be understood in order to comprehend the student's personal growth in college.

College students are still at the doorstep to adulthood. Adolescence is just coming into fruition, and students are grappling with issues of self-discovery and quasi-adulthood. Levinson (1978) calls this segment of development between the ages of seventeen and twenty the preadult years. At the same time, he classifies it as the years of the "early adult transition." It is not, as Levinson describes it, until sometime after the age of twenty-two that a person enters what he describes as "early adulthood." This will last until approximately the age of forty, when the person begins midlife transition to "middle adulthood." It should be noted that Levinson's developmental stages or eras in the life cycle are generated from research done on men. Women, however, follow a similar pattern.

Three Theories of Development

Many theorists have written about the early adult transitional period that occurs during a student's college years. They share in common many of the same principles and generally group similar characteristics together, but they differ in their groupings and adherence to the sequential characteristics of development. Three of these theories are reviewed here.

Coons's Five Stages of Development

The first theory is that of Frederick W. Coons (1974), a psychiatrist who was formerly director of the Psychiatric Division of the Student Health Center at Indiana University and associate professor of the Department of Psychiatry at the Indiana University School of Medicine. Coons identifies five stages of development occurring in the college years.

1. Resolution of the Child-Parent Relationship

The first stage of development is a break in the child-parent relationship. Prior to this time, a student's identity and dependence have been tied directly to the family. Moving to college allows the student to establish a new relationship with his parents. Though for many years the student has been experiencing increased freedom and autonomy, the actual move away from home into the college environment is both a physical and psychological transition that helps ensure independence from the parents. This break in the child-parent relationship is actually more the establishment of a different relationship with the parents.

It is a difficult transition for both parents and child. In cases where parents have been restrictive, the student could have difficulty in establishing a new relationship with parents. Though it may take years to establish a more adult-to-adult relationship, a new relationship does exist when a student enters college that allows the student to develop increased independence and autonomy.

2. Solidifying a Sexual Identity

In the second stage of development, Coons hypothesizes that the student begins to solidify a sexual identity. This is differentiated from identifying a particular sex-role, which happens much earlier, but instead is a process of understanding the nature and needs of being a man or a woman. This is the time of identification with appropriate sex-roles, which as Coons points out is based upon past parental relationships and sex-role-modeling prior to adolescence.

3. Formation of a Personal Value System

The third stage of development is the formation of a personal value system, which Coons sees as a process of moving from values imposed primarily by parents, church, schools, and the community to an internalized set of values.

4. Development of the Capacity for True Intimacy

The fourth stage of development is the development of the capacity for true intimacy. This is based upon a history of establishing close personal relationships in the past with best friends or "chums." It is a process of establishing an essential degree of comfort in human relationships, a sense of shared personal warmth with another individual, and the development of sensitivity and awareness of feelings necessary in any human relationship.

5. Choosing a Life's Work

This is more than choosing a vocation. It is closely aligned with exploring the world of work in a given area of interest. Actual decisions about a life's work may not be made until several years after college. Essentially, the college years are seen as an opportunity to explore a particular area of interest that might eventually become the start of a person's occupation.

Prince, Miller, and Winston's Developmental Tasks

The second major theory is advanced by Judith Prince, Theodore Miller, and Roger Winston, Jr., (1977) in their conception of the "Student Development Theory." The theory sets out three major tasks that need to be accomplished as a student develops. These three major tasks are accomplished

STUDENT DEVELOPMENTAL TASK INVENTORY
(Revised, Second Edition)

TASK 1: DEVELOPING AUTONOMY	**EMOTIONAL AUTONOMY (EA).** Students who have accomplished this subtask are free from the need for continuous reassurance and approval from others, especially from their parents, and have a reduced dependency upon family, peers, and social agencies (such as a need for grades as a study motivator, or the need to be policed concerning out-of-class assignments, etc.). Evidence of maturity on this subtask includes changes in one's relationship with parents, moving increasingly from that of child-to-parent towards adult-to-adult relationships (that is, relationships of reciprocal respect). Students see their parents more realistically as persons with their own needs, virtues, and shortcomings. **Descriptive characteristics:** Self-confident, assertive, self-directed, self-motivated, self-reliant, manages emotions in appropriate ways. **INSTRUMENTAL AUTONOMY (IA).** Two major characteristics describe students who have accomplished this subtask. These are (1) the ability to carry on activities and cope with problems without undue help from others, yet also knowing when and how to seek help, and (2) possessing the ability to be mobile in relation to personal needs and desires. Students advanced in this area feel able to make their own livings and plan their activities and time in ways to maximize the outcomes. **Descriptive characteristics:** self-sufficient, self-supporting, problem solver, geographically mobile, manages time, money and other resources well, brings about desired changes when needed. **INTERDEPENDENCE (ID).** Students who have accomplished this subtask can be described as having developed "mature dependence." They realize that they cannot dispense with their parents, that they cannot receive the benefits from others and society in general without contributing in return, and that they cannot feel comfortable accepting continuing support without working for it. Recognizing that loving and being loved are complementary and that there is a direct relationship between one's own behavior and community welfare in general are basic attitudes of students who have accomplished this subtask. **Descriptive characteristics:** supportive, good citizen, cooperative, does own share, helper, responsible, collaborates effectively with others.

STUDENT DEVELOPMENTAL TASK INVENTORY—*Continued*

TASK 2: DEVELOPING PURPOSE

APPROPRIATE EDUCATIONAL PLANS (EP). Students who have accomplished this subtask have formulated well-defined educational goals for themselves and are able to see the relationship between academic study and the other aspects of their lives. They are aware of the educational setting (both resources and limitations), have made accurate assessment of their academic abilities, know the requirements for graduation, and are generally able to cope with the demands of the higher education environment. They are either personally satisfied with their educational experiences or are taking steps to meet their goals in other ways. **Descriptive characteristics:** goal-oriented, self-directed learner, educationally motivated, seeks indepth educational experiences, enjoys college, takes advantage of all available resources to enhance learning.

MATURE CAREER PLANS (CP). An awareness of the world of work, an accurate understanding of one's abilities and limitations, a knowledge of requirements for various occupations, and an understanding of the emotional and educational demands of different kinds of jobs are evidence of accomplishment of this subtask. Students who have high achievement on this subtask have been able to synthesize their knowledge about themselves and the world of work into a rational order which enables them to formulate vocational plans and which allows them to make at least a tentative commitment to a chosen career field. They will have taken at least the first steps necessary to prepare themselves through both educational and work experiences for eventual employment. **Descriptive characteristics:** tentatively committed to a career field, knowledgeable about self as a worker, seeks experiences related to chosen field, knows how to utilize available career information.

MATURE LIFESTYLE PLANS (LP). Achievement of mature lifestyle plans includes establishing a personal direction and orientation in one's life which balances vocational interests, personal values, learned skills, hobbies, and future family plans. Plans need not be highly specific nor committed to an absolute, but must be of sufficient clarity to permit identification of appropriate present steps and reflect thoughtful long range goals. Students who have accomplished this subtask will have a general orientation that leaves open a wide range of future choices, but which provides a sense of direction and meaning to present activities. **Descriptive characteristics:** self-aware, purposeful, committed, thoughtful, future-focused orientation.

through successful completion of nine subtasks as explained on the accompanying diagram. The Student Developmental Task Inventory summarizes the theory. The three major tasks to be completed are listed.

Task I: Developing Autonomy

Similar to Coons's theory, autonomy is tied to a reciprocal adult-adult relationship with a student's parents. It moves through understanding, independence, and acceptance of independence—both financial and conceptual.

Task II: Developing Purpose

The development of purpose is primarily concerned with the student's career and vocational interests. Here the student moves from defining educa-

STUDENT DEVELOPMENTAL TASK INVENTORY—*Continued*

<table>
<tr>
<td rowspan="3" style="writing-mode: vertical-lr;">TASK 3: DEVELOPING MATURE
INTERPERSONAL RELATIONSHIPS</td>
<td>

INTIMATE RELATIONSHIPS WITH OPPOSITE SEX (IRS). Students having accomplished this subtask will have developed the sensitivity and awareness of feelings necessary for establishing close, meaningful relationships with members of the opposite sex. Mature intimate relationships reflect mutual support and commitment. They represent less a means of self-discovery and self-enhancement and more a means to achieve unity with another human being. Hopes, fears, aspirations, doubts, feelings, and thoughts are shared through frequent private conversations and other shared experiences. Involved in this subtask is the ability to love as well as to be loved and the testing of the ability to make long-term commitments. Differences of opinion and beliefs do not weaken the integrity of the relationship or the individuals. **Descriptive characteristics:** honest, caring, concerned about partner, supportive, aware of and expressive of feelings, sensitive to the needs and well being of the relationship.

MATURE RELATIONSHIPS WITH PEERS (MRP). Having accomplished this subtask, students will describe their relationships with peers as shifting toward greater trust, independence, and individuality. Their friendships survive the development of differences and episodes of disagreement; these friendships persist through times of separation and noncommunication. The need for many casual friends decreases in favor of spending more time with a few good friends. **Descriptive characteristics:** trusting, dependable, supporting, accepting of differences, warm, open, aware of the needs of others.

TOLERANCE (TOL). Respect for those of different backgrounds, habits, beliefs, faiths, values, and appearances describe students who have high achievement in the tolerance area. They respond to people in their own right rather than as stereotypes calling for conventional responses. There is an increasing openness and acceptance among students who have accomplished this subtask, which enables them to be flexible when interacting with others. It should be kept in mind, however, that tolerance does not mean either an improved capacity for teeth gritting and tongue biting or the development of screening devices to shield one from the values and behaviors of others. **Descriptive characteristics:** respectful, understanding, flexible, accepting of diversity, able to effectively and objectively interact with many different kinds of people.

</td>
</tr>
</table>

tional goals through an understanding of his/her own abilities, interests, and values to a level of commitment toward future vocational and life plans.

Task III: Developing Mature Interpersonal Relations

In this developmental task, the student is primarily concerned with, the establishment of interpersonal relations, which includes identifying with a sex-role, moving toward the development of intimate relationships with others, and tolerance of differences among people. As in Coons's theory, this is a move from a more authoritarian prospective to a more relativistic view.

Chickering's Seven Vectors of Development

The third theory is that of Arthur W. Chickering (1969), a psychologist, university administrator, researcher, and scholar. He hypothesizes seven developmental "vectors" that form a developmental continuum occurring during the span of the college years from approximately eighteen to twenty-five years of age.

1. Achieving Competence

Competence is analogous to the confidence that an individual has in his own ability to achieve successfully what he sets out to accomplish. One must develop confidence in his ability to achieve intellectually, physically, and so-cial-interpersonally.

2. Managing Emotions

In this vector of development, the student comes to understand and con-trol his emotions. This occurs first through becoming aware of feelings and then learning to trust them. Chickering (1969) declares that "emotions have to be experienced, to be felt and perceived for what they are" (p. 10). The student learns to manage the basic impulses of aggression and sex through developing more useful and effective modes of expression which tend toward the achievement of a genuine freedom of emotions that can exist with confi-dence in the individual's ability to manage them.

3. Becoming Autonomous

"To be emotionally independent is to be free from continual and pressing needs for reassurance, affection, or approval. The first step toward emotional independence is, of course, *disengagement* from the parents" (Chickering 1968, p. 58). The development of emotional independence moves from this disen-gagement from parents to interaction with the individual's own peer group, and finally to personal autonomy. *Instrumental Independence,* the second component of autonomy, is both the ability to carry out activities self-suffi-ciently and the ability to come and go as one desires. Chickering points out that one of the major obstacles to developing autonomy in this stage is the financial dependence many students have upon their parents. The final stage in developing autonomy is *interdependency*, which Chickering describes as the "capstone of autonomy." In interdependence, students come to recognize their parents as complimentary to their existence, but that their existence is not dependent upon their parents. They recognize that their existence is separate from their parents, and that they must work to support themselves. Chickering (1969) summarized the development of autonomy as follows:

> Change occurs along three major vectors, emotional independence, instrumental independence, and recognition and acceptance of interdependencies. Development of emotional independence begins with disengagement from the parents, and re-belliousness in relation to them, to other adult authorities, and to established in-stitutions. During this period, relationships with peers and sympathetic adults

provide transitory emotional support. Maturity in this vector comes when relationships or reciprocal respect and helpfulness are developed with parents and peers such that the strengths and weaknesses of self and others are recognized and mutually satisfying relationships are sustained through vagaries of distance in disagreement. (p. 77).

4. Establishing Identity

Chickering notes that the establishment of identity is in many ways the combination of the six vectors and is to a large extent dependent upon the successful completion or development of these other areas. He suggests that much of the developmental process during the college years is really a resolution to an "identity crisis," but at the same time he suggests that no one "small umbrella" could cover the multitude of activities taking place during this period of development. Discussing identity, Chickering says, "The primary element remaining is that solid sense of self that assumes form as the developmental tasks for competence, emotions, and autonomy are undertaken with some success and which as it becomes more firm, provides a framework for interpersonal relationships, purposes, and integrity. It is . . . the self, the person one feels oneself to be" (page 80). Much of this experience has to do with psychologically coming to accept one's appropriate sex-role and an understanding of oneself as a man or a woman. It is a process of self-discovery of who one is as a person.

5. Freeing Interpersonal Relationships

Through this vector of development, a student moves from an authoritarian, intolerant mode to a sense of increased tolerance and acceptance of different people, their life-styles, backgrounds, opinions, and beliefs. A shift toward a more open, intimate, and sincere relationship with close friends and intimate acquaintances follows.

6. Developing Purpose

Chickering describes this phase as "formulating plans for action and a set of priorities that integrate three major elements: (1) a vocational and recreational interest; (2) pursuit of vocation; and (3) life-style issues, including concerns for marriage and family" (p. 108). In the vocational/recreational interest phase, the student begins to shift interest from recreational pursuits toward more serious pursuits as he comes to clarify vocational aspirations. In the next phase of the pursuit of a vocation, the student is primarily concerned with the selection of a vocation after college. Through experiencing different classes, exposure to different life-styles, and encountering different people, places, and things, students begin to integrate their interests and narrow their range of vocational choices. In the final stage, students are concerned with a style of living, of family, marriage, and intimate relationships. This is a period of compromising one's vocational aspirations with basic life-style considerations and coming to grips with realities about oneself, one's career, and the future.

7. Developing Integrity

Chickering (1969) describes the development of integrity as "the clarification of a personally valid set of beliefs that have some internal consistency and that provide at least a tentative guide for behavior. Such development involves three overlapping stages: the humanizing of values, the personalizing of values, and the development of congruency" (p. 17). In humanizing values, the individual moves from a rigid set of absolute rules to a more relativistic view. Values the student brought with him/her to college are questioned, modified, and gradually expanded in scope to be generally more liberal. This is accomplished through objective analysis. As the values come to be viewed as more relativistic, it is necessary for the individual to personalize the value, and by doing this, the person adds some stability and self-commitment to these values and accepts them as his/her own. Internal consistency and congruents are often challenged. Constantly throughout life, a person must seek new sources of strength in personal behavior and in others, in order to renew these values.

As can be seen from this analysis, Chickering's theory differs from the other two in that each of his vectors is in many circumstances, occurring simultaneously and represents simply an issue of development through college. The accomplishment of one is not always contingent upon the other; however, each is integrated and may be tied to others, so that the humanizing of values is tied to the establishment of identity. They are, as Chickering describes them, vectors for development.

The Progression of a Student's Development in College

The important thing to note from these theories is that the development of an individual involves a very complex system of interrelationships and experiences based on physiological maturation, environment, and personality factors. None of these developmental stages takes place in a void. No two people move through them at the same pace or with the same experiences. As an RA, it is important that you understand the types of development that are taking place.

It is easy to identify the common factors in the three different theories just given. Students in this period of adjustment to college must wrestle with issues relating to their parents and their autonomy, relationships with their peers, discovering who they are as individuals, the integration and acceptance of a workable value system, a career and life direction, and establishing an ethical and moral base of reasoning.

Development is a continuous process and has no absolute starting and finishing point. It is a loose-knit, fluid interchange of events, circumstances, and developmental cycles. We can work with this stage-development theory; try to understand the basic developmental cycles, and develop an approximation of when each would occur during development in college. Coons (1974) points out that the particular developmental task most in evidence at a given time will define much of the student's relationship to the institution. If we can identify *which* developmental task is most in evidence at a particular time, we should be able to anticipate the adjustment difficulties a student will be experiencing in the residence hall at that time. Your ability to recognize the developmental stages and to understand the experience the student is going through in general terms should help you better understand what to expect, and how to help a student through his maturational crises.

The three theories of development that have been briefly reviewed reveal a pattern of growth during the college years and beyond. The next section is devoted to transposing the developmental stages into a pattern of experiences evident in each of the undergraduate years. It is designed to draw particular attention to the adjustment problems in college and the residence hall environment. As we set out the overall scheme for this chronological development, it is important to remember that individual students vary in the pace of development or in areas of crisis.

We can divide the college experience into three general areas. The first area we shall call the "beginning years." It includes the freshman year and, for most students, part of the sophomore year. The next general grouping of development we shall label the "middle years." This stage begins sometime in the middle of the sophomore year and lasts until sometime in the junior year. The final stage of development in college we shall refer to as the "ending years." This stage starts sometime in the junior year and lasts throughout the senior year and beyond college.

Beginning Years (Freshmen/Sophomore Years)

Attending college for the first time is a threatening and frightening experience for many students. The familiar environments of home and high school are gone. In place of these is a new and formidable experience. College professors with doctoral degrees, maps to find one's way around the campus, a library with hundreds of thousands of volumes, and thousands of new fellow students confront the entering freshman, who is thrust into this environment and expected to survive. This experience challenges the individual's personal security, need for acceptance, and need for physical comfort. Not only are the new students uncertain of this unfamiliar environment, but they are filled with doubt as to whether they will be able to succeed in meeting the expectations of their parents, teachers, friends, and the expectations they have for themselves.

Many students, upon entering the residence hall environment for the first time, project the attitude that they know everything there is to know about that environment. It is not easy to admit to other people that one is simply not knowledgeable about a new situation, such as the residence hall, and perhaps a little frightened about the new experience. For men this seems to be especially true. Men, as defined by our culture, are supposed to be self-reliant, independent, and to have the ability to confront new tasks with little difficulty. It is often difficult for the new freshman male to admit that he really does not understand all there is to know about what is happening. To ask simple questions such as "Where is the dining hall?" or "What do I do if I get locked out of my room?" is an admission that he is not in control of his environment. When one's ego is fragile and one's self-image is closely tied to the perceptions of other students, a person may be reluctant to ask some of the most simple and basic questions.

This new environment presents a major adjustment for students. It is often the first time they have been on their own away from their friends and families. They want to be accepted by their peers and want to make this a successful experience.

Students, in these early days of meeting other people, tell other people who they are through their past experiences and through what their parents do. Students use these reference points because their identity has been tied to these things for so long. Students who are dissatisfied with their background, dissatisfied with themselves, or who wish to enhance their images will embellish their backgrounds and experiences when they describe them to other people. They may claim that their parents are much wealthier than they really are, that they were tremendous athletes in high school, or that they were heavily involved in some recognition group for intellectual achievement. By communicating this to other people, the student hopes to establish a more favorable impression and to gain the acceptance and approval of others.

Almost all students go through an adjustment phase when they enter the residence hall environment. Most will be secure enough to adapt and establish an open and honest relationship with their peers. Some will rely on various forms of embellishment to bolster their identity and enhance their security. Sautter (1974) explains the trauma of the new freshman in making a transition to college this way: "It should be pointed out that the transition to college is a real trauma for many freshmen. . . . The 17 or 18-year-old freshman probably does not have a very realistic idea about college. . . . The resident is probably self-conscious and a little confused, even somewhat homesick. . . . He or she does not understand the tremendous organization of the university, nor how to use the facilities available to him/her. The resident may have no friends. He/she does not know how to relate to upperclassmen, what activities to try to enter, or the meaning of the residence hall organization" (pp. 5–6).

Psychological and Emotional Development

In this first transitional move into college, students go through what Rossi (1964) has identified as an adaptation phase of somewhere between four to eight weeks. In this period, the student makes some major transitional adjustments to set a pattern for future interaction, values, and success in this environment. As Rossi concludes from his study:

> massive socialization effects occurred during the initial few weeks of entry into the institution in question, that effects were greatest among those individuals who were most oriented toward their peers, and that changes beyond the early weeks were relatively slight, as long as the individual remained in the institution in question. Indeed, the major shift in value emphasis occurred during the period between September and November indicating that socialization to the normative system of the school occurred in a short period of time and involved changes of considerable magnitude. Changes of similar magnitude did not occur among upperclassmen, sophomore, junior, and senior classes being essentially alike in their value orientations. . . . Thus, one major finding was that the major socialization processes taking place in college were occurring during the earliest period of entry into the institution. It certainly looked as if students came into college with a set of expectations which they were willing very rapidly to change into conformity. (pp. 3–4)

This socialization process appears to be faster for female students than for male students and tends to effect actual academic performance by shifting grades downward.

Meeting the expectations of the peer group is an important developmental factor for the new freshman. In these first few weeks of adaptation to the new residence hall environment, freshmen learn to conform to the normative modes of interaction in the living unit and to emulate roles set by their peers. These patterns of interaction or models of how to cope with this new environment are set by upperclass students in the residence halls. Coelho et al. (1968), through their research explain the experience of the freshmen in college in this way: "most students dealt with the perplexities of the new system by actively seeking information and taking cues from upperclassmen. . . . In effect, upperclassmen helped in learning new academic skills or improving standards of performance as to meet institutional demands and personal level of aspiration. . . . Upperclassmen in the residence hall may also expose the adolescent to new aspects of himself by suggesting alternative acceptable uses of time and energy. . . . By actively using upperclassmen, the adolescent is free to experiment with role images of the developing freshman" (p. 336).

Thus, the new student learns from the more experienced student how to act, what to say, and what to do. Freshmen conform to the group standard by emulating the behavior of the older and more experienced students. As these standards of behavior are set during the first few weeks, they come to form the expected role behavior within this new environment. Another way of viewing this adaptation process of conformity or patterning is to view it as "habits." People are creatures of habit and soon develop a routine of studying, eating, sleeping, and socializing at predictable times each day. Much of a successful cafeteria operation is dependent upon this routine or habit. Probably the cafeteria manager at your institution can tell you with precision when the meal hour will be the busiest, approximately what percentage of the total number of students eating in that cafeteria will eat a particular meal, and even the approximate number of servings of each entree that will be requested for a given menu combination.

Students who develop the habit of studying between certain hours every evening and in a particular location every evening will tend to continue this pattern of behavior throughout the year. Likewise, people who exercise at a particular time during the day will tend to continue this pattern of behavior as long as their schedule permits. Once the pattern is established, it becomes difficult to break.

This has some interesting implications for what you as a Resident Assistant can do during the first few weeks after the new student enters the residence hall. If the environment the student enters is one in which studying is respected and offers a supportive community of openness and trust, it is likely that this will begin to form a pattern that will serve you and your residents throughout the academic year. Programs and other activities that help integrate the floor during these first few developmental patterning weeks would be very useful. Likewise, if noisy, disruptive, and otherwise prohibited types of behavior are allowed to go unchallenged during these first few weeks, it is probable that this will establish a pattern of expected behavior and create an entirely different type of living environment.

Peer-Group Influence in the Residence Hall Environment

The single most important influence on students' development in college, upon values, career aspirations, and over-all adjustment is the peer group. The peer group sets the standards for interaction, acceptable behavior, and approval, and serves as a mirror to reflect the images that students have of themselves. It is a key factor in helping students determine who they are and what they wish to become.

Newcomb (1960) describes peer influence as second in importance only to those personality traits and background experiences that students bring with them to college. During the college years, he believes that the peer influence has the greatest impact upon the student. As Newcomb points out, "in so far as we are interested in the study of formal peer groups . . . it seems clear that they are likely to be found wherever local arrangements—of living, dining, studying, engaging in student activities—result in very frequent associations among a given group of students. Not all of those whose association with each other are frequent will necessarily be subject—and certainly not in equal degrees—to the effects of the norms that inevitably develop under such conditions, but a large proportion of those who are influenced by such norms can probably be best discovered" (pp. 12–13).

The residence hall floor is likely to form some important peer groups that will significantly influence the development of students during their college years. Coelho et al. (1968) confirm the importance of the residence hall environment through their research with college freshmen. They explain this influence as follows: "friendships in the early period were formed usually on the basis of physical proximity. They were useful, especially to freshmen going to large universities, in preparing him to meet various new socio-academic demands and to learn his way around the campus maze. They help to combat initial feelings of loneliness, to provide tension relief as students talk about their concerns together, and to give orientation to classes, teachers, types of courses, through the impromptu bull sessions that arose in the dormitory unit" (p. 338).

In the very important freshman year, with the patterns being set, the peer group takes on special importance. People living in the residence hall living unit, in close proximity, will be one of the primary influences upon an individual's first year in college. The type of interaction and the support found in the interaction with peers in this environment, and how that is facilitated by you as the Resident Assistant, can be an important step toward students' success in their first year in college.

Part of the interaction in the living unit is controlled by the physical environment. If the living unit is constructed in such a way as to form small isolated groups in the unit, chances are that smaller groups will form the initial peer groups for individuals. Chickering (1974) states it this way: "(1) the friendships and memberships in various groups or subcultures influence development, and (2) the interior design in architectural arrangements concerning placement of living units and the nature of their location in relation to one another, influence the choice of friends, the groups joined, and the diversity of persons with whom significant encounters can occur" (p. 80).

Precollege acquaintanceships, similarity of attitudes, common interests, size of the group, the homogeneity of the group membership, and the relative isolation of the group will contribute both to the formation of the peer group and to the degree of influence it has on its members. The peer group is a significant influence in the lives of new freshmen making the transition into college and will help set a pattern of behavior within the first few weeks that will greatly influence their direction during the first year in college.

Tolerance

The new freshman is described by Coons (1974) as an authoritarian personality. Freshmen tend to view situations as either right or wrong. Students who have not learned to share, to compromise, and to accept other people's views will experience interpersonal conflicts. The residence hall is one of the best places for a student to learn to be tolerant. Learning to live with others in such close proximity, to accept the necessary inconveniences of noise, regulated eating hours, and other people's annoying habits all contribute to helping the individual become more tolerant.

Tolerance is a necessary step toward maturation. Unless a person can learn to compromise, accept other people's views, and express his satisfaction or dissatisfaction with the behavior of other people, he will have difficulty moving to a level of maturity and personal identity.

Independence

As students adapt to their new environment through conformity with peer expectation, they begin to break with the world of the family and parents and enter a new world defined by their peers. The establishment of independence is a necessary step in discovering one's identity. To be independent, one must establish an identity apart from the past—an identity that is not tied to parents and high school relations, but a new identity that demands self-discovery and self-reliance.

The move for independence encompasses several different levels. First, the student must develop an identity spearate from that of his parents. As Coons (1974) explains, "if there is a typical freshman problem, it is probably the student who has become bogged down in his attempt to resolve the child-parent relationship. He will frequently complain bitterly of his overprotective, excessively involved parents who insist that he call home twice weekly and inform them of his every move" (p. 6). Though the individual undoubtedly has been testing his autonomy for some time, entry into college is often the instrumental freedom that is necessary to sever the relationship with the parents and to begin a new identity separate from that of the parents.

Powell et al., (1969) explain the cycles of this transition with parents as follows:

> Almost inescapable during the transition from high school to college is a change in perception of one's parents. It begins, generally, when parents are seen as having attributes such as usually being right, being somewhat different from other adults, and having some peculiar power and influence over one's behavior. Then uncertainties about the parents and their ideas arise—some ambiguity about how controlling or permissive they are going to be during the first year of college, some questions about dependence and independence relating to them. Parents are generally seen more and more realistically, feelings about them which were previously

suppressed find expression, and the relationship changes from that of child to parent to that of adult-to-adult. The parents are perceived more objectively and compared with parents of close friends. The student's attitude toward them moves in the direction of understanding and acceptance in spite of their failures, weaknesses, and biases, which are now more evident than before. (p. 102)

Freshman women have a much more difficult time establishing this independence or autonomy than do men. Much of this is set by the sex-roles assigned to men and women in our culture. Men are culturally expected to be more independent than are women, and they are usually given more freedom and more independence in making decisions at an earlier age. Females, on the other hand, more often are protected and sheltered by their parents, though this is changing as the role of women in our culture changes.

Lieman (1968) notes that most men and women during their four years of college are "weaned from home" and become independent. He describes this autonomy as follows: "They [students] developed greater confidence to deal with new problems, became more responsible for their own behavior, less dependent upon their peers for behavior patterns. . . . It would appear that these changes are . . . a reflection of the maturation process" (p. 385).

This new-found independence carries with it new-found freedom. No longer does the student need to report his whereabouts to parents. No longer does anyone challenge or monitor the student's behavior. Freedom, independence, and self-determination are all dropped upon the student in a relatively short period of time.

One of the most common problems you will experience with new freshmen is their reaction to this freedom. They need to test the boundaries of their freedom through trial and experimentation. Signs of this new freedom are observable. You will see it through declarations that they wish to have an apartment off-campus, a car on-campus, and other visible signs that confirm their independence. An apartment, free from almost all control, seems to be the ultimate sign of independence. When they have their own apartments, they seem to make a declaration of true autonomy and independence. An automobile is one of the earliest signs of independence a person achieves in today's culture.

Value Exploration

Students enter college with the values that they have learned through their home-lives and other experiences prior to college. While in college, students explore many values. Seeking a sense of belonging in their peer group, they explore the value systems of their peers and experiment with different beliefs and attitudes. College offers an opportunity to try out different attitudes, beliefs, and values, to experiment with them and to find those that fit and modify those that don't. This is a time when students reach out to discover what they believe. In doing so, they blend their feelings, attitudes, and beliefs into a system of values that will help guide them as they interact with the world.

In general, parental influences still prevail in the first year or so and tend to dictate the student's values in the more important areas of moral beliefs, social beliefs, and general behavioral standards. Peer influences tend to have a liberalizing influence on these values, but they have their greatest effect in more superficial areas, such as dress, dating, and politics. As Newcomb (1960) pointed out, the major influence on a student's success in college is the background the student brings with him to college. The peer influence and the tutelage that the student will receive in college, although they play an important part, are nevertheless secondary to the eighteen or nineteen years of moral and intellectual shaping and development that have taken place prior to college.

Most students have had experience in making decisions for themselves that involve an assessment of their beliefs and values, or they have found occasions in which they have had their values and beliefs challenged. These experiences force students to make decisions about why they believe the things they do. A few students, however, have not had many of these experiences, and when they are placed in a new environment, apart from the security of their parents and home-life, and are confronted by values and beliefs that clash with those that they hold, they often experience value conflicts. On the one hand, the student wants to be accepted by his peer group, wants to have their admiration and respect, wants to conform and be like the others. On the other hand, the student has been taught that many of the values that are being expressed by his peers are morally wrong. If the student is unable to justify or rationalize the difference between what he has been taught and the values being expressed by peers, the student can undergo a collapse of his value system. Coons (1974) explains it as follows:

> A student who has had no practice in listening, weighing, and discriminating may be overwhelmed. There is also the tendency to rebel against the authoritarian parents and the possibility that the whole house of cards may come tumbling down about his ears is a very real one. The total collapse of the value system is a catastrophe of major proportions. The student may cease to function both academically and interpersonally within as short a time as forty-eight hours. The anxiety is intense, and he complains vigorously of a total loss of meaning and purpose and feeling "like an empty shell of a human being." "There is no purpose to getting up in the morning, going to bed at night, attending classes, or, in fact, doing anything." (p. 11)

One of two things could result from this total collapse of the value system. First, the student may need to undergo psychological therapy and be removed from the environment until he has developed sufficient coping mechanisms to deal with the conflicts in his values. The second alternative is for the student to seek a new value system and adopt it. Such students are drawn to some of the fundamentalist religious groups, special religious or cult groups, and charismatic groups where they no longer need to make value decisions for themselves. The group prescribes what is correct and why it is correct, and it provides emotional support and a sense of belonging that reassures and reinforces the values offered by the group. Life becomes simpler, and the student is again able to function.

Social-Sexual Development

The social-sexual development of the student is the process by which the student comes to realize what it means to be a man or a woman. This is really a process by which the individual comes to establish an ego identity. Chickering (1969) describes this development as follows: "issues of sexual identification intimately interact with concerns for bodily appearance and self presentation. Discovering what it means to be a man or to be a woman, coming to terms with some of the behaviors and roles required, and developing a position consistent with one's own peculiar blend of masculinity and femininity is an absorbing and complex task" (p. 83).

Our culture has one basic stereotype for masculinity. Men are supposed to be physically strong, sexually virile, daring, independent, and have the capacity to drink great quantities of alcohol. These attributes are looked to by young males seeking their own identities as men. Much of the freshman/sophomore years is spent grappling with this issue of masculinity in an attempt to discover a suitable role-model for the individual. Professors, a father, an uncle, and often older students serve as role-models. The young man may find that he is more like the rather intellectual professor in his sociology class than the football coach. He may find this intellectual model more suitable for his particular blend of personal identity.

This process is gradual. Upon entering college, one does not start looking for role-models. The process of developing a sexual identity has started much earlier than college; however, interaction within the peer group and the new independence in the relationship with parents pushes the individual into confronting these changes in his life. At times like these, a person looks to others he would like to resemble and begins to model his behavior accordingly. Erickson (1950) explains the process in this way: "the integration now taking place in the form of ego identity is . . . more than some of the childhood identifications. It is the accrued experience of the ego's ability to integrate all identifications with the vicissitudes of the libido, with aptitudes developed out of endowment, and with the opportunities offered in social roles." (p. 261)

The relative consistency of our cultural expectations for the sex-role of men does not guarantee a long-term and easy transition into an appropriate male ego identity. Mussen, et al., (1969) describe some of the transition difficulties in this way:

> It [an extremely stereotyped masculine identification] appears less likely to lead to a diffused sense of identity than an extreme feminine identification, but it would appear that the most desirable identification is one that, while basically masculine, allows for some flexibility and avoidance of extreme stereotypes. . . . In adulthood, personality characteristics that may have developed partly as defenses among less stereotypically masculine youths in adolescence—such as, efforts to be sociable and sensitive to the interests of others, development of introspectiveness and inner-resources, and a need to probe one's self—may contribute to social and vocational success, and hence may result in increased security, socially and vocationally, and a confident adjustment. One is reminded of the "big man on campus" who never again finds the world so rewarding or compliant and who becomes an increasingly pathetic example of the "perennial sophomore"—really happy only at college or school reunions. In contrast, one recalls the "invisible undergraduates," unrecognized and, perhaps, somewhat lonely in school or college, who go on to become leaders in business, science, and the arts. (p. 692)

Among the demands placed on men in this stage of development is the rather inflexible cultural view of male sexuality. To be a man, our society defines that one must be heterosexual—not simply sexual but, specifically, heterosexual. Many young men experience a crisis because of demands placed on them to demonstrate their masculinity by having sexual relations with women. Take, as an example, a new freshmen who enters the college population for the first time in either the residence hall or in a fraternity house. He enters a situation where men are openly discussing their sexual experiences—both real and imagined—in great detail. A young man who has not achieved this level of sexual intimacy may begin to view himself in some way sexually inadequate. If he has not had these sexual experiences—as allegedly all of the other young men have, then there must be something wrong with him. Our society leaves him only one option—he must be homosexual. If a young man is more in touch with his feelings, more sensitive, and more easily given to signs of emotions, this sensitivity may lend to confirming for the student, and perhaps for others, the question of his homosexuality.

Frederick Coons (1974) writes about this dilemma of sexuality in describing the young college freshman or sophomore as follows:

> Our society plays a very dirty trick on its males by telling them that they must either be heterosexual or homosexual and they must make this choice at about age 16 or 17. The other assumption is that if one is not heterosexual, one must be homosexual whether there is any conscious awareness of sexual attraction toward the same sex. . . . The homosexual panic of the college freshman or sophomore

usually arises in such a predicament. . . . On listening to a student, one hears nothing about overt homosexual behavior, or indeed, the predominance of homosexual fantasies. . . . He may confess some mutual sexual exploration with friends during adolescence, but no behavior identifying any homosexual adaptation. One is then in a position to point out his apparent heterosexual retardation and ponder with him whether he has not confused heterosexual retardation with homosexuality. (p. 9)

Coons goes on to point out: "much of the college male's concern about homosexual feeling and behavior is a result of his confusion of intimacy and tenderness with genital sexuality. It seems that the American male is taught from birth that every time he begins to feel a warm glow and a desire for physical closeness with another person of either sex, he must have an orgasm if he is going to be a 'real man' " (p. 16).

Many young men in this period of discovering their sexuality may experience some homosexual contact. Kinsey (1953) and other studies have pointed out that homosexual experimentation and homosexual relationships are not unique and vary with both intensity and longevity. The problem is in making a number of unwarranted conclusions upon a solitary or infrequent experimentation with homosexuality and a person's sexual preferences. Chickering (1969) explains this danger as follows: "the danger is premature assumption that a homosexual affair signifies lasting homosexuality. Particularly where relationships with the opposite sex are difficult and anxiety provoking, such an experience and such an assumption may reduce still further the frequency of heterosexual contact and the possibilities for finding satisfaction in such relationships. Thus the unwarranted assumption sets in motion events which eventually make it valid" (pp. 84–85).

Female students experience virtually all forms of sexual behavior less frequently than do male students (Mussen et al. 1969). Our society allows them greater latitude in defining their sexuality and in showing their sensitivity and emotions. Women have several roles that are legitimate options from which they may choose. A woman may choose a domestic career and find this a satisfying identity relative to society's expectations. At the other extreme, a woman may feel more comfortable taking on a somewhat more businesslike orientation and find that this sex-role is viable within the confines of the image identified with the more liberated woman. Mussen et al. (1969) explains the sex-role stereotype option and resulting ego identification for women as follows: "there are more ways, even in adolescence, in which a girl can successfully establish a feminine ego identity than in the case with boys, although, not necessarily with less difficulty. For one thing, . . . the girl is permitted considerably more freedom as a child to engage in cross sex behaviors. There is also increasing evidence that the traditional feminine role is in a state of transition. This means that the girl may be exposed to conflicting social rewards and punishment" (pp. 692–93)

Women are given greater freedom in expressing emotions, sensitivity, and compassion toward one another. It is not surprising to see two female roommates cry with emotion and become very sentimental at the end of the school year. The same emotional behavior expressed by two male roommates would be viewed as unusual.

The basic needs to be comforted, held, and to express one's emotions are reserved in the male and relegated to heterosexual contacts. Dating behavior serves as the initiation for this establishment of satisfying heterosexual contacts. Initially, much of the dating relationship centers on having an appropriate personality interaction, being a "good date." Good conversation, the way one dresses, a nice personality, and other more superficial signs in the dating relationship are important in the initial stages. The dating relationship has a positive effect upon the individual's human-relations development. Specifically, it teaches such things as good interpersonal skills with members of the opposite sex; it develops social courtesies and skills; it aids in discovering more about one's own identity; it provides occasional sexual experience; and it fosters a level of intimacy that would not otherwise be available (Mussen et al. 1969).

Dating relationships, which begin in high school and seem to blossom in the first years of college, become a major influence in the person's development, self-image, and esteem. Dating relationships can be anxiety-producing situations for both men and women. Questions of physical attractiveness, personality, status, and other issues related to one's identity and image are drawn into question. Not having a date for the weekend can be a traumatic experience for both the man and the woman. Developing the self-confidence to request a date, with the possibility of being rejected, is sometimes difficult for the young man still developing his identity and self-image. Of equal difficulty for the woman is waiting to be asked for a date or not having socially acceptable means to make contact with a young man whom she would like to know better. At present, some of these stereotype roles seem to be breaking down, permitting both sexes greater latitude.

Intellectual Development

William Perry (1970) described the intellectual development of the college student as a move from what he calls basic dualism to a level where the student is able to accept a plurality of different views, interpretations, and value systems. In the initial transitional stage in college, the freshman and sophomore years, the student moves from this system of viewing things as either right or wrong to a stage in which he is able to accept a modified, dualistic view of the world.

The student comes to recognize that there is a plurality of answers and points of view and that people have a right to their own opinions, yet the plurality is nevertheless perceived as an aggregate of discreets not having an internal structure of external relation, with the implication being that no judgments among opinions can be made.

The freshman, being an authoritarian personality, has a very rigid view of things. For him absolutes do exist. There are right answers and there are wrong answers. The new freshman is more inclined to accept the right answers from his instructors based upon the authority that they have as instructors.

The student in this initial stage learns a number of other skills in this transition to college. Coelho et al. (1968) describe some of the other skills they discovered in their research with freshmen:

> the freshman year data indicate that they were able (a) to look ahead and see clearly what was expected of them so that they could organize a block of time; (b) to distinguish between primary and secondary demands on their time, subsidiating minor interests to major academic goals; (c) to study for long stretches of time without feeling bored, imposed upon, or resentful, or to recover quickly from periods of negative effect, particularly through brief rewarding contacts with peers; (d) to concentrate under difficult conditions or to rectify external conditions to improve their concentration efforts; (e) to diagnose the interest and attitude of their professors; (f) to formulate intermediate goals that were attainable within a sequence of long-range work responsibilities. Not all students showed all these abilities in extraordinary measure, but each of them was clearly revealed in some students. These tasks include: learning new academic skills and intellectual competencies required by the higher educational process; developing close and meaningful relationships, as well as productive work relations with one's peers; dealing with physical separation from one's family and regulating one's need for autonomy and relatedness to parents; extending one's heterosexual interests and feelings in preparation for courtship and marital decision. To the adolescent in transition from high school to college, these tasks are problematic. They are meaningful and ego involving, for they include what is expected of him by his peer group, the college faculty, and his parents; they also include the self expectations he has developed earlier in the course of becoming an adult. (p. 331)

Common Adjustment Problems in the Beginning Years— (Freshmen/Sophomore Years)

The transition to college makes many adjustment demands on students. Each of the following sections focuses on a common problem that freshmen and sophomores experience and offers some suggestions on how you can help with their problems.

Self-Esteem Needs

Self-esteem is generally described as the gap between one's self-image and one's self-expectations. When one moves into a new environment, one's image and expectations often change. It is important in the transition to college that the person retain a strong ego-identity and a strong sense of self-worth. One's confidence can be easily undermined in a new environment in which basic security and self-esteem needs can be challenged by peers and the threats prevalent in the new environment. Students need to feel the comfort and support of other people to reaffirm their self-worth and positive self-image. You, as an RA, can be of assistance by adding support and encouragement to students. Opening up yourself as a friend and a supportive agent could be a critical step to the student in helping him maintain a positive self-image and increase his self-concept.

Roommate Reaction

On the first day of move-in, students who have not specified a particular roommate get to meet the persons assigned to them as roommates. This can be a tense situation, particularly if the new roommate is of a different ethnic or racial background. Having parents along during this first encounter generally complicates any problem between the roommates. There might be a justification for not allowing parents into residence halls on move-in day. It has been the author's experience that students are often able to work out apparent or imagined conflicts within the first two weeks after move-in, because once the students recognize that they have many of the same interests and many of the same apprehensions, they learn to share experiences and often become friends. This, however, is not always the case. Some roommate matches are just not as agreeable as others. Sometimes the life-style differences are too divergent for the two students to reach an equitable compromise. In these cases, a roommate change will be needed. But the outside observer can only speculate as to whether or not, during the first week or two, the two individuals will reach a compromise situation.

As an RA, you can best assist in handling these situations by assuring all parties involved that the university will seek to reach a workable solution for everyone at a reasonable time after the move-in rush is completed. Undoubtedly, your university will have some policy regarding these conflicts. You can be of great assistance by knowing the policies and following the procedures that the university has outlined. Most importantly, you need to know the rationale behind the policy. Parents especially will question you on this issue. Though it is likely that they will seek out higher authorities to challenge any decision or interpretation you may make, you can lend credibility to yourself and to your superiors if students or parents approach higher authorities. Most importantly, you may lend support to students involved in the roommate reaction. Once the parents are gone, attempt to discuss the situation openly with the students. In the subsequent days, attempt to involve the students jointly in common experiences that would help them get to know one another. Athletic events, discussion groups, dining together, and other mutual experiences may reinforce their common interests and encourage the relationship.

If it is obvious that the two students are unable to get along with one another after a period of time together, it serves no purpose to have them reside together. It is disruptive to them as individuals, to their development, growth, and possibly to the living unit as a whole.

Conflicts

Roommate conflicts and interpersonal conflicts with other students in the living unit are common for freshmen and sophomores. For most students, this is the first experience they have had in living in a small group situation. Often the lack of privacy and the irresponsible acts of a few individuals come into conflict with individual needs for privacy and the basic need to retreat from the stress and congestion of college. Conflicts will arise naturally in any group situation but seem to be accentuated when groups of students are asked to live together in close proximity to one another with the primary focus of attention on themselves. This basic group intensity infringes upon a person's territorial needs and basic desire to have maximum control over his environment. As students develop greater tolerance and greater interpersonal skills in relating to other people, conflicts will be more quickly resolved among the students in the living unit. Patterns of acceptable behavior will emerge naturally from the group as group norms become established in the living unit. The conflicts that arise between roommates are usually over minor things, often reflecting an underlying interpersonal difficulty or a difference in personality types.

Academic Adjustment

Adjusting to the new academic environment with its demands for studying, more intense academic competition, and enhanced critical thinking skills is both frightening and anxiety-producing for students. The anxiety and apprehension surrounding the freshmen's first college examination can evoke a number of common anxiety-stress behaviors. Stress, frustration, fear, and questions of self-worth can manifest themselves in outward behavior to expel this anxiety. Such behavior as excessive drinking and disruptive actions are common. Other stress reactions, such as depression, panic, and avoidance are also common.

Reaction to Freedom

The search for autonomy and independence can create a reaction to this new-found freedom. Students who have not had much freedom from parents may not have sufficient experience in disciplining their own behavior and abuse this freedom. Frequently, such behavior is disruptive to the living unit and/ or personally destructive. As the RA, you can assist by maintaining a positive peer relationship. If a student expresses negative social behavior, usually other members of the living unit will discourage it. There is a high probability that, through this reaction to freedom and lack of self-discipline, the student's grades and other academic interests will suffer. This can be used as a basis for initiating counseling intervention to explore with the student his current behavior and lack of self-discipline relative to his academic goals.

Problems with Parents

Certainly the most common problem for most freshmen and many sophomores is the break in the child-parent relationship. This becomes especially difficult because many students must rely on their parents for financial support. Because students generally lack financial independence, they are subjected to at least some control by their parents. As students mature and learn to handle greater degrees of freedom they learn to respond on a more adult level to their parents. This does not mean that parents will respond likewise; parents also must learn to accept the new relationship with their children. The more protective and involved the parents are with the student, the longer this adjustment will take. Many students, however, are able to resolve this parent-child conflict by the end of the sophomore year. Some students will take longer. In either case, the resolution of this conflict is necessary to a student's growth and eventual maturity. As the RA, you may support students in establishing a more positive adult-to-adult relationship with parents by sharing with them some of your personal experiences with your parents and how you have progressed in this development.

Homesickness

Common to most freshmen is a sense of loss or feeling of "aloneness" that has been termed "homesickness". It stems from an absence of attachment within the family unit where love, belonging, support and reinforcement are abundant. A melancholy state of depression can emerge as a reaction to this sense of loss. Though most students experience some "homesickness", few students are willing to admit it. Students seem to equate homesickness with a lack of maturity and with ties to the affirmation of the child-parent relationship. Most students are able to overcome this homesickness through a short weekend visit at home or through love and support of close friends at college. Those who are unable to cope with the depression of homesickness can develop a sense of complacency about college life and may need to return home until they are emotionally ready to make the break from that familiar and secure family environment.

Extreme Introversion and Extreme Extroversion

Some students having difficulty in establishing relationships may exhibit one of two common behaviors—extreme introversion or extreme extroversion. Introversion is a common reaction from the student who has difficulty establishing relationships with peers. The simplest solution, as the student may interpret it, is simply to remove himself from the group. It is easy to do. The introverted student may keep to himself, spending much of his time away from the living unit or spending much time alone in study, watching television, or simply alone in his room. The student may be somewhat insecure and perhaps somewhat frightened about the college experience. Some students simply take longer to establish positive peer relationships. They may be somewhat shy and retiring toward the beginning of the year but soon learn sufficient skills to interact within a supportive group of peers. Some students, however, never seek this interaction, and they are hence not afforded the opportunities to learn important social skills necessary for their development and maturity. Simple things, such as how to engage others in conversation, how to tell a joke and how to participate in a group are all part of the social skills a person learns through interaction with peers. Perhaps most importantly, the student will not experience the important support that peers can offer and the important reflection of the student's image as perceived by others.

Extremely extroverted students are the other side of the coin. They wish to participate in the group so much that they try too insistently. Through their extroverted, sometimes compulsive, behavior, they force themselves upon other individuals to the extent that some groups begin to ostracize them. Often these students have what are best described as "awkward social skills," in which they do or say inappropriate things within the group. Unfortunately, the harder these students try to become part of the group, the more apprehensive the group becomes. These students can develop a reputation for being overbearing and obnoxious and are left out of many group activities. While a student may establish many contacts at the beginning of the year, as people get to know the extremely extroverted student, they move further and further away from him. As with the introverted student, the extroverted student has not learned an acceptable style of interaction within the peer group and tends to overcompensate for deficiencies.

As the RA, you are in a position to observe both types of students and to assist them in developing positive skills that will benefit them in their interactions with others. All too often, the outstretched hand of the RA is clung to permanently by students with social-skill problems who have been ostracized by the group. They come to sit in the RA's room for prolonged hours, occupying much of the RA's time and inhibiting other students from making casual contacts. Much of your free time can be consumed by these students because you are the one person who seems to care about them and who has extended a hand of friendship. By becoming their constant companion, you may not be assisting them in developing necessary social skills. Though they will undoubtedly pick up important skills through you from role-modeling behavior, their close contacts with you may be an escape from establishing more positive relationships with other people within the living unit.

In this situation, talk with the student about his interaction with other people in terms of developing appropriate social skills and interpersonal relationships. The discussion should center on alternatives and ways in which he might positively learn to interact with the group. Suggestions related to group activities, informal discussions, and similar common experiences may be shared among members of the living unit and will increase contact for these students and assist them in beginning to develop better relationships. Some of these students may need assistance from a professional staff member to assist them in acquiring the necessary skills and confidence to deal with other people. Do not be afraid to discuss the situation with your residence hall director or other professional staff members at your university.

Difficulties with the Opposite Sex

During this period of late adolescence or early adulthood students are discovering their own sexual identity. It is not uncommon for a student to experience some difficulty with the opposite sex. The college social situation places an emphasis upon dating and establishing intimate interpersonal relationships with members of the opposite sex. Part of a student's self-concept and "self-esteem" in this stage is defined by his relationships with the opposite sex. In developing relationships, students do not always have the capacity to achieve a compassionate relationship of personal intimacy, and often lack the depth and emotional vitality that they are seeking. Students may have a number of brief, unsatisfying encounters with members of the opposite sex.

As an RA, you will see much stress and anxiety about the dating relationship among the members of your living unit. Some students will be confident in themselves and will frequently have positive social interactions with members of the opposite sex. Others will consistently have difficulty establishing such contacts. These students may lack self-confidence, have a poor self-image, or have not developed good social/dating skills. Simply put, the student may not know how to meet somebody of the opposite sex or may not have occasion to meet someone of the opposite sex in a setting that would lend itself to the initiation of a date. Prescribed social roles in dating for men and women compound this situation. On the one hand, a man may be reluctant to ask a woman out for fear that she may be dating someone else or that he may not have enough money to support the type of dating relationship that he believes is appropriate. The female student may be in a worse predicament in that she may be reluctant to contact a man for a date, for fear of seeming too forward. It is socially acceptable for the cost of the date to be shared, and for the women to initiate a date by asking the man to a group social function.

You may be able to talk candidly with students experiencing difficulties in establishing social relationships. You can tell the student that deceptive tactics, witty "one-liners", and contrived schemes are often viewed as somewhat "corny". The open, honest and straightforward approach with an individual usually works best.

Fears of Homosexuality

Men in particular undergo a crisis in discovering their sexuality that often includes wondering whether or not they may be attracted to other males. Some may experiment through casual sexual contacts with other males, and some may overcompensate by continually declaring loudly and publicly how heterosexual their relationships are. Though the majority of students are able to establish a satisfying sexual identity, some students experience more anxiety in coming to grips with their own sexuality.

One view of the homosexual issue is to see the individual in terms of how satisfied the individual is with himself. People are sexual: some people are heterosexual, some are homosexual and some are bisexual. It would seem that the important thing is that a person is satisfied with his sexual identity and is comfortable with the life-style it presents. When there is a conflict between what the student believes he wants to be and what the student perceives he is, then there is a difficulty that the student must resolve usually through professional counseling. By being an understanding listener, you may help the student better understand some of the questions surrounding this issue of sexuality. If, early in the year, you begin showing bias and bigotry about homosexuals or defending your own sexual identity to students in your unit, you may lose a student who needs to talk with you.

Suicide

The difficulty of handling autonomy and independence in this new college environment may cause students to cry out for help through attention-getting devices such as suicide. In a later chapter, we discuss the issue of suicide in college. You should be particularly aware of this problem relative to the initial stage of development within the residence hall situation, though it is present among college students throughout their education.

Other Problems

Illness, family problems, financial difficulties, and general personal problems are always present among students. In today's high-pressure college environment, few students can afford to miss more than one week of classes and hope to catch up. These problems are not specific to freshman/sophomore years, but they may present special problems for students who have never had to cope with them independent of the support of their parents. Think back to the time you were first sick in college and your parents were not available to comfort you. It is rather frightening to be ill and on your own in school.

Financial problems are also frightening to new students. While at home, although you may have had certain financial constraints, you probably were never faced with worrying over whether you would have enough money to eat. The student who has irresponsibly spent his/her money in the first few weeks of the month—depending upon the cafeteria eating arrangements at your institution—may not have sufficient money to buy food for the rest of the month. Though some students may be able to borrow money or to get additional funds from their families, some students are not able to. Personal problems related to roommate conflicts, exams, a physical impairment, or having to spend a birthday alone for the first time can be a mild trauma for a new student.

All of these things and more, the student will experience in this initial stage of development. It is at this time that you as the RA are sensitive to these needs and lend your support, assistance, guidance, and experience in guiding the student through these difficult new experiences.

Middle Developmental Years—(Sophomore/Junior Years)

As students reach the end of the sophomore year and start the junior year, they should be well on their way to having defined a new relationship with their parents, established a sexual identity, and begun to examine questions of what they believe and what they value. They should have established some tolerance and the ability to interact with other members of the peer group. Intellectually, they should have begun to move into a less authoritarian frame of reference and a more open-minded acceptance of other points of view.

Students are now beginning to question what they have accomplished and what lies ahead. Most students are starting to study in their chosen major fields having completed most of the core course requirements. They have successfully been able to stay in college until this point and have learned much about existence within the system, including such things as how to register, how to select classes, and how to use the college catalog and bulletin. Students should feel somewhat more comfortable with the environment and should have established a positive peer support group of friends on whom they may rely. If they have defined no other identity for themselves than that they are "college students", they have an interim identity that will satisfy their need for the time being. High school seems far behind now, and there might even be some disdain toward those people who inquire about who they were or what they did when they were in high school. Their identity and self-concept at this point is tied to their college or university. Many students by this time have begun to single out attainable role-models in the educational community that they would like to emulate. They are more confident in their ability to cope with the new environment and more secure in what lies ahead and what they have already accomplished.

In this middle developmental period, sometime in the sophomore or the junior year, the student will experience growth in many areas and, in particular, emotional growth and growth in the maturing and clarification of their values.

Emotional Growth

As students come to understand themselves better, they increase their capability to move from responding only to their own wants and desires to accepting others in an intimate and sharing relationship. As students mature, they learn to free interpersonal relationships, enhancing their ability to share with others, and to become less self-centered and more other-centered. As Erickson (1950) explains: "what I have in mind is that late adolescent need for the kind of fusion with the essence of other people. The youth that is not sure of his identity shys away from interpersonal intimacy; but the surer he becomes of himself, the more he seeks it in the forms of friendship, combat, leadership, love, and inspiration" (p. 114).

As a person comes to feel more secure in his/her relationships with the opposite sex and as an interpersonal intimacy occurs, greater security and confidence in this relationship lessens the need for outward signs of physical affection. As Chickering (1970) points out, "although the interpersonal ties are stronger—again with persons of both sexes—they are considerably loosened and less binding. Couples do not have to walk with arms around each other or even hold hands. Public necking—that vehicle for personal declaration of attractiveness and likability—and mutually supportive commitments and assurances are no longer required. Physical intimacy plays its important part. But again, for most students the context is one of respect, commitment, and love. Sexual intercourse in the absence of such feelings is infrequent" (p. 105).

The development of this capacity for intimate contacts and a sense of loving between people carries a concomitant ability not only to love but to know how to accept love from other people. The student begins to accept other people in a common union of understanding and mutual commitment. People become more secure about releasing more intimate and personal information about themselves. The student learns to share his own life and experiences, desires, needs, wants, and frustrations with others in a union of caring and emotional support.

This period of emotional development takes time. The person moves from a level of self-commitment and self-exploration to a new level of personal acceptance and need for sharing and union with another person. This state of intimacy is not an absolute, but a period of growth that often leads to marital plans.

Value Clarification and Identification

By this time the student has identified many attitudes, beliefs, and values that he has either defended, questioned, abandoned, or has more often than not been confused. In this period from the sophomore to the junior year, the student will attempt to find a resolution to some of these value questions, sorting out what he believes in and why. Vital issues of the day and questions about drugs, sex, religion, and politics take on increased importance in the late-night discussion groups as students attempt to sort out how they feel about given issues. Lehmann's study (1968) using instruments measuring beliefs, values, and dogmatism suggests that this period between the sophomore and the end of the junior year is a critical time in value changes and adjustment. Feldman and Newcomb's (1969) study confirmed this change in values from a conservative, authoritarian position to increased liberalism to an eventual melding of the two into a value system similar to that of the parents—with the important differences that by this time students have internalized the value system as their own. Though students emerge with a value system somewhat more liberal than that of their parents (Astin 1978), overall it tends to be most similar to their parents values.

In this period, the student is attempting both to sort out and to integrate an internally consistent value system that will serve as the basis of an ethical system of personal integrity that in later life will dictate his interaction in the world. Very closely tied to this is the person's intellectual development and an increase in his critical thinking ability.

Intellectual Development

As the student moves into this middle stage of development, he moves toward making a conscious act of commitment to certain values based upon the affirmation of these values in a world recognized as relativistic. The student's ability to analyze and define problems, recognize important unstated assumptions, and draw valid conclusions is enhanced in this stage of development.

The student may become increasingly motivated by having the opportunity to explore areas of interest within his chosen academic major. By this time the student should have learned to balance academic demands with the personal demands placed upon his time. In essence, the person has learned to function within the academic community in sufficient capacity to attain acceptable academic standards and maintain other personal needs.

Common Adjustment Problems in the Middle Years— (Sophomore/Junior Years)

Intimacy

The need to be loved and to love is an important factor in human relationships for the student in this middle stage of development. Problems that students often experience will be those of intimacy. The student may experience great emotional trauma as a result of a break in relationships with the opposite sex or peers, or a sense of loss in the absence of such contacts. Breaking up with a boyfriend or girlfriend seems to be quite prevalent in this stage of development. It takes on new and increased meaning, however, when one's innermost feelings seem to have been betrayed by the rejection of the opposite sex peer. Often, where the relationship had been satisfying at a particular interpersonal level, as the two students mature, one may find the relationship less fulfilling and meaningful than the other person. This leads to conflict, and often a break between the two individuals.

As an RA, you will no doubt see many students experiencing these feelings of rejection. When the student is closely tied to another student by feelings of emotion, intimacy, and compassion, the break in this relationship can sever much of the student's self-esteem, and security. The loss and feeling of rejection can become all-consuming. It can, for all practical purposes, halt the forward progress of the individual and bring the person into an emotional crisis that may impede his functioning. Common behavior that is manifest in these situations includes such things as failure to attend classes, lethargic attitude about life, feelings of depression, feelings of loneliness, despair, frustration and abandonment, and often feelings of revenge and hatred in reaction to what the sufferer perceives the other person has done to him.

Your contact with the student in a counseling relationship, discussed in the next chapter, may be the only assistance you can offer outside of referring him for counseling from a member of the professional staff. It is important for you not to become an intermediary between the two parties. You will soon find this role an untenable position in which you can become locked into the center of the controversy. You can be of the greatest assistance to the student by remaining objective, not taking sides, and helping the student think through the situation. Offer empathy but not pity. Offer support but not advice. And be very careful about agreeing with a negative appraisal of the other individual, no matter what your personal feelings are. Remember that the person did care for that individual at one time or he would not be so hurt by his friend's absence.

Value Conflicts

Students experiment with a number of different values, attitudes, and beliefs during this period of development. Hair length and life-style vary as the student tries on different roles from conservative to liberal. Style of dress, length of hair, and rebellious or activist expressions are evident. Religious conversion and a sense of disorientation and confusion about beliefs may exist. As mentioned in the discussion of the initial stage (freshman/sophomore year), the student may experience in this value conflict a total collapse of his value system. As Coons (1974) pointed out, this may manifest itself through either a total collapse, in which the student may cease to function, or it may eventually culminate in the identification with a total value system, such as is found in some fundamentalist religious groups or some cult groups.

Sophomore Slump

Somewhere toward the end of the sophomore year, many students experience what is sometimes called a "sophomore slump." This is best described as a sense of depression or a questioning of some primary values about being in college. With approximately two years of college behind them and at least two more years of college ahead, many students begin questioning the basic worth of their education and what they wish to accomplish in life. One of the primary questions for many sophomores at this halfway point centers on the utility and application of material that they have already learned. They question what worth some of the information they have acquired has, and at the same time feel greater independence and self-confidence to meet new challenges. For those students who are uncertain about completing college, this is a time of reappraisal and reevaluation as to what degree the college environment—now that it is no longer a mystery—meets their needs in life.

Students usually resolve many of these questions themselves. As an RA, you must be careful not to put yourself in a position of attempting to sell any one point of view. Often the RA believes he is doing a student a service by attempting to convince him that he ought to stay in college, when what might really be best for that particular student is to experience some things outside of college for a time. Often students "stop out" of college for a year or so after their sophomore year in order to experience other aspects of life. Many return; others find greater satisfaction in life outside of college. The important thing is that the student be able to work through some of these issues for himself. As an RA, you may help the student define the problem and assist him in the decision-making process without giving advice about what he should not do.

The Apartment Quest

Many colleges and universities have what is called a two-year parietal policy that requires students to stay in residence halls for the freshman and sophomore years—or until they achieve a given number of academic credits. There are two prevalent philosophies supporting this two-year parietal rule. One philosophy contends that at least two years of residential learning provides the basic foundation for social skills and other important developmental skills for the greatest majority of students. A second philosophy maintains that the greatest learning of these social/developmental skills takes place in the freshman year and in part takes place through interaction with upperclassmen, such as sophomores. In short, the sophomores role-model appropriate behavior for the incoming freshmen, who in turn pass it on the following year to the freshmen. Thus, the retention of the sophomores in the residence halls becomes a way of transmitting the positive developmental environment from one generation of college students to the next, even though when looking at returning sophomores one often wonders.

In either case, by the end of the sophomore year many students are seriously considering a move from the residence halls into apartments—that is at institutions where such off-campus living is permitted. Though students undoubtedly justify their move by blaming the food in the cafeteria, the fact that they cannot study in the residence hall, or the assumption that it is less expensive to live in an apartment than it is to live in the residence halls, the underlying issue is really an extension of independence and automony separate from the control and supervision of any authority. There is nothing that seems a more outward sign of independence and autonomy than having one's own apartment. It presents a new freedom, a new life-style, and a new experience that heretofore the student could not claim. In the opinion of the authors, for most students, it is probably a useful step in their development. It offers them a new experience and demands of them the development of some new skills in working with other people in the apartment and meeting the demands of the outside world including such things as paying utility and telephone bills, purchasing food, cooking for, and cleaning for themselves.

The one thing that may help retain the student in the residence halls, if that is what he wants, is a need for a sense of community or a sense of belonging that he may have found in the living unit. Students who have enjoyed the experience of associating with other members of the living unit may envision the same type of interpersonal community environment the following year. If this is strong enough, they may choose to stay in the residence hall. Like most other things, it must be an individual decision. If the student has made up his mind to move off-campus, your greatest assistance may be in helping him identify possible off-campus living arrangements. You may wish to invite someone to speak at a floor meeting about apartment living and fending for oneself during the spring semester when most students begin their apartment search. Consumer protection agencies, the student ombudsman' office, a student government committee, or dean of students office personnel who work with off-campus living might be good resource persons to invite for a program. There are, after all, important things that a student should know about contracts, leases, damage deposits, subleasing, pets, utilities, vacations, and landlords.

Ending Years of Development in College—(Junior/Senior Years)

As the student completes his junior year and begins his senior year, he should be in the stage approaching what Levinson (1978) describes as "early adulthood". At this point in a person's life, he should begin to feel pretty comfortable with himself and be on his way to clarifying his values, be accepting a personally comfortable sex-role, have established an adult-to-adult relationship with his parents, be on his way to sharing intimate feelings in an unselfish and compassionate way, and have developed tolerance and acceptance of different life-styles. Intellectually, the student should begin to relate to the world around him in relative terms. The student's critical thinking and analytical abilities ability for handling complex questions and abstract thinking should all have increased. Most students by this time are absorbed in their academic work, which most find intellectually stimulating. This is really a period when much of the student's "search for identity" is solidified or consolidated relative to the college experience. The end of four or five years of college by no means heralds the end of the search for identity. People continually discover new things about themselves and continue to learn and grow throughout their entire lives. The period of adolescence and early adulthood is really a time when people come to grips with who they are. To establish an identity is not an end in itself but a process in self discovery that seems to be most heavily concentrated in adolescence and the early adult years.

Career and Life Planning

Much of the solidification period in college in the latter part of the junior year and throughout the senior year is concerned with the selection of a career and life work. Students often enter college with a concept of what they believe they would like to do and use college as an opportunity to refine their general interests into a specific career orientation. During the latter part of the junior year and into the beginning of the senior year, the student has generally entered a major field of study and further defines or narrows his occupational interests. Students can see the world of work looming only a short time away, and a degree of career anxiety and feelings of vocational expediency grip many students with a sense of fear, apprehension, and anxiety. This career anxiety or career exploration and vocational direction do not suddenly emerge in this stage of development. There is a pattern that Super et al. (1957, 1963) suggest occurs as early as age fourteen and continues until around the age of twenty-five. This period of exploration within vocational interests that Super describes follows a six-step pattern of development as follows:

1. Crystalization of a vocational preference.
2. Specifying a vocational preference.
3. Implementation of the preference.
4. Stabilization in the chosen vocation.
5. Consolidation of one's status within the vocation.
6. Advancing in the occupation.

The first three of these generally occur in college. The trauma of the senior year is the trauma often associated with implementing the vocational preference. Miller and Prince (1976) describe this maturing of career and vocational plans as follows: "Career planning includes examining the world of work, understanding the abilities, interests, and values that are needed in various occupations, synthesizing facts and knowledge about oneself and the world of work, and committing oneself to the career and beginning to implement a vocational decision. Finally, a plan for the future that balances vocational aspirations, a vocational interest, and family concerns must be developed along with a sense of direction to identify next steps and make a tentative commitment to future plans" (p. 13).

The careers and vocations that people select are based upon a combination of many factors. One of the recent motivating factors has been the job market. Colleges and universities experienced an increase in the number of students interested in the sciences and engineering when the job market called for more engineers and scientists. A similar increase in the number of students entering the field of education occurred when there was a shortage of teachers in the occupational market. In the later 1970's, the interest seemed to be in accounting and functions related to management and business. The job market, then, plays an important role in helping someone select an occupation. However, of equal importance is how the person feels about himself and what he thinks he can accomplish. It is unlikely that persons who see themselves as shy and retiring will view themselves in an aggressive occupation such as sales and marketing. People come to make decisions about their vocations on the basis of many factors, including their self-perceptions, the availability of jobs, their status needs, other people's expectations of them, and previous role-models with which they have identified.

Many students enter college with the impression that college is primarily designed to teach a vocation or occupation. As the student experiences college, he quickly comes to recognize that the intent of college is not to train one for a specific occupation, but to provide opportunities for the individual to develop both mentally and personally. Lehmann (1968) found in his research that a proportionally larger number of seniors, in comparison to their views as freshmen, no longer believed that the major aim of college was to prepare them for a vocation, but that students should be provided with a liberal education.

As an RA and a student yourself, you are no doubt aware of the frequency with which students change careers. Astin (1977) confirms this as follows: "A substantial literature on career development during the undergraduate years indicates that students frequently change their plans after they enter college. . . . These changes are more systematic than random; students who change majors or career plans usually change to related fields. Fields differ markedly in their retention and recruitment of students, with business and law generally showing the greatest gains and science and engineering the greatest losses in the undergraduate years" (p. 135).

Astin, reporting on a study conducted in 1974, found that ten major career fields—business, college teaching, engineering, homemaking, law, medicine, nursing, school teaching, scientific research, and social work—account for approximately 64 percent of the career interests of undergraduate students, excluding those students who have undecided majors. It should be noted that one of the primary influences upon the career a person chooses is sex. Men have a tendency to move into the more traditional male occupations associated with law, engineering, medicine, and the sciences, and to move away from the more traditionally feminine fields such as school teaching. Women similarly have moved from the more masculine fields, such as law and medicine, into more traditionally feminine occupational roles (Astin 1977), although recent trends show more women moving into occupations historically dominated by men.

Values

From the freshman to the sophomore year, the student moves from values of idealism to values of increasing realism. As the students' experience increase, they gain a better perspective and recognize the limiting variables in resolving complex issues. This might be described as a period of learning to accept the world around them with an increasingly realistic perspective. Astin (1977) suggests that this increasing realism in students' value patterns may be somewhat impeded by the college experience in certain areas such as status needs, which "decline markedly after college but which decline substantially less among persisters and among students heavily involved in academic pursuits or in campus life" (p. 54).

This increasing sense of realism is also reflected in a decrease of rigid, inflexible views of issues and the world around them. Lehmann (1968) found in his study comparing the effects of college over a four-year period, that students became more flexible, less rigid, and less authoritarian during their four years in college.

It is on the basis of developing this valid set of attitudes, beliefs, and values that the student acquires an internally consistent set of values. An emergence of this personal integrity or sense of moral and ethical reasoning develops over a period of time in an invariant sequence of developmental steps (Kolberg 1970).

Acceptance of an adult role is beginning to emerge in the student in the latter part of the junior year and throughout the senior year. Levinson (1978) describes this transitional period as a period of entering the adult world. It involves a number of basic processes: exploration of self and world, making and testing provisional choices (cautiously or with a great enthusiasm which masks their provisional quality), searching for alternatives, increasing one's commitments and constructing a more integrated life structure. This period usually begins about the age of twenty-two. It lasts about six years—never more than eight or less than four—and ends at twenty-eight or twenty-nine (Levinson 1978).

Intellectual Development

By this time, most of the student's critical thinking and analytical abilities have been developed. It is a commonly held belief that most people's intellectual capabilities reach a peak somewhere between the ages of eighteen and twenty-five. Tony Buzan (1976) states it this way: "It is normally assumed that IQ scores, recall ability, ability to see special relationships, perceptual speed, speed of judgment, induction, figural relations, associative memory, intellectual level, intellectual speed, semantic relations, formal reasoning and general reasoning, etc., etc., decline after reaching a peak at the age of eighteen to twenty-five" (p. 58). Buzan attributes much of this decline in mental ability to the failure of the current educational system to help people understand the process of learning—where the "mind [is] continually used and its capacities expanded" (p. 60).

Intellectually the student should be at the point where he begins making commitments to values based upon a relativistic view of the world. The internal consistency of these values and the commitment to them conforms to what Chickering (1968) describes as integrity. It is on the basis of this personal integrity, or clarified internally consistent value system, that people form the ethical basis on which they relate to others, reason, and make decisions.

Common Adjustment Problems in the Ending Years—
(Junior/Senior Years)

As you might expect, most of the adjustment difficulties associated with the latter part of the junior year and the senior year revolve around career decisions and career anxiety. The person is being presented with what for most could be described as a threat to their basic security and basic identity. After all, for many students, their entire lives during the previous three or four years have revolved around the university community. A student's identity is tied very much to being part of the collegiate environment. In the past four years, the student has come to know the environment, to depend upon the environment, to identify himself in terms of the category (college student), and to develop a sense of security within that community. Now the student is presented with a threat to his basic security. Within a period of a few months, the student will be in some new location or environment.

Often the student tends to view his entire success or failure in college relative to his ability to find a place in a particular occupation. This can become especially threatening for an arts and science major who perhaps was more interested in acquiring a liberal education than in pursuing a specific vocational interest. Fears of getting into graduate school—especially law school and medical programs—tend to raise the stress and anxiety among senior classes. Students in other fields opting for a limited number of positions in business management and related areas may become very competitive. Reports abound of students violating university procedures in the placement office to assure a scheduled appointment with a favored firm. The anxiety preceding and following interviews can create very real stress. As you know from your own experience, people have a tendency to relieve this stress and anxiety through heightened reactions to situations and people. Interpersonal relations among people in these stressed and strained situations can be aggressive, competitive, and difficult.

Career Decisions

Students who, for a long time, have delayed the inevitable choice of what they are going to do after college are now faced with that decision. The student who has always wanted to become an advertising agency executive finds that most of the jobs in marketing are actually in basic sales positions. The student who wanted to go into medicine finds that the medical school he was interested in rejected his application and instead he opts for dentistry. Much of their image and career aspirations and hopes and dreams seem to culminate for many students in the junior and senior years.

Job Anxiety

Job anxiety is an extension of career decision problems. The anxiety is centered around pending decisions of other people. Will a student be offered a job with a particular company or be accepted in graduate school with an assistantship? Or will he need to take a job of lower status or attend a graduate school of lower status? Job anxiety mounts even for students who have been offered positions or graduate assistantships at their chosen institution. Often they are reluctant to accept these, hoping that something better will come along. The anxiety, stress, and tension mount as the year progresses and the jobs appear to be fewer and fewer. The news media often carry stories about how many college students will be out of work this year; at the same time, one begins to hear about friends who have acquired responsible positions. This is a difficult and stressful time for all. Many students are gripped with a type of panic that affects other students as the anxiety of one student feeds off the anxiety of others.

Fear of the Adult World

Most students who are completing college find their college experience generally satisfying. They recall with nostalgia their freshman days, their first date, and memorable moments on campus. After all, for the past four years much of their lives have been directly related to the campus environment. It has been their home. They feel warm and comfortable and very good about the college environment as a whole. They may question different aspects of their education, disdain the administration, and curse some of their instructors, but most will look upon their time in college with very fond memories. The student begins experiencing a sense of loss in leaving this comfortable, warm environment and may experience apprehension about his future. Many will suddenly be plunged into entirely new situations that will challenge and test them in new ways. Some students may feel a sense of relief in finally leaving, but most will feel a sense of loss as they depart from close friends and recall their college experiences.

Self-confidence

The anxiety, stress, and emotional involvement in departing from college can attack a person's self-confidence. The student's self-image, self-esteem, and status needs as well as other people's expectations of him all seem to come together at one time. If the student has had many positive, reinforcing strokes from interviews and friends, this may have a tendency to accentuate his self-confidence and encourage him to go beyond. Often, however, the opposite is true. The student may have one or two very stressful job interviews, parents are calling with questions about what he will do after college, relatives and friends have expectations of the student's success and the student has expectations of what he should be able to do. His self-confidence is laid on the line. If the self-confidence is overly attacked, the student may retreat from certain situations and question his own self-worth. Depression often sets in. Students in this period need emotional support to make it through some very anxious situations.

Security Needs

Because students are moving away from the environment that they have been a part of for so long, the security they felt in that environment is also being taken away. There is a basic fear or apprehension of the unknown. Questions of identity, autonomy, dependency on parents, and financial independence all come to bear as the student looks to what lies ahead. What if the student will not be able to locate a job right after college? What does this mean for the student? Will the student need to rely on his parents for financial support? If the student does rely on his parents, what will this be saying about the student's independence, and what will this say about how the parents perceive the student's success or failure in college? All of these questions confront the person on a continual basis and threaten his basic security. When security needs are threatened, other higher-order developmental needs go unfulfilled as the person attempts to ensure his future.

Marital Plans

Many students plan marriage immediately after college. Much of a person's emotional dependency and security is tied to completion in this area. A traditional pattern for men and women is to get married and start a family. The anxiety surrounding the decision to get married, compounded by the job experience, compounded by the probability of relocating, plus general difficulties in completing the senior year in college and successfully graduating can unduly complicate an individual's life to the extent that professional intervention/counseling is needed. Commitments, plans, expectations, and a myriad of other tasks all seem to need to be completed at one time. The graduating senior faces many decisions. It is a real trial of his emotional stability and coping mechanisms.

General

Because so much of a person's identity and self-image are tied up in successes and failures during this period of time, it is evident that this is a high anxiety and stress producing period for the seniors. Stress and anxiety are self-perpetuating. When one or two individuals in a group become stressed and anxious, they often release this stress and anxiety toward other people. Thus stress and anxiety can become contagious and trigger similar feelings in other people. As an RA, you need to be cognizant of the pressure that is confronting the juniors and seniors and to make yourself available to them for emotional support as well as for counseling. You have to be careful in assessing when it is appropriate for you to inquire about the professional and other decisions that may be confronting them at that particular point in their lives. Often merely asking questions can produce heightened anxiety. Having to disclose to other people that one may not have been as successful in job placement activities as they would have liked is difficult for many people.

Perhaps the best things that you can do are to make yourself available for assistance when students need it and to show your concern and interest. Make these students aware of the counseling opportunities on campus and of any career-planning and placement workshops that may be available to assist them with some of these decisions. They will need your support and friendship and your positive reinforcement during this time of stress and anxiety.

As an RA, you need to be aware that you too will experience some of these same anxieties and crises as you move into your senior year. You will find that your interest and maturity level exceed those of many of the students in your living unit. So it may be very easy to lose patience and become intolerant of certain activities. Be careful not to take your anxieties and tensions out on the students in your unit. You will need to find some personal coping mechanisms and support within your peer group to assist you with the decisions and frustrations that may be confronting you throughout the year. Some schools do not permit graduating seniors to assume the position of RA for this very reason. The best way to decrease anxiety about job placement and other related graduation plans is to plan early. Put together a résumé, contact the placement office, and do your job search and review early. These things will help ensure some confidence for yourself as you approach job interview situations. As other people's anxiety mounts, you will be able to maintain confidence in your preparation and will have a "jump" on many late starters.

CHAPTER 6
Peer Counseling

Many RAs join a residence hall staff expecting that they will become full-time counselors. There are a few hall directors who also believe this.

RAs do some counseling in the form of active listening. They do some advising in the form of providing information, and they do some referral counseling to help students seek assistance from a professional counselor or psychologist. RAs do not do psychological analysis or clinical counseling, and it is unfortunate that many psychology majors view this helping relationship as an opportunity to try out their ability to diagnose and assist troubled students. The skills necessary to do this take many years to develop, and no RA is expected to do it—nor should attempt it.

The RA is best viewed as a peer counselor, a helper, or a good, skilled listener and facilitator. Many of the skills needed to perform this counseling role cannot be taught in the short time that most students remain in the RA position. For this reason, RAs should be chosen particularly on the basis of their human relations skills. Sensitivity toward others, an ability to work in groups, a positive, accepting personality, and a desire to help others are the qualities needed to fulfill the counseling responsibility. Every RA must have these qualities to some degree. You can teach a person the operational procedures needed to manage the residence hall, to report emergencies, or to apply first aid, but in the short time that a person holds the RA position, you cannot teach her to develop a personality that makes other students want to know her and the sensitivity to work compassionately with another student in a time of emotional crisis.

If you did not possess these qualities, in all likelihood you would not have been chosen as an RA. However, having these qualities is not enough. The key is knowing how to transform these qualities into skills. This chapter will help you to do that by providing you with some techniques, some strategies, a counseling model, and a number of tips.

Complaints about Counseling

The most common complaints heard from RAs about counseling are: (1) most of the student contacts the RA has are for relatively trivial, routine things like unlocking doors or asking students to turn down their stereos; (2) they are not always certain when they are counseling a student and when they are simply having a good discussion; and (3) they are given too much theory and not enough practical information. These complaints are supportable. Let us start by looking at the first complaint.

Most of the requests that an RA receives are for routine things, like opening doors or a request for information. Nevertheless, these requests are important. How you handle them can either demonstrate to the student that you are willing to assist or that you would prefer not to be bothered. It would be easy for the student to assume that if you are too busy to help with little things, you are too busy to help with something major. It comes down to establishing a basis for trust and confidence. You must demonstrate to students in your living unit that you are interested in them as individuals. If you fail to do this, it is unlikely that you will have students interested in seeking you out for any assistance.

Though it is not really very important to define the specifics of a counseling contact as it differs from a discussion, many RAs seem to need to establish some clear parameters for their own peace of mind. For our purposes, we shall define a counseling encounter as an act of helping another person cope with an emotion, a personal problem, stress, or a crisis by assisting her in decision-making and helping to return the person to an improved emotional state. These counseling contacts will come from one of three sources: (1) the student will initiate the contact; (2) you will observe behavior in a student that indicates the need for some form of counseling intervention; or (3) a resident of your living unit or another staff person will inform you of behavior that indicates the need for counseling intervention.

The third complaint heard from RAs is that they are given too much theory and not enough practical application. A modification of this complaint is that the techniques they have been taught are superficial, simplistic, and artificial. Some of this is no doubt true. It is difficult to teach people how to transform personal qualities into skills until they have some basic understanding of exactly what it is they need to do. On the other hand, a review of major counseling theories and counseling approaches is best reserved for those who are interested in counseling as a profession. It is easy to become bogged down with conflicting theories and schools of thought on counseling; yet, there needs to be a pattern or model to follow.

The helping-skills or counseling model we will use is composed of three phases. The first phase is to become aware of your own feelings, motivations, values, strengths, and weaknesses in preparing yourself to help others. The second phase is to establish yourself with the residents in your living unit in a way that will encourage students to seek you out for your assistance with their personal problems. The third phase is a five-step helping-skills model. In the last two sections of the chapter, the model is modified to suggest a method for giving advice and for making a referral for professional counseling.

Helping Skills: An Overview

Most of the problems that a student experiences in college are common problems that reflect maturation, adjustment to a new environment, and the stress brought on by the college experience. Few of these require the assistance of a professional counselor. General depression, anxiety, stress, disappointment, rejection, and the feeling of loss brought on by the death of a friend or relative are the kinds of feelings that you, as an RA with skills in helping, should be capable of handling. These problems will be brought on by many of the same experiences that you have had. Whether a problem stems from a feeling of personal inadequacy, difficulty with class assignments, problems with parents, money, or a member of the opposite sex, it can usually be discussed and some methods of coping with it or possibly resolving it can be uncovered.

Most problems that students experience can be worked out alone or with the help of a friend. Simply talking over the problem with another person can be all the help needed. There is something special, a type of emotional catharsis, in sharing a problem with another person; it is almost as though one no longer carries the burden alone. The sympathy and understanding that another person expresses can usually help a troubled individual cope with the problem.

At the same time, you should realize that not all students in your living unit who may experience deep emotional stress or conflict resolve it by themselves. Though individually you may never be confronted by a student who is contemplating his/her own death, the probability that this will occur in your unit is higher than you may realize. It is quite probable that one of your residents will experience some type of serious emotional problem during the year as a result of breaking up with a boyfriend or a girlfriend. Your ability to respond to these situations may be crucial to the student's ability to function. Many of the skills you develop through your RA training will be used daily. Some, however, are really preparation for the one or perhaps two times that you may be called upon for some serious counseling during the year. These one or two times might make the difference between life and death for the student involved.

Preparing Yourself to Help

Confidence

The very nature of the helping relationship in counseling places you in a position of authority. The student comes to you seeking assistance with a problem. Many undergraduate RAs, not having previously been exposed to this degree of responsibility, feel a sense of ambiguity. They lack the basic self-confidence to enter into an exchange with the student for fear that they may say or do something that will make the student's situation worse.

This is a reasonable reaction but, for the most part, unfounded. There is very little that you, as a reasonably prudent RA, could say that would do irreparable harm to the student. Most of the situations that you will encounter will be situations within your frame of reference. The types of problems that students experience in college are similar to the types of problems that people experience in all walks of life; most of them are not unique, special, or overly serious. It is important that you keep a perspective on these things, recognizing that by virtue of your position and training, students have confidence in you. However, there will be situations that you may encounter during the year for which you will not have the necessary skills. As you come to recognize your ability to help students, you must also recognize your limitations. Later in the chapter we shall discuss conditions under which you should seek the support of a professional counselor in making a counseling referral. For now, remember that you can help students most of the time. In situations in which you are uncertain, ask the hall director for guidance.

Attitudes, Beliefs, and Values

As an RA, you are in a position to influence the attitudes, beliefs, and values of a number of students during a time in their lives when they are discovering their values. This in itself is a heavy responsibility. In a counseling encounter, the influence is magnified by virtue of the counseling relationship, in which you are viewed as a person with the ability to help. It is for these reasons that you must accept one of the basic canons of counseling—do not judge other people's values by your own.

At most institutions, RAs are selected because they have certain personal skills, motivations, and values that coincide with the institution's approach to working with students in residence halls. Except in the case of some religiously affiliated institutions, RAs are not chosen to teach beliefs or values. Though the RA may reflect her values in her day-to-day interactions with students, she generally does not have the responsibility to promote a particular set of beliefs.

To enter into a helping relationship with a student, you must first become aware of what you believe, not superficially, but what you *really* believe. Issues such as sex, religion, politics, interracial dating, and similar topics will confront you in many forms through your contacts with students. If you do not approve of interracial dating or perhaps premarital intercourse, you are entitled to these beliefs, just as the students in your living unit are entitled to theirs. When a student comes to you for counseling, she is not coming to you to have you judge her behavior by your own standards. She is coming to you to receive help with a problem. Let us take an example.

A woman in your living unit becomes pregnant and believes she wants an abortion. You personally find abortion unacceptable. How can you best help her? Will it help her to have you condemn her for what she is contemplating or for you to try to prevent the abortion? You have two choices. First, you could try to remain as objective as possible and facilitate the student's own decision-making process, helping her consider the choices available to her and their ramifications. Or, second, you could tell the woman that you personally have some very strong feelings about this decision, and refer her to a person who could be more objective.

Either of these approaches is acceptable. Sometimes we have such strong feelings about a particular topic that we cannot be objective. We sometimes cannot free ourselves from values that judge the right or wrong of other people's actions. In these situations, our only option is to be open about our feelings and tell the person that we cannot be objective enough to help with the decision.

The counseling relationship should be as value-free as possible. You can never free yourself from your values, but you can refrain from expressing them and judging others by them.

It is not always easy to remain nonjudgmental. Sometimes we think we are helping people when we are actually attempting to push our view of the world and what we value them. Perhaps the classic example of this is presented in a counseling encounter with a student who is contemplating resigning from school. When the student seeks out the RA to discuss the issue, the RA takes the position of trying to convince the student to stay in school. This position is based upon the premise that it is better to attend college than not to attend college and that it is bad to drop out. This may or may not be true. Undoubtedly, the RA sets out upon a well-intentioned quest to help the student stay in college. The person who should be making this decision and who should be in the midst of the evaluation is the student, not the RA. Not only is it presumptuous of the RA to assume that she is more capable of determining what is best for the student, but it places the RA in the position of assuming responsibility for the actions of the other person.

If you are to help other students with their personal problems, you must know yourself and know what you believe and how strongly you feel about these beliefs. Becoming aware of yourself is a continual process and may require you to participate in some self-discovery workshops with other staff members and students. Once you know what you believe, you can work to control these beliefs in your counseling encounters.

Motivation

What is the motivation to help another person with a personal problem? Ideally, it is associated with a basic sensitivity to others, the desire to alleviate suffering in others, and perhaps the knowledge that the other person trusts you enough to share his/her problem. Thus, there are rewards. It is ego-satisfying to help others with their problems and to have the knowledge that they wished to share something of themselves with you.

It can also be addictive. Often RAs find that they want to help so much that they come to assume responsibility for trying to solve the student's problem. They cross the line between helping the student make her own choices and telling the student what they believe the student should do.

The helping role of the counselor is primarily one of an understanding, often sympathetic, facilitator of the student's own ideas. Many times you will feel as though you could simply dispense your wisdom on the particular topic and resolve the student's problem. Seldom will this be acceptable.

It is easy for an inexperienced RA to confuse the role of counselor with that of problem solver. There is much ego satisfaction in resolving other people's problems. In the long run, however, this is not an effective method of helping a troubled student, who is left with the solution to a particular problem and not the necessary skills to resolve similar problems in the future. One of your goals as a counselor must be to help students develop these skills for themselves. If they do not, they will contact you with every problem that arises. Though some RAs may find that this enhances their personal esteem, it does not best serve the students' personal development.

Remember, it is always simpler to give advice than to stimulate ideas in others. If you find yourself falling into the role of guru, consider who is receiving the most benefit from the relationship—you or the students.

Objectivity

There are many demands placed on your time as an RA. If you are well liked and trusted by your residents, they will bring you a number of their problems. People who are sensitive to the needs of others are also susceptible to falling into the trap of accepting other people's problems as their own. If you are going to remain a viable resource for the students in your hall, you must remain objective and retain some degree of emotional detachment. You can never accept responsibility for someone else's problem or someone else's decision. It is the student's responsibility to resolve the problem, not yours. Most people do not have enough time or emotional fortitude to accept responsibility for the problems and actions of an entire living unit of college students. You will be of help to your residents only so long as you can be objective and assist them with their own decision-making.

Conclusion

Think about these questions carefully before you enter into a counseling relationship with a student. It is important that you understand yourself, your strengths and limitations, your values, and your motivations. Recognize that you are capable of helping students with most of their problems, but that you should not try to solve the students' problems for them. Help them work through their own problems, recognizing that not all problems have a solution. You will be of help only so long as you retain some emotional distance from the problem.

Establishing Yourself with Your Residents

No matter how well you have prepared yourself to help students with their problems, unless students are willing to discuss their concerns with you, you may not have an opportunity to use those skills. The opinion that your residents have of you is important to your success in counseling. If they view you as a person solely concerned with the enforcement of college policies, concerned only about yourself and your friends, or concerned only with the prestige and authority of the RA position, this will effect their willingness to share their concerns with you.

First Impressions and the Start of School

What happens during the first few days of the academic term can be critical in establishing yourself with your residents. The first impression you make upon your new residents will have a lingering effect; it will either lay the foundation for further contacts or create barriers to them. Some RAs begin this process during the summer, before the school year, by contacting each of their residents by mail. Though this is a time-consuming process if you have responsibility for a large living unit, the early expression of concern may pay off in improved relationships later.

Make an aggressive attempt to contact your residents as they arrive. Within the first week, you should have met and learned something about each resident. Many RAs make a list of the residents' names and room numbers on a floor diagram and keep it with them until they have committed it to memory. The list can also be used as a check to ensure that you have met each of the residents. By the time of the first floor meeting, you should have met and talked with each person in your unit, if only briefly.

In the following few weeks, you should make a point to stop at each student's room for a few minutes to become more familiar with them. People like to talk about themselves and what they do. Share things about yourself. Tell them about your hobbies, your interests, your college major, and anything else that makes you seem more like a person.

Part of what you do in establishing yourself is to develop a sense of belonging among the members of your floor. You do this by finding ways for people in your living unit to interact. Dinner is always a good opportunity to have a group of your residents get to know one another. Make certain, especially during the first few weeks, that you invite some of the new residents in the unit to have dinner with you and any of the other residents with whom you usually dine. It is important that you make an effort to establish all residents in your living unit as part of the group.

Once you have made the initial contact, follow up with each student throughout the next few weeks. If a resident tells you that she is taking a math class or is trying to locate a particular building, when you next see her, if only in passing, make certain that you ask about the particular thing she brought up. You really have several goals to accomplish during these first few days. First, learn the names of your residents. Second, learn their backgrounds. Third, learn something unique about them as individuals. And, fourth, learn something you can follow up on later. This follow-up is an important way to demonstrate that you care about them.

These initial contacts will be important in helping you establish the respect of your residents. This respect can be more easily lost than acquired. Continual contact, recognition, reinforcement, and similar forms of support will be necessary throughout the academic year.

Establishing and Enforcing Policies

Students are not compelled by college policy to contact you for assistance, to respect you, or, for the most part, to follow your directions. Your residents do not report to you, and you do not have supervisory responsibility for them. Instead, your authority in the living unit is derived primarily from the authority that the students are willing to give you. To the extent that your residents respect you, recognize your competence, and come to you for information and assistance, you have authority in your living unit. It is true that you can make a disciplinary referral, but chances are that any other student at your institution can make the same referral.

Perhaps the case for not having authority is a bit overstated. You do have some authority by virtue of the responsibilities assigned to you and the fact that the institution recognizes your authority to intervene in certain situations. The point is that your effectiveness in the RA position is very dependent upon how students view you in that role. If you attempt to set yourself up as perfect, unapproachable, always correct, and puritanical, it is likely that few of your residents will come to you with their concerns for fear that you will condemn them or at least lose respect for them. On the other hand, if you conduct yourself in a drunken, rowdy, and slovenly manner, it is likely that students will feel that you are unable to handle your own problems, let alone theirs.

The respect of your residents is an important element in performing your job. It is not always easily gained, but it is easily lost. Being respected and being liked can be two separate things.

The issue of being liked and being respected always seems to play a critical role in the area of policy enforcement. Some RAs confuse being liked with being lenient about the enforcement of policies. Once you have explained the policies, the rationale behind them, and the institution's instructions to you on their enforcement, you have taken the first step in establishing the expectations for enforcement of these policies.

One good way to undermine your credibility at this point is to inform your residents of the institution's policies and then add your commentary on the policies with which you agree and those with which you do not agree. "The University told me to enforce the marijuana policy, I personally disagree with it, but I have to enforce it." You are sending out a dual message to your residents. You have told them that you are doing something in which you do not believe. This is a difficult position for other people to respect. An easier position to respect is "the university has this policy, the reason for this policy is. . . ." If somebody asks you if you agree or disagree with the policy, your stock answer should be, 'My personal beliefs about these policies are not an issue" or, "Yes, I believe in this policy and I have found it to be supported by most of the other staff." The fact that you agree or disagree with a particular policy is not really the issue. If you have accepted the responsibility of the job, you have accepted the responsibility to carry out the policies and enforcement that go with the position.

During the first few weeks, some students will feel the need to challenge your enforcement of policies. This is a testing period. Students will try to determine how strict you are, how sincere you are about enforcement, and what the real behavioral boundaries are. This testing is like testing the enforcement of the speed limit in a new town. The speed limit may be posted at 55 mph, but chances are good that one will not be arrested until traveling 60 to 65 mph.

Many students need to determine what the limits are for behavior. If you allow Frisbee wars in the hallways at the beginning of the year, or allow people to shoot golf balls in the hallway, play soccer, play their stereos too loud all evening, flood the hallway with water to slide on or throw toilet paper from the bathroom windows, then be prepared to permit this kind of behavior throughout the year. It is much easier to set reasonable limits at the start of the year than to stop this kind of behavior once it has gotten started.

It is more important that people feel that you treat everyone equally, that you are consistent, and that you are fair, than to have them believe you are doing them a favor by letting them do what they want. What needs to be communicated to your residents is that a small group living situation carries with it special duties to respect the rights of others. This means some restrictions on personal freedom. In a community living situation, people simply do not have the personal freedom to play their stereos as loud as they wish until whatever hour of the morning they wish. There will be some students who are selfish and will not want to acknowledge this limitation on their freedom. Chances are that your relationship with them will become somewhat strained as you help them develop this understanding.

Availability

Being available to all of the residents of your living unit is a complex task. If you spend the majority of your time with a small clique of people, you run the risk of alienating other segments of the unit. The same applies to spending most of your time with other staff members, as is often the case. It is not easy to balance your personal needs of comradeship with the needs of your residents.

Students are sensitive. If they continually see the RA in the company of other RAs, they begin seeing the RA as a member of an elite club in which they cannot participate. This is difficult for the RA, who often finds that her closest associations are with other RAs. It is equally difficult for the hall director, who wants to establish a spirit of unity among the staff yet wants to ensure that the needs of the building residents are met. If all the RAs congregate in one or two of the RAs' rooms, it is apparent that they are not spending their available time with their own residents. The RA will then be looked on as an outsider who only comes to the living unit to deal with problems, to change the bulletin board, or to enforce regulations. The RA must become part of the living unit, a part of the team. It is not an easy job. It takes time and continued effort.

Confidentiality

Confidentiality is essential. There is probably no quicker way to lose the respect of your residents and to ruin any opportunity to help students with personal problems than to begin sharing a person's personal problems with other members of the floor. Though the individual to whom you are speaking may feel good about the fact that you have taken her into your confidence, he/she will be wondering if you share what she tells you with others.

Inevitably, if you violate a student's confidence, it will eventually get back to that student. Not only will that person probably never trust you again with any important information, but chances are that her friends will soon learn not to either.

The only person with whom you should legitimately share these confidences should be the hall director. Occasionally some information may be shared with other members of the RA staff, but only when there is a legitimate reason for them to have this information. The indiscriminate sharing of information can quickly generate a lack of trust among the residents in your unit. This is another reason why continual association with the other RAs in the building develops a feeling that the RAs are an exclusive group who get together and share information about their units. No one wants her personal feelings, beliefs, or confidences shared with large groups of people. If the person chose to share information with you, she did not necessarily choose to share it with every other person on the staff. Again, the only appropriate person with whom to share confidences is the hall director. Though there may be no need to share certain confidential information with the hall director, the confidential information that you receive should be considered available to your hall director. You do not keep secrets from the person who hired you, has responsibility for your actions, has trained you, and who is interested in achieving the same objectives you are. If you do not feel that you can share certain confidential information with your hall director, you either should not have agreed to accept the information or you have a problem in your relationship with your hall director that must be resolved.

Conclusion

The best way to establish yourself with residents in your living unit is to be yourself. After all, one of the things that gained you the position was your personality and your ability to get along with other people. Let that come forth. Be sincere and honest about yourself as an individual. Do not try to put on any superficiality about your job, what you will be doing during the year, or your authority. Be open, be yourself, and be available.

Remember that not everyone will like you; but, after all, this is not your goal. Your goal is to let everyone know that you care and are concerned about them as individuals, that you are willing to help, that you have information and training that can help them if they choose to take advantage of it, and that you are available to them.

Counseling Model

The goal of any helping-skills encounter is to help the student make a positive self-directed choice about her own life that will aid her development and return her to a state in which he can again cope with the college experience. There is a five-stage model you can use in bringing about this goal. The five stages are: (1) precounseling stage, (2) listening stage, (3) problem identification and analysis stage, (4) resolution stage, and (5) the follow-up stage.

Precounseling Stage

This is the stage in which the student has either sought you out for assistance with a problem, someone has told you about a problem a student is experiencing, or you have observed something about a student about which you would like to talk with her. In the latter two situations, you will be initiating the counseling. In these circumstances, you will need to explain the purpose of your inquiry. These statements of inquiry can be simple expressions of the behavior you have observed. For example: "John, I have observed that you have been very depressed and moody recently. Is something bothering you?" Or: "John, is everything going all right for you? I have observed that you have not been attending classes recently."

These statements give the student the opportunity to discuss a particular problem, if there is one. They also indicate that you care. When someone has told you about a problem that one of your residents is experiencing, it is appropriate for you to explain by saying something like, "I was talking with X the other day, and she told me that you and your boy friend broke up. How are you feeling about that? Is everything all right?" Or: "The hall director told me that you were not pledged by the sorority in which you were interested. I was sorry to hear about it. How do you feel about what happened? How do you feel about yourself?"

These questions will enable the student to understand how you came to observe the behavior and what behavior you have observed. An open-ended question will invite more than a yes or no answer. If the person wishes to talk, offer her the opportunity. In both these cases, you can do a little preparation beforehand. You can think of some areas you may wish to explore with the student and, most importantly, you can plan the time to make the contact to deal with the problem.

If the student approaches you with a problem, you will not have the opportunity to think about the problem beforehand or possibly to set the time and place for the discussion. You do, however, have the right to request the student select another time. You may find yourself in the middle of an important class assignment, late for an important meeting, or so frustrated that you simply cannot assist the student at that particular time. You should not feel that every time a student comes to you with a problem you must drop everything and deal with it at that precise moment. You will quickly learn that some students will come and sit in your room and simply spend time procrastinating. This wastes both your time and theirs. There are other students who run to the RA with every petty little problem they have. Soon you will find such students running to you on a continual basis to check the most minor issues.

You will need to decide whether you need to see the student immediately or whether the problem could wait until a more convenient time. Each decision needs to be made independently, based upon what you know about the individual, her emotional state at the time, how often she comes to you with problems, and how important the completion of your own work is at that moment.

You must also assess some things from the person's tone and physical manner at the time. A woman who continually runs to you for emotional support, often crying, may not need your attention as much as a woman who does not come to you often and is somber and lacks much emotion. You must begin making some subjective decisions about the individual and how important the particular problem. Chances are that the first encounters will be the most meaningful. If a student comes to you for the first time with a problem, if at all possible try to see that student and help her with the problem. Try using these general guidelines to make your assessments:

1. Is this the first time you have seen this student or does this student run to you with every type of problem?
2. What is the observed emotional state of the student when she makes the inquiry about talking with you and is this state out of the ordinary for this individual?
3. How much time will the problem actually take to resolve? Is this simply a request for information that you can resolve in five or six minutes?
4. What is your relationship with the person? Is it a positive relationship in which the person trusts you already or is it one in which you are still attempting to establish trust?
5. How serious a problem does the person feel it is?

It is appropriate, given the aforementioned criteria, to inquire whether the student feels that her problem requires your immediate attention or whether it is something that can wait until you have more time or are better able to assist. Remember that you will not be able to give your full attention to helping if your attention is focused upon studying for an examination or completing a paper. You will be trying to get the problem resolved so that you can move along to what you really want to do. Instead, it is better for both of you to set a time later—that evening if at all possible—to discuss the problem. Most students will understand if you explain that you have something that must be completed.

There is no rule that your personal goals must always come second to the desires, whims, needs, or problems of students in your living unit. You will find that they usually do; however, there are times when you must recognize that you also have things that must be accomplished. The trick is to have a balance. To turn people away from your door regularly will soon earn you a reputation of not caring enough and not being interested in your residents. When you think it appropriate, based upon your evaluation of the situation and some basic inquiries, make the decision to talk with people about problems they are experiencing when there is a time that is acceptable for both of you.

Assuming that you decide that the student's problem is important enough to set aside what you have been doing, your first step in the counseling exchange is to make the person feel welcome. You would probably do something like this anyway, whether you had invited the student to your room to discuss an observed problem or if the student just stopped by your room. Making the person feel comfortable requires just a little more effort when the purpose is counseling.

Set the environment for the exchange. Close the door, physically push what you were doing previously aside, and sit directly across from the person. If another person is in the room when the student comes in and is not discussing an important problem with you, it is legitimate to ask the other person to leave. The visitor, understanding your role, will not be offended. In no case should you try to discuss a serious subject with a student in front of another person. If the telephone rings during the conversation or if there is a knock at the door, answer it but be very brief with the caller and tell her that you have someone with you now and that you will contact her later. This is a way of reinforcing to the student with a problem that she is the central focus of your concern. There is probably nothing more irritating for a troubled student discussing a serious problem than to have the conversation interrupted by a telephone call and the person with whom she is sharing the information spend an extended time on the telephone. This conveys a clear disinterest.

Be conscious of the nonverbal clues you are sending. If you lie down on your bed and stare at the ceiling or sit behind your desk, you could be nonverbally communicating disinterest or placing a barrier to intimacy between you and the other person. The same applies to assuming any physically superior position relative to the student seeking help. If you sit on the desk or tower above the person, you are conveying a superiority that may further inhibit the student from expressing her feelings.

The proper counseling posture is to sit directly across from the student. Your posture should be open—meaning that neither your arms nor your legs should be crossed. Nonverbally, having your arms or legs crossed could communicate that you are closed off from the other person. Your eyes should focus on the other person's face. If you have trouble looking into the other person's eyes, try looking just slightly above them at the eyebrows. You may find this less intense. Try to project a feeling of being relaxed and open, yet attentive and interested in the other person. Your voice should be calming, tranquil, and soothing, but not a whisper. Your entire demeanor should convey acceptance, comfort, and understanding. This mode will help the person feel more comfortable with you and more willing to share her problem.

Listening Stage

This is the stage in which the student talks and you listen. It is an opportunity for the student to describe how she views the problem. You in turn are periodically relating back to the person how you are interpreting the situation being described. You will find that the person will describe fairly clearly how she is viewing what is happening. (This mode of counseling incidentally, is called client-centered counseling.) You are trying to get into the student's frame of reference in order to understand the view being described. It is not important whether or not you agree with the viewpoint being presented; the important thing is that you listen and understand what is being said. In this communication you need to determine what is seen as the problem, what is viewed as the reason or cause, and how the student is currently coping. To determine these things you first must be a good listener.

Communicating is a difficult process. It requires the person sending the message to confirm that the message she is sending is received as it was meant to be received, and it requires the receiver to confirm that what she has received is the message that was intended. Thus, good listening is an active process. Messages are sent, received, and confirmed by each of the parties.

To do this you must know how to listen. There is a difference between hearing what somebody is saying and truly listening to what is said. This two-way process means that you must check the meaning of certain words. If the student says his roommate hates him, that only tells you that the student perceives a conflict with the roommate. The appropriate question for you to ask in this situation is "What specifically do you mean?" Or: "How do you know that to be the case?" What you must try to establish is what this person means by the word hate. Communication only takes place when you both understand and have a common meaning for the words, phrases, and situations that are being described.

The techniques you use in the listening process are as follows:

1. Be yourself—be natural, be comfortable, be confident with yourself. Act naturally and express an interest in what the person is saying.
2. Talk less and listen more.
3. Ask questions that clarify the communicated message.
4. Use open-ended questions that call for more than a yes or no answer.
5. Help the student stay on track and away from tangents.

Being yourself means exactly that. Be natural about your actions and your relationship to the other person. Do not try to be overly psychoanalytical, try to use complex terms when they are unnecessary, or attempt to impress the person with your knowledge. The student is looking for a friend and someone who can help her work through a problem; she is not looking for a psychoanalyst. You should refrain from giving the impression that you are doing a psychological counseling session. Your goal is not to make a diagnosis but to help the person cope with the problem. Talk less and listen more is a good rule of thumb. This is a chance for the student to paint a picture for you of what is happening and for you to understand. The student at this point is the teacher instructing you. You, in turn, are trying to understand the subject matter or the view that the student is painting. You can only do this if you give the student time to discuss the problem.

The amount of time, however, is not the issue. Some students will be able to paint a clear and accurate picture for you in a relatively short time. Others will need to add a quantity of elaborate and nonuseful detail. You have a right to help the student move through the explanation with questions such as, "How does that particular event affect the problem?" Or, "Yes, I am familiar with that area, go on."

One of the important techniques to learn is to ask questions that clarify. This is a simple technique, but it is an important method of communicating to the student what you are hearing her say. Feed back the information that has been given you. Some stock questions you should make part of your listening vocabulary are "What I hear you saying is . . . ," "If I understand you correctly, you are saying . . . ," "Did you say . . . ," "What do you mean by . . . ?"

These are questions that clarify and, most important, give the student information on what you are perceiving. Sometimes this will be enough for the student to gain perspective on the problem. You are asking questions that help the student clarify the situation by feeding back or reflecting what she has said. This reflection of ideas and perceptions is important in gaining a mutual understanding of what is being said as well as in establishing a different viewpoint for the student.

The use of open-ended questions is a good technique to help the student elaborate in more detail areas you do not understand or areas in which you feel the student has made some incorrect assumptions. The difference between an open-ended and a closed question is that closed questions can be answered with one or two words. Open-ended questions need a more complete response. For example, if you ask a student, "What is your major?" the student may easily respond, "My major is. . . ." You could ask that same question and receive more information by asking, "Why did you choose your current major?" Open-ended questions are best for follow-up information. Follow-up questions are questions like, "Could you tell me more about . . ." or, "How do you believe the situation would have been different if you would have . . . ?" Remember, most of the counseling session will be spent with the other person doing the talking and working through the problem. You will be asking appropriate questions to help her clarify the problem.

Be careful not to deviate from the subject being discussed. As we said earlier, it is appropriate for you to help the student keep to the problem at hand. When asking your questions, ask only those that directly relate to the problem. This will help eliminate diversion and help the student focus more clearly on the problem.

While talking with the student, you must have good attending skills—that is those nonverbal or subverbal indications by which you let a person know that you understand. Good attending skills are essential. They confirm that you understand what has been said. The following are some attending skills that you should practice and that you should use in a counseling session:

1. Nodding your head communicates that you understand and are soliciting more information, or that you are giving approval to the individual. If you want to see this technique work, sit down across from a friend and, while she is talking, nod casually and somewhat continually throughout her discussion. Part of the way through, simply quit nodding and only look at her. You will find that very quickly she will either begin going into more detail or may ask you if you understand what she is saying. In our culture, we need to know that the other person is actually hearing or understanding what we are saying. We need reassurance or confirmation. The nodding provides this.
2. Supporting hand gestures, such as the rotation of one hand in a certain way, expresses the feeling of approval, come on, keep going, etc.
3. Facial expressions, smiles, frowns, and similar expressions are also ways of expressing to the person that you understand and approve or disapprove. It is not necessary to say anything, just show the appropriate facial expression to get the person to continue talking.
4. Subverbals such as "uh huh" or another similar form of subverbal humming sound in our culture communicates understanding.
5. The open accepting posture discussed earlier conveys interest and sympathy.

If used appropriately, these techniques will aid in the communication process and facilitate listening. If you are acknowledging the receipt of information and asking questions of clarification, you become an active participant in the listening process. As a participant, you contribute as well as receive by confirming the information that is given. This interchange is essential to effective listening.

Problem Identification and Analysis Stage

Once the student has had the opportunity to explain her perception of the problem, what she believes to be the cause, and how she plans to cope with it, and you understand and believe you have a fairly accurate picture, you can then begin to analyze the elements of the problem. In this stage you will be helping the student direct her thinking to specific elements of the problem. The basic technique used is questioning and sharing of personal experiences.

There are three steps to be accomplished in this problem identification and analysis state. First, you should reiterate or review the problem as you view it with the student. Establish your perception of the problem, confirming with the student the three basic elements of the cause, the perception of the problem as the student sees it, and how she is currently coping with it. You are trying to confirm that you are talking about the same problem and, that you understand.

Second, you need to determine whether the student's perception is accurate. This should be done through a series of questions and confrontations. Let us examine each one of these techniques.

Through questioning and answering you attempt to have the person acknowledge practical realities that may be in conflict with the persons perception of the event. Never assume that you know more about the problem than the student does. You do have a base of personal experiences on which to draw and it may be appropriate to point out that what the student is experiencing is not abnormal and that many people have expressed similar problems. Be careful, however, when expressing this, that you do not minimize the student's problem. An example in point might be the student who has received a poor grade on a paper. The student may feel that the professor has always had bad feelings toward her, so she may try to shift the responsibility for her performance to the professor. Questions you might appropriately ask would be, "What makes you believe the professor picked on you specifically? Have you spoken with the professor about the situation? Do you personally feel that this is the best example of your work? Do you feel that the paper could have been better than it was? Have you had an opportunity to see anyone else's paper? Are you certain that no one else has received a similar grade for a similar performance?"

Use confrontation to point out inconsistencies in what the student has said. Such statements as "On the one hand you have said _____, but on the other hand you have also said "_____" are attempts to establish a consistent line of reasoning. This will help students gain a clearer perspective on the way they are viewing the problem. You have the advantage in that you have some distance from the problem and can be more objective. When students become emotionally involved in a problem, they can lose perspective and not always realize the inconsistencies in their reasoning. In our example of the student who received a poor grade on a paper, you may have inquired earlier how she had previously performed and found that he had done well. You may suggest the conflict in logic as follows: "You have done well on all your past examinations and papers, yet you say that the professor is out to get you, why is that? Does that seem consistent to you?"

In analyzing the problem, there are three possibilities: (1) the student may be relaying accurate information and is perceiving the problem correctly; (2) the student may be relating distorted information and has a distorted perception of the problem; (3) the student may have related accurate information but may have misperceived the problem.

Once having helped the student analyze the problem, the next step is to identify the problem and to develop alternatives and the consequences of those alternatives. In analyzing alternatives, there are five things that you need to establish:

1. Does the student have any control over what is happening? A good case in point might be the student who is experiencing frustration and anxiety because of financial problems created by the late arrival of a financial aid check. The student has little control over the cause of the problem. However, she may have alternatives that you could explore.
2. Is any action on the part of the student necessary or indicated? Sometimes the best course of action is to do nothing. This is always an alternative.
3. If some action could be taken to help the situation, what types of action are possible? In the case of the student who is experiencing financial problems because of not receiving a financial aid check, other courses of action might include a part-time job, a loan from another source, or an extension on payment.
4. What are the resources the student can bring to bear on the situation?
5. What are the consequences of the alternative actions proposed? What is the worst that could happen, the best that could happen, and the probability of each?

In this stage of discussing the alternatives, you may make some suggestions, but most suggestions and alternatives should be analyzed by the student. Do not fall into the trap of trying to answer the questions, "What do you think I should do?" or "What would you do if you were me?" The student is asking for your advice and for you to make a decision. This is usually inappropriate within the framework of this helping skills model. Your response should be, "The question is what do *you* think you should do, not what I think you should do." Appropriate questions are, "Now that we are at this point, what do you believe you can do about the situation? What alternatives do you see available? What resources do you have to deal with it?" Suggestions that you might make could be derived from your experience within the university. Such suggestions as, "Have you considered trying to get an emergency student loan from the Dean of Students Office?" Or, "I know there are part-time jobs available in the cafeteria, have you considered working there?"

The last step in this analysis stage is to determine with the student what he believes would be the ideal outcome and whether this outcome is realistic. Specifically, what would it take to achieve this desired or ultimate outcome? Does the student have the resources to achieve it? Is it actually within the realm of probability?

Resolution Stage

In the resolution stage, you want to have the student reiterate the alternatives, how she intends to implement action if necessary, and to develop a time-frame in which the action will be initiated. You will confirm with the student the action that will take place. When the student leaves your room, she should feel that several alternatives are available and that she has a definite course of action. This is the ideal situation. Sometimes it will not be possible to reach this desired end. The student should feel satisfied that he/she has worked through his own problem with your help.

Make sure that the student understands that you have a continued interest in what eventually happens to her. Invite her back to talk with you after she has taken the action proposed. What you wish to do is establish a foundation for the follow-up stage.

Follow-Up

This is a check to ensure that the student has attempted to implement the course of action she identified. Confirm with the student again that you care and have a continued interest. This follow-up should be informal and might be acccomplished by stopping by the student's room. However, *you* are the one who should make the effort. That may mean asking the student to have dinner with you or making a point to ask her to stop by your room for a few minutes.

The follow-up need only be a one-time encounter for most situations. For some students who are having prolonged difficulty, it may be necessary to continue these follow-ups. This is particularly true with people who are under severe emotional strain, such as might occur when breaking-up with a boyfriend or girlfriend they have been dating for a long time. Your continued support and interest will be helpful. Be careful, however, not to reinforce that depression or sorrow. If the student finds that she is getting attention for this, it may reinforce the behavior. If enough people reinforce depression and similar emotional states, the student could continue that particular state and may become more depressed.

Many of the emotional problems that students undergo simply take time for them to work out. If you observe in your follow-up that the student is not coping with the problem effectively and that it is impairing her ability to function, you should initiate a counseling discussion with her for purposes of referring her to another person at the university (i.e., a professional counselor or professional staff person). These people ahould be able to give the student some additional help in coping with the situation.

Counseling Tips

Listed below are a few helpful techniques for counseling students with this helping-skills approach.

1. RAs sometime have difficulty responding to students' crying. They feel uncomfortable when others start to cry. With men, the emotion is viewed as unmasculine because our society tells men that they must bottle up these emotions and not let themselves be seen expressing sorrow. Society permits women to express emotion through crying more openly and freely. If a student begins to weep when explaining a problem, do not be embarrassed or ignore what is obvious to both of you. Offer the student a tissue and some consoling words to confirm that this expression of emotion is acceptable and is nothing about which to be embarrassed. Crying is a natural emotion for many people and can be a healthy way of relieving the tension and anxiety of a difficult situation.

2. Listen carefully to what a person says. If you listen, you will find the person will tell you exactly what is troubling her. It is not necessary to become hyperpsychoanalytic and to look for hidden meanings. This, after all, is not the real reason that the person came to talk with you. Being a good listener and a sympathetic friend as an RA are the key elements of being a successful counselor.

3. Learn to empathize with the student. Empathy is an important medium of support. It not only helps you understand what the person is experiencing, but confirms for the student your concern. Many counseling tips can be summarized by simply learning to empathize with other people.

4. Be confident in your ability to work with the student. You were selected because of your skills in working with people and with groups.

5. Do not evaluate how well you are liked on the floor by how many people come to you with personal problems. The occasion to help a student with a personal problem may arise only a few times within your living unit in an academic year. It is important that, when it does arise, you are trained and confident in your ability to handle the situation.

6. Remember that most problems students experience are normal everyday difficulties related to depression, fear, anxiety, stress, self-confidence, interpersonal relationships, and rejection. Each of these could be a crisis for the individual. People learn and grow from solving crises

in their lives, and the ability to solve and handle one's crises helps one to handle future problems. These crises represent development and growth in the individual.

7. Be aware of your feelings about a student whom you are counseling. Hostility toward the person, recent problems you have had with her or stereotypes you have about the individual will color your perception of what the individual tells you. Try to erase these images and listen to the student. This will help enable you to see the picture that the student is painting for you.

Seeking Professional Help

A referral to professional counseling should be made when it becomes apparent that the student is experiencing a severe emotional problem with which she cannot cope. Behavior that you observe, that is reported to you by another person, or that the student describes may indicate such a referral.

Your goal in working with a student who has apparent need for professional guidance or who is experiencing an emotional crisis with which you cannot assist is to have the student agree to see a professional and actually keep the counseling appointment. Many students are reluctant to seek professional assistance for fear that they may be viewed as mentally ill. Though this label serves no purpose within the context of a helping relationship, it may be one of the greatest barriers you will need to overcome in having the student seek professional counseling.

The three elements in making a referral for professional counseling are: (1) recognizing the signs for referral, (2) helping the student recognize and accept the need for professional counseling, and (3) making the referral.

Recognizing the Signs for Referral

As has been pointed out already, students will be able to resolve most of the difficulties they experience with the assistance of a friend or with some help from you. There will be, however, some students who need professional help with their problems. It can be particularly difficult within the college environment to identify these students, since the college environment naturally lends itself to the acceptance of behavior that in another environment would be out of the ordinary. Students are undergoing a number of conflicts and crises in both their identity and their values. Some of the common signs of emotional problems, such as erratic sleep patterns and erratic eating habits, are difficult to interpret within the college environment. Below are listed some of the signs people use to signal a need for assistance. This is by no means meant to be a definitive list or the only criteria on which to base a decision to make the referral. The behavior listed is intended solely to assist you in developing a commonsense approach to identifying signals for help in the unique environment of the college residence hall.

1. Poor emotional control can be exhibited in different forms. Open hostility and belligerence toward people for no apparent reason, exaggerated outbursts of emotion diaproportionate to the event, and uncontrolled crying or laughter at unexplained, inappropriate times are some common signs of poor emotional control. It is not one or two of these incidents, but the repeated or prolonged occurrence over a several-day period, that may signal the need for help. This is especially true when the behavior deviates radically from the person's normal personality or is tangential to or follows a difficult emotional time, such as the loss of a parent or rejection by another significant person.

2. Excessive moodiness or worry is another sign the person may be experiencing a problem. Anxiety, stress, and depression are normal outlets within a person's emotional cycle. A person who is anxious and feels under stress during final exam time may be expressing a very normal emotion. It is natural for her to worry. Extreme cases are people who spend an inordinate amount of time worrying about very trivial or insignificant matters, such as whether there will be enough forks in the cafeteria line. Preoccupation with or unnatural attention to detail is often a sign that the person has some need of assistance.

3. Sleeping and eating habits that change dramatically are also a sign that the person is experiencing some problem and is attempting to avoid dealing with it. A student who suddenly begins sleeping eighteen to nineteen hours a day and missing classes is probably experiencing some difficulty. The opposite is also true. The student who develops insomnia and begins taking catnaps during class or at other times is also experiencing some problem. Eating sometimes is another sign—either excessive or continual eating or abstaining from food for prolonged periods of time. Some of this erratic behavior may occur naturally. The student who has been studying or partying for three days may need to get some additional rest. The person who is crash-dieting may not eat for several days. It is important that you recognize this behavior within the context of the surrounding situation and in relation to the individual's normal pattern.

4. An unnatural preoccupation with personal health may be a sign of needing help. The person constantly complaining about the most minor ailment and continually seeking pills and medical advice from other residents may have emotional, rather than physical problems.

5. People who seem to express a universal mistrust or paranoia about others may need help. This severe form of insecurity in which a person may claim that people are continually talking about her or trying to injure her, or similar unsubstantiated claims, is probably a sign that the person needs help.

6. Persistent and continued depression for a prolonged period of time—more than one week—is generally not normal. This could be serious if the person stops talking about the future and begins viewing life as holding only more of the same joyless existence. A student reaching this state of depression is in serious need of attention and is very possibly suicidal.

7. Students who talk openly about doing away with themselves are signaling a need for professional help. Such discussions are to be taken seriously and are a call for help and support.

Questions to ask yourself:

1. Does behavior that the student exhibits seem out of the ordinary?
2. Do you believe you can deal with the particular problem, or do you believe it beyond your skills at this particular time?
3. Is behavior that the student is exhibiting getting worse, less frequent, or better?
4. Does the behavior place anyone, including the person in question, in a life-threatening situation?

Use these questions to help analyze a referral situation. If the answers to any of these questions indicate that the student needs help, work to make the referral. Always include your residence hall director in the information you have about the student and her behavior. Share with the residence hall director your perceptions and evaluation and gain her assistance in helping you to work with the student. Remember, the psychological health of the student and her active progress toward growing and accomplishing both academic and personal goals are the main purpose and objective for which both you and the residence life staff will be working.

Helping the Student Recognize and Accept Professional Counseling

As in the helping-skills model, the listening stage is the opportunity for the student to provide you with a picture of her experience. The questions and techniques you use in gaining a perception are the same as the ones used in the counseling-skills model. In general terms, you are trying to determine if this person's overall perception of his experience is realistic. Be careful at this stage not to get into a controversy with the student, but at the same time be careful not to accept gross distortions of reality as being within the realm of possibility. For example, if a person tells you that she is seeing pink elephants, it serves little purpose to talk about how large the elephants are and hold out the possibility that they may in fact be an accurate perception of reality.

Listen to the student with the same interest and empathy shown in the helping-skills model. Do not encourage the person if she talks of bizarre or strange events that are taking place in her life or bizarre actions that she may like to carry out. Your goal in listening is to determine a frame of reference from which to help the student reach a decision about seeking additional help.

Specifically, question the student about the behavior that she has exhibited. Inquire as to whether or not she feels satisfied with what is taking place in her life and if she would be interested in improving. Never argue with the person or in any way try to convince the person that your perception of reality is correct and her perception is not. Confront only with logic and understanding.

You are not attempting to diagnose the actual cause of the problem, but trying to help the student reach a decision about seeking further help. The same techniques of confrontation, open-ended questions, and questions related to the student's goals are appropriate. Reiterate the behavior the student exhibited and ask how she specifically feels about the behavior. During this entire stage of questioning, you will be attempting to have the student acknowledge a willingness to seek additional help.

If you believe that professional counseling help for a student is needed, talk over this perception with your hall director. In most situations, your hall director should be involved, if only by confirming the institutional referral procedure or suggesting a particular counselor to whom you may make the referral.

You will need to accomplish two things in making the referral. First, the student will need to understand that seeking assistance from a professional counselor is not an indication of mental illness. To overcome this reluctance to see a professional on campus, you may need to reassure the student that all records kept by the counselor are confidential and protected by federal law. The institution will not remove the student from school nor will it record on any of the student's transcripts that she has seen a professional counselor. A common fear is that a decision to seek help will become public and that the seeker will subsequently be viewed as unstable. It is a breach of professional ethics for a counselor to discuss a student's problem with anyone other than another professional, unless the student seems likely to harm herself or others.

The second thing that the student must accept is that she needs assistance. If you can help alleviate the stigma of seeing a counselor by accomplishing the first item well, you will have a better chance of getting the student to acknowledge that he may need the assistance of a professional.

Making the Referral

Once the student has accepted the idea of seeing a professional, have the student state the specific action she will take. It will, in most situations, be the student's responsibility to make contact with the counselor. Though there may be some occasions in which you will want to assist the student by literally accompanying the student to the counseling center, for the most part you want the student to take the necessary steps in making the appointment and going to the counseling center.

One technique to confirm the agreed-upon behavior of seeing a counselor is to have the student state the specific behavior she will accomplish in the time-frame during which she will accomplish it. For example, "I will call Dr. Smith for an appointment to discuss my problem tomorrow morning, and I will attend the counseling session we agree upon." Have the student repeat this in exact terms. This then becomes a kind of verbal commitment or bond between you and the student.

You will need to follow up with the student to assure that she has kept the commitment. If she has not, it will reinforce this verbal bond and may prompt the agreed-upon action. Sometimes this follow-up will offer the student the needed opportunity to share with someone else the events of the counseling session. You can supply some feedback to the student and simply listen to what the student has to say about the counseling session.

Contact with the counselor, once the referral has been made, is generally not a good idea unless the counselor asks you for your help or feedback on the student's behavior. What transpires between the student and the counselor should remain limited to them, unless the student chooses to share the information with you.

Advising

Advising is the act of giving information and suggesting a specific course of action for an individual to take. There are times when you, as a resident assistant, will be doing just this. Advising should be done infrequently, but there are some obvious times when it is necessary.

It is appropriate for you, as a resident assistant, to advise someone when she comes to you with a request for specific information. An example might be, if a student asks you the best way to get to a particular classroom building, you advise her by providing specific information. If a student asks you what to wear to a certain event, say a football game or a semiformal dance, you should feel comfortable in advising her by providing information based on your past experiences. You can share other types of information, such as not to take an overload of academic hours in the spring quarter, when there are many activities. Other areas in which you might advise are directly related to personal safety and security, such as not walking alone at night in dimly lit areas or not keeping large sums of money around the room. These are appropriate areas in which advice is worthwhile.

As a general rule, you should advise only when the student requests specific information, when the person's safety or security is at stake, when the issue is of no emotional consequence, or when the results of your advice cannot injure or harm the individual. These general rules about giving advice may help you analyze when it is appropriate and how to give it when asked:

1. Do not give advice to people who do not seek it or who do not want it. Often your interjection of "what I would do if I were you" is not at all welcome. It is better to wait until your opinion is asked and then to give it only if it is appropriate.
2. If a person does ask for advice and it is appropriate to give it, do so in confidence. This allows the person to disagree and does not make the person feel as if she is following directions.
3. Never give advice using such words as *don't* and *shouldn't.*
4. Present advice as suggestions. Use phrases such as, "Have you ever thought about trying . . ." or "You might try. . . ."
5. Use personal experiences in making suggestions. This provides the listener with a base for your authority in making the suggestions, and it reveals some personal information about you.
6. If you choose to give advice, give it cautiously and sparingly. Remember, no one likes to be told what to do or how to do it.

It is interesting to note that people are always ready to give advice, yet so few people are willing to accept it. Even though many people solicit advice and suggestions, people seldom put them to use.

Summary of Counseling Tips

1. Develop the skills of empathy, acceptance, attending behavior, and reflection.
2. Be confident in your ability.
3. Learn to listen to what the person is actually saying.
4. Never take notes.
5. Make the person feel comfortable.
6. Learn to ask open ended questions.
7. Learn to give feedback responses.
8. Develop skills in confrontation and assertiveness.
9. Care about the person with whom you are talking.
10. Share personal experiences when appropriate.

11. Be authentic and sincere about your emotions and express them to the student.
12. Do not act shocked or upset.
13. Observe things about the person, learn to be a good observor.
14. Do keep confidences.
15. Do not make decisions for the individual.
16. Show acceptance of the individual.
17. Do not give advice except when called upon to do so.
18. Do help the student to understand that feelings are normal.
19. Do acknowledge responses that the student makes such as crying.
20. Counseling is not a substitute for discipline.
21. Help students develop responses to assist them in dealing effectively with their emotions.
22. The goals of most counseling situations are to (a) help the student learn and grow from the experience; (b) to assist the student in developing positive coping mechanisms; and (c) to return the student to a state of previous emotional stability or improved emotional stability.

CHAPTER 7
Interpersonal Communication

Most of your skills in working with students in the residence halls are based upon your skill as an effective communicator. Whether this communication takes place in a counseling framework, in a disciplinary encounter or in helping to motivate students, it is based upon your ability to verbally express yourself in a way that accurately transmits your thoughts to another person. Communication is a process by which we share our ideas, concepts, thoughts, emotions, and feelings with another person through the use of verbal and nonverbal symbols. The primary function of communication as we will use it in this chapter is to control one's environment so as to realize certain physical, emotional, economic, or social rewards. This definition is not meant to imply that the control function of communication is exclusively for self interests. It is possible, such as in a counseling situation, that the desire to stimulate another person's thought thus influencing her behavior, is done from a purely unselfish and caring perspective.

Three Levels of Communication

Most communication is noninterpersonal. It is either at a cultural level, or a sociological level that we most often communicate. By cultural communication we are referring to forms of communication that are defined by our culture. Such communication situations as initial meetings, governmental functions, talk at cocktail parties with strangers, and other rituals and ceremonies of our culture provide a standardized or formalized way of communication. By virtue of living in this culture, we internalize the communication pattern accepted within our society. In meeting with strangers in which we may choose to communicate, our topics of conversation will start at the cultural level of things we share in common. The weather and sports are topics that might be discussed at this level.

Communication at the sociological level is communication defined by a person's membership in a particular social group. Social groups are defined by characteristics such as socio-economic status, race, education, geographical region, religion, and the interaction of these and other factors. These social factors are combined within society to make-up subcultural groups. Subcultural groups have accepted patterns of communication behavior just like those at the cultural level. Communication at this level is a function of increased knowledge about the beliefs, attitudes, and behaviors of the person with whom you are communicating. It may be said that cultural level communication and sociological level communication as the two forms of noninterpersonal communication demonstrate our varying abilities to predict and understand the communicative exchange with another person. If the only knowledge that we have of a person is on a cultural level, then our ability to predict that person's behaviors, attitudes, and beliefs for the purpose of sharing common experiences through the symbols of language is lessened. On the other hand, if we share with that person membership in a particular subcultural group, we increase our ability to predict the extent to which we can share our thoughts and ideas through mutually recognized symbols based upon commonly shared experiences.

The third level of communication is interpersonal communication. In actuality, very little of our communication falls into this category. It is the most intimate level of our communication in which our predictions in the communicative process are based upon knowledge of a particular individual's learning experiences and commonly shared understandings. We can distinguish noninterpersonal communication from interpersonal communication on the basis of whether or not the process of our communication is based upon our prediction on a general group level or upon an individual psychological level.

Interpersonal communication is the act of sharing personal, intimate, and valued experiences with another person. It differs from interpersonal relationships in that interpersonal communication is the process by which one person provides personal information to the other, whereas with an interpersonal relationship, both individuals exchange information at a personal level. An interpersonal relationship is characterized by trust and intimacy exchanged with another person. It fulfills an emotional need within each of us to be close to other people, and serves to help us define ourselves, explore interests, and receive feedback from a person with whom we share trust and closeness. Some contend that all forms of communication should attempt to move to the interpersonal level, where others suggest interpersonal communication as an alternative form of communication not as a goal in itself. The authors support the latter view. Interpersonal communication is not required for successfully communicating in all of our intereactions with people.

Establishing Interpersonal Communication and Relationships

Interpersonal communication is most gratifying when it is part of an interpersonal relationship. It is rare that we move into interpersonal communication with a person whom we have just met. An exception to this rule may be if you go to a psychologist to talk over a problem, or sometimes a dating relationship in which there is a mutual attraction and both parties are engaged in learning about the other. Although the establishment of an interpersonal relationship is not necessarily a prerequisite to interpersonal communication, it is the most appropriate and satisfying vehicle for the sharing of this information.

The residence hall is an environment that lends itself to the establishment of these most rewarding relationships. As students spend more and more time sharing the experience of living together, attending classes together, and other things that occur throughout the year, they increase trust in one another and gradually move to a level of sharing on an interpersonal level. The more interaction these students have with one another, the more information they have about the other person and the better they are able to understand the other person's behavior.

Interpersonal relationships in a residence hall—given shared space, frequency of contacts, and similar experience—are stimulated during periods of personal crises. When students experience crises, whether with parents, dating relationship, or classes, they are most likely to seek someone that they trust and with whom they can share their feelings. When presented with a crisis, people feel vulnerable and need the support of others. Although the RA is sometimes sought-out because of the position, and hopefully as the result of positive past contacts, most often the student will seek out a person with whom she has shared a mutually rewarding relationship. This person will hopefully lend support and shared experiences providing comfort and acceptance to the student in crisis.

Interpersonal deprivation is another crisis that stimulates interpersonal communication. People have an optimum number of stable friendships they need to maintain in order to feel comfortable. When a person enters a new environment, such as moving into a residence hall for the first time, this transition usually alters the number of stable relationships, and the person will seek to reestablish this optimum level by increasing interpersonal communication with individuals to establish new friendships.

Consistent with the observation that people have an optimum level of friendships, it is interesting to note how students associate in small groups of five to six students who tend to spend the greatest amount of time together. One might characterize the typical residence hall living unit as a group of groups. New students transferring into the unit midway through the academic year often find it difficult to enter into these small groups because of the level of stable relationships maintained by the group. These groups are generally based upon those things that we mentioned earlier (time, shared space, frequency, proximity of rooms, etc.). The students become friends, tend to support one another, share mutual experiences, and support one another's likes and dislikes. If the RA can win the confidence of one or more of the students in these groups, the RA can more easily win a similar relationship with other members of the group. One way to utilize this information is to analyze your living unit in terms of these groups, and target some of your energies into maintaining positive relationships with key individuals within each of those groups.

Interpersonal Communication Skills

Although most interpersonal relationships come about naturally, it is possible to make an interpersonal relationship happen. It probably would not be very successful to walk up to people with whom you have limited contact and inform them that you wish to establish an interpersonal relationship. Such behavior would be viewed suspiciously because it violates our cultural expectations of how relationships are formed. You can stimulate these relationships, however, by showing interest in another person, what they do, and what they say. People generally appreciate being sought out for advice. This is a rewarding process acknowledging that the other person's opinion has value. People tend to remain in relationships they find rewarding. If the relationship is not rewarding, people leave the relationship. Thus the stimulation and maintenance of a relationship is based upon giving and receiving rewards through communication. These rewards take various forms, depending on our knowledge of the individual. Many of these rewards are intangible. The acknowledgement that you are in some way important, and that this person enjoys your company may be the total sum of the reward expected or needed in maintaining the relationship.

In sum, interpersonal relationships and thus interpersonal communication is most likely to occur when the quality of our relationship with another person is such that it is mutually rewarding. It is sustained through the period of time in which it is mutually satisfying, we trust and enjoy the other person, and that relationship serves a common need. Relationships dissolve or are modified when they cease to become rewarding.

The ability to empathize with another individual is closely associated with interpersonal communication. It is the ability to attune yourself to the sensory and verbal cues expressed by another person to the extent that we experience someone else's feelings as our own. We do this by projecting ourselves into the experience of the other person. Our ability to empathize is based upon our ability to understand and accurately read cues individuals give us as to their internal state. Verbal symbols and expressions of emotions are cues we use to interpret how a person is experiencing a particular internal issue. Of equal importance, are nonverbal cues. Nonverbal cues such as eye movement, body language, voice inflection, and key word phraseology provide a deeper understanding of another person's communication. By accurately reading a person's eye movements, a trained therapist can determine if the person is thinking, remembering, is sad, embarrassed, or happy. Having this information aids in interpreting and responding accurately to the experience of the other person. The more information we have about a person, the more accurately we can understand the internal state of experience being communicated.

There are two steps to empathizing. First, we must be able to predict and understand the motives and attitudes of the other person. The prediction must be based upon an understanding of the individual, and what rewards, behaviors, and experiences this person has had and finds satisfying.

The second step is learning to communicate what we understand the person to be saying. This feedback has the quality of reaffirming what you are hearing, and what you are seeing. Not only must this communication provide understanding; it also must be rewarding. The reward comes in the knowledge that the other person understands and shares those feelings. This means that if the person is relating a sad, stressful situation, the person empathizing with that experience may feel a similar emotional state. They too may feel depressed, perhaps cry, or get angry. It is at this psycho-physiological level that the deepest empathy takes place. It can be said then that empathy takes place when two people share in the same sensory experience at an emotional level.

Cross-Cultural Communication

As we noted in an earlier chapter, higher education has changed significantly since the early 1920s when college students came from basically the same socio-economic background and had similar kinds of social and cultural experiences. There were few international students, and few minority students in higher education. As higher education has grown over the years and become more egalitarian, institutions have moved from this homogeneous group to a more diverse student population. Within recent years, many institutions have purposely recruited minority and international students. It is not unusual on large campuses to find a wealth of students from different cultural backgrounds. This variety and richness of cultural backgrounds and experiences also presents increased complexity in human relationships inherent in a group living situation. This is one of the important opportunities students have to learn from people of various backgrounds and experiences. In a residence hall, students are forced to interact at several levels. Outside of the residence hall or in their hometown community, issues tend to segment cultural groups and inhibit opportunities to understand and share an appreciation for what that culture has to offer.

Studying about a culture, or learning the language is only a small step in developing an understanding and appreciation for that culture. This is not to say that it will not be possible to establish an interpersonal level of communication with somebody from another culture, but only that it will require a conscious effort at understanding the person's background and experiences to do so. There is great value in developing an understanding and appreciation for another culture. It not only permits you to enter into what might be a rewarding interpersonal relationship with a person, but also helps provide you with the skills to work with people from varied backgrounds.

Language is an integral part of both our self-concept and our psychological processes. Our view of the world and our relationships with other people rest within our language and our ability to use it to control our environment. The development of our identity, one of the primary issues in the college years, is tied closely to our ability to use our langauge to control our environment. Our success in being able to control our environment through language begets more self-confidence. It is through language that we get feedback about ourselves, and are able to communicate our innermost feelings to other people. If we must communicate in our secondary language or dialect in order to receive feedback and to control our environment this presents an additional burden and inhibits our success in receiving the rewards and controlling our environment.

Basil Burnstein, as sociolinguist (1975), identifies two forms of communication. One he describes as an elaborated code of communication which employs complex syntax, written rules of grammar, elaborate lexicon, and the use of complex sentences to express ideas. The second language code he identifies as a restricted code. This code is based upon an understanding of commonly shared symbols and minimizes the use of complex and elaborate symbols. Standard English, that particular system of language heard on the six o'clock news and taught in high schools and colleges is an elaborated code. Valley girl talk, street talk, and some forms of interpersonal communication are restricted codes. It uses many commonly shared symbols and mutually shared experiences that need little explanation. We typically use restricted codes within the family and with close personal friends. Anyone who is able to communicate has access to some form of restricted code. The use of elaborated code, however, is available to many but not all speakers within a culture. One code is not necessarily better than another code. They are separate, and serve different purposes in our communication patterns.

Speakers of Black English who are also able to use standard English are considered to be functionally bidialectic in that they can speak Black English in situations appropriate to this communication pattern, and switch to standard English when it is necessary to communicate in this dialect. It is sometimes assumed that Black English is a substandard English form. This is not true. Black English is a separate linguistic system, with its own grammatical rules governing usage, a rich lexicon, and an intricate set of nonverbal and verbal intonational communication symbols. Black English is a separate language system or unique dialect. A student who is a competent speaker of Black English enters the university environment, predominated by the use of both elaborated and restricted forms of standard English. This student must communicate at a competent level both in Black English and standard English at a sophisticated level among both groups. Native speakers of standard English who come from a traditional White middle class background must also learn to improve their use of the elaborated form of standard English for use in the classroom, however, they are not required to switch between two separate dialects.

Other subcultural groups must also learn to accommodate the special demands placed on them in a standard English situations. The Cajun French of Louisiana, as well as people coming from isolated low-income rural areas in Appalachia must be able to shift to a new language dialect.

Language is one of the most visible signs of cultural differences inherent in the melting-pot present in residence halls. When cultures vary, values, habits, hygiene, food preferences, social customs, and a host of other things associated with a culture also vary. It is easy for Americans to sit in judgment of other cultures, using our culture as the standard. There is a tendency for us to ignore people who are different or to ostracize them because they do not share the same experiences. It stems from a need to be in homogeneous groups, to be close to other people, and to develop an interpersonal relationship with others. We recognize implicitly that it is more difficult to establish these relationships when our cultural experiences are uniquely different. Although different, it is not impossible and if achieved can provide one of the most rewarding friendship experiences a person can have.

There are some things that you can do to improve cross-cultural communication on your floor. First, you must spend time with a person from a different background; for the purpose of getting to know them and to develop an understanding of their unique experience. With international students you may wish to treat yourself to spending time learning about their country, where they went to school, what things are different between their country and yours, and finding things in their culture that you value. Often a student will be interested in sharing these experiences with other students in the living unit who are interested in learning about other cultures. A floor program on that particular country, or inviting the international student to participate in late-night discussions are ways to obtain that person's participation in the living unit and to diffuse cultural prejudices and biases that may be building. Second, if the student is exhibiting some behavior you find to be questionable, or seems to be particularly distraught over something, take the time to inquire. Males from middle-eastern countries as one example, are not reluctant to hold hands in public. In our culture, two men holding hands suggests that they may be homosexual. In the cultures of the mid east, it may only suggest that they are acquaintances. If you wonder about some type of behavior, religious practice, or other aspects, take the time to ask and find out what is going on. If the particular behavior is disruptive and causes conflicts or resentment in the living unit, this is a reason to talk with the student about the behavior. It is more than likely that the student will appreciate your inquiry and be interested in how her behavior could be viewed in the American culture.

Never sit in judgment of another person's experiences or culture. Cultures are different. One is not necessarily better than another. To a greater or lesser degree, we are all products of our environment. The freedom that you have as an American, the liberties and socially acceptable patterns of behavior that you know from our culture, may be completely unacceptable in another situation.

Be sensitive to how you would feel if the situation was reversed. Try placing yourself in the other person's situation. You might feel alone in a culture separate from what you are accustomed, using a language that you can speak but with which you still may have difficulty. A group of young people can be very authoritarian, overly involved in themselves, and searching for their own identity. It is obviously not an easy situation.

This same cultural sensitivity applies not just to people from other countries, but also to people from other subcultures within this country. There are some experiences unique to the Black community that are different, not better or worse, than the predominant middle-class white cultural experience of most university campuses. Take time to know and understand this experience. Also understand that students may feel more comfortable in relationships with people from their own subcultural backgrounds. In the Black community in particular, many students experience sanctions for participation or emulation of the dominant white culture of the university. This tends to be true for some American Indians, Chinese students, and certain religious subgroups such as students of the Islamic faith, certain fundamentalist Christian groups, and members of the Hispanic community.

Understanding the cultural differences, and getting to know more about the individuals in these subcultures will assist you in breaking down the cultural barriers and stereotypes identified with these groups. By diffusing these racial and cultural stereotypes you may be able to avoid some of the bigotry and cultural conflicts that occur when people live together without taking the time to know one another. Part of a student's education in the University should be developing an appreciation for other cultures. Each has something to offer.

SECTION 3

Confrontation and Crisis Management

CHAPTER 8
Behavior Problems, Confrontation, and Counseling

Counseling is never an excuse for discipline, yet the way you approach a disciplinary situation can still be within the framework of a counseling model. Some students undoubtedly feel a need to explore different college policies or simply to act out certain behaviors, sometimes to the point of breaking rules or infringing upon the rights of others. As an RA, you have an obligation to the institution and to the other students in your unit to enforce the policies that the college community has agreed upon to guide its standards of interaction. Though it may not always seem that a particular policy that you are enforcing is helping the student adjust to the responsibilities of college, in the long run learning to interact within this special living environment will aid the student in both accepting accountability for his action and developing respect for other people, their property, and their individual rights.

Types of University Policies

Before examining the disciplinary encounter, it is important to have a perspective on what the disciplinary process attempts to teach and how it has come to exist in its current state. At one time, universities had a caretaker, or *in loco parentis* (in lieu of parents), philosophy about the relationship between students and the institution. Educators perceived their responsibility to the students as one of making rules and regulations similar to those that parents may institute when educating their children. The federal courts at one time agreed with this educational philosophy (*Gott* v. *Berea College,* 1913) noting specifically that a duty of the college was to act *in loco parentis*. Though some institutions may still retain *in loco parentis* based rules and regulations, the majority of colleges have abandoned most of these in favor of policies based upon a community standard of behavior in five major areas: (1) regulations related to the health, safety, and well-being of the college community; (2) landlord-lessee policies; (3) federal, state, and local laws: (4) regulations designed specifically for the unique situations provided by a small-group living situation within a residence hall; and (5) regulations related to the academic mission of the institution. A key element in working with students in disciplinary encounters is for you, as the RA, to understand and communicate the reasons behind each of these institutional policies.

Health and Safety Regulations

A college has a responsibility to protect the health, safety, and well-being of students, faculty, and staff. This is a special obligation that must be ensured for the institution to be able to fulfill its educational mission. Policies in this area relate to security within individual buildings, possession of dangerous weapons on campus, state health codes, state fire regulations, and similar security or safety precautions. The rationale behind the prohibition against hot plates in student rooms, as one example, is probably determined by fire code regulations.

Most residence halls have operational policies that require doors to be secured at a certain time each evening and that visitors of the opposite sex be escorted by a resident of the building, and prohibitons against students having duplicate keys made for their rooms and the exterior doors of the building. These policies are directly related to the security of people in the building. In the past few years, a number of colleges and universities have reported rapes that have taken place within the residence halls themselves. Thefts of private and college property are not uncommon in residence halls where there is little or no security. It is simple to see why institutions must enforce these regulations.

Landlord/Lessee Regulations

The second category of regulations are landlord/lessee regulations. These are provisions of the contractual relationship between the student and the institution when the student is provided with housing in return for payment of a fee. Such regulations as not permitting students to keep animals in the residence hall may be both a health regulation and a contractual obligation that the student assumes when entering the residence hall. Other landlord/lessee policies relate to students paying for room damages or damage to public areas, check-in and check-out procedures within the residence hall, contract periods of the room (such as requiring that the room be vacated during academic vacation periods), and the right of the institution to inspect rooms for the purposes of enforcement of health and safety regulations. Most of the policies in the landlord/lessee relationship may be considered extradisciplinary, in that many institutions have chosen to regard them not as disciplinary violations, but as contractual violations that may carry the imposition of a fine. Noncompliance with the regulations could mean termination of the contract or a similar penalty.

Federal, State, and Local Laws

Educational institutions generally accept responsibility for enforcing federal, state, and municipal laws through various means and with various degrees of dedication. The major crimes related to theft, battery, possession of dangerous drugs, extortion, and similar violations are most commonly enforced by institutions. State institutions have an obligation to reflect the standards of the citizenry of the state, the interest of the alumni, the interest of the faculty, as well as the needs of the students. All of these groups play a part in the total university. The state has an interest in the university because of the funding it provides and because of the type of education that the people of the state want to see provided for their children. The alumni have an interest in the university because its reputation reflects directly upon the degrees that they received there. The faculty obviously have an interest in the university because their professional careers are reflected by the reputation of the institution. And of course students have an interest in the university, in that it is the education at that institution that they are purchasing and the reputation of the institution that their degrees will represent. Most state institutions will state, within their institutional philosophies that certain types of behavior related to legal violations are in opposition to the best interest of the institution and the students. However, an institution may not believe that it is the appropriate role of the resident assistant to enforce such policies. The area in which this is seen most clearly is in the area of laws related to alcohol and to the possession and use of marijuana.

Within the last decade, laws regulating the use of both alcohol and marijuana have undergone dramatic changes. The drinking age has been lowered in many states to eighteen, and marijuana in many circles has become a socially acceptable drug. Universities are placed in a paradoxical situation. On the one hand, they do not want to place the RA in an enforcement role within the residence hall, yet, on the other hand, they wish to provide an environment that is educationally sound and that reflects the basic educational interests of all members of the university community. This is a difficut task. Some institutions enforce both marijuana and alcohol regulations rigorously. They believe that this is consistent with their educational mission and will provide the type of living environment that is most conductive to the educational goals of the students. The reasons given for the enforcement of these regulations are (1) that the institution must follow through on its obligation to the state, the alumni, the faculty, and future student generations; (2) not to enforce these policies gives tacit approval for the violation of institutional policy and the law; (3) failure to enforce policies related to drug use encourages such behavior and promotes an environment that is not conducive to the educational interests of the institution and the students as a whole; (4) the university must stand for certain values and principles, both in theory and application;

(5) nonenforcement of laws related to marijuana and other drugs encourages the introduction of other more dangerous behavior related to drug trafficking and the influx of undesirable elements into the campus community.

Other institutions have taken an opposing philosophy, asserting that it is • not the institution's duty to monitor an individual student's behavior and that there are more important concerns of the institution than victimless crimes such as the use of marijuana or alcohol. The reasons given for defending this policy are: (1) marijuana is a socially acceptable drug to the majority of college students; (2) the purpose of the RA is counseling and not the enforcement of state law; (3) RAs are not trained as police agents and, therefore, should not involve themselves with the identification of and enforcement of law violations, except to protect the immediate well-being, safety, and security of residents in the unit; (4) the use of marijuana is a victimless crime in which no one suffers; (5) the use of the substance is basically a personal choice that a student must reach independently; (6) the university cannot enforce such rules and regulations, because it does not hold police power or have the technical or legal capability of enforcing such policies; and (7) since students are adults, it is the duty of police agents to enforce such laws as they would for any other adult members living within the community at large.

Either of these philosophies may be defendable within the context of the individual institution.

Small Group Living Regulations

The fourth area in which institutions often make regulations is in residence halls. This unique style of living requires regulations to help maintain an environment consistent with the mission of the institution. Policies related to quiet hours, conduct in the hallways, noise, and similar courtesy regulations are designed to enable all students to benefit from the environment without infringing upon the rights of any individual student. This is the area in which most of an RA's time is spent—helping people cooperate and learn to live together. Some students believe that they have a right to express themselves, even to the point of infringing upon others' rights. This does not necessarily mean that the RA must personally enforce all policies. A good case in point is the situation of a person playing a stereo too loud. It is generally considered best for the student who is being disturbed to first ask the other student to turn down his stereo. Too often people come to rely on the RA to fight all their battles and they begin to feel that the RA is employed to do nothing but enforce these kinds of rules and regulations. The first response that a person should have is to ask the offending student to comply with some reasonable noise level so that the complaining party can complete his or her studying. Only when this first course of action has failed should the RA actually become involved by making a similar request.

Academic Regulations

The last area in which the university makes rules and regulations related to its mission as an institution is in the area of academic standards. These rules and regulations seldom come under the purview of the RA. They are generally related to such areas as academic honesty, cheating, plagiarism, falsification of information, disregarding lawful directions of college officials, or failure to comply with certain rules related to the process or function of the institution.

Goals of Disciplinary Counseling

The process by which the university community educates students who violate the community standards is through disciplinary counseling. The goals of disciplinary counseling are as follows:

1. To educate the student by explaining the reasons for the community standard.
2. To bring the student's behavior into compliance with the community standard.
3. To have the student maturely accept accountability for his/her behavior.
4. To help clarify the student's values as they are related to the behavior in question.
5. To assist the student in making a more positive self-directed choice that will better enable him/her to assume later adult roles.
6. To help the student consider in advance the consequences of his/her behavior.
7. To determine with the student the reasons for his misconduct.

These seven goals can be said to provide the framework on which the disciplinary encounter takes place. Through a dialogue using techniques similar to those used in counseling, the RA attempts to bring about the accomplishment of one or all of these goals.

Confrontation Skills

There is no set of exact rules to tell you how to respond to a particular disciplinary encounter. You can, however, develop skills in confrontation that will be of assistance to you in many of your personal interactions. RAs find the first few confrontations with students difficult. They, however, do gain self-confidence in their ability to handle these situations as more of them arise. Few ever feel totally comfortable or enjoy the actual exchange.

One way to feel more comfortable is to develop your assertiveness. Assertive behavior is that behavior in which a person confirms his individual rights in a nonthreatening, nondefensive, interpersonal manner. It is behavior that is open, honest, direct, nonaggressive, and communicates to the other person the speaker's beliefs or opinions. The behavior does not demand other social skills such as compassion, empathy, or persuasion. It is most simply viewed as a statement of the individual's rights, beliefs, attitudes, feelings, opinions, and similar forms of personal expression.

Assertiveness is a personal exchange. Many people use it as part of their basic communication pattern. It is not a special technique used only in confrontations; it is communication that expresses how you actually feel. Examples of assertive communication behavior are given in such exchanges as the following: "Excuse me, but I would like to finish what I was saying." Or, "No, I will not run to the main desk to get you a room key. I need to be alone to complete this research project, could we talk later?"

Assertiveness is different from aggressiveness or passivity. Aggressive responses attack the other person or in some way infringe upon his rights. The passive response permits another person to take advantage of your rights. To be put upon or to be compelled through some sense of duty or tradition is to be passive in some situations. It is perfectly acceptable to let people take advantage of you if you are willing to accept the sacrifice of time or duty. If somebody inconveniences you by asking you to perform a special favor, being assertive does not necessarily mean that you must refuse to do the favor. It only means that if you feel that it will impose an inconvenience on you, to the extent that you do not wish to comply with the request, you state this and do not comply with the request. It indicates that you are in control of your own life and that you are not compelled to perform special services for individuals that unreasonably infringe upon you. Because you are an RA, there are certain duties that you will be expected to perform that may inconvenience you. The acceptance of these duties is not being passive. It is simply following through on the expectations of your position.

There are three assertive techniques that you should make part of your disciplinary counseling skills. The first is called the assertive confrontation. (Based on a model by Lange and Jakubowski, 1976) It follows a simple four-step pattern as follows: (1) describe the person's behavior in objective terms; (2) describe how this behavior affects you or the others within the unit; (3) describe how you feel about the behavior; and (4) describe what you would like to see the person do to correct the behavior.

Some examples of this are as follows:

"John, your stereo is very loud. The noise is preventing people on the floor from studying. I feel the stereo is too loud, and I would like you to turn it down."

"John, I saw you put glue in the lock of another student's room. Unless it is cleaned out before it hardens, a locksmith will be called to repair the lock at your expense. John, I do not think you have a right to damage university property or to inconvenience this other student. I would like you to clean out the lock and ensure that it is in working order. I will discuss this situation with the hall director for possible disciplinary action."

Another form of assertive confrontation emerges when a student has made a commitment for a certain type of behavior and then does not comply with the commitment. This may follow a discussion that you had earlier with the student about his behavior. Examples of this confrontation would follow a very similar format as follows: (1) statement of the behavior observed; (2) statement of the student's commitment; (3) presentation of contradication; (4) statement of how you feel; (5) statement of behavior you would like to see take place; (6) statement of steps you will take. An example of this form of confrontation would be as follows:

"John, I observed you smoking marijuana in the floor lounge. The last time this took place, you gave me your word that it would not happen again. I do not understand why you gave me your word if you did not intend to follow through. I am upset and angry that I cannot trust you and accept you at your word. I feel disappointed that you are unable to comply with your commitment. I would like you to stop this behavior immediately and get the marijuana out of the residence hall. I intend to discuss this situation with the hall director and to refer you for disciplinary action."

These two forms of assertive confrontation can be useful in your exchanges with students. They can also be useful in other interpersonal exchanges in which you feel that your personal rights have been infringed upon.

A third assertive technique is called the broken record technique. (Based on a model by Fensterheim and Baer, 1975) It is the simple assertion of your belief, opinion, or request. Your response to any remark is the same until the person complies with your request. Simply put, you repeat the same demand or request over and over and over in a broken-record type response. An example of this is as follows: (Paul is the RA. John is the student.)

Paul: John, I see that you have furniture in your room from the floor lounge. You know that this furniture should not be in your room. I would like you to take it back now, please.

John: I need it in my room for studying.

Paul: Unfortunately, there is not enough furniture for everyone, and the lounge furniture is to be in the lounge. Would you please take it back now?

John: I am studying right now. I will do it later.

Paul: I understand that, John. However, I would like you to take it back now, if you would, please.

John: But the furniture makes my room look so much better.
Paul: That may be true, but you will have to take it back now, please.
John: I would really like to keep it.
Paul: Yes, I understand, but please take it back now.

The exchange shows that Paul is requesting over and over that the same action be taken. Eventually, John will probably comply with the request, or the two will reach a compromise in which John may take the furniture back after he has completed studying. One thing that Paul, as the RA, could have attempted was to offer to help John take it back at that moment. The goal, after all, was to get the furniture returned to the lounge and to make John aware that the furniture did not belong in his room. If Paul could have accomplished this by grabbing one side of the piece of furniture and offering to help John carry it, this might have accomplished the same end.

Eye contact, body posture, the gestures you use, facial expressions, voice tone and inflection, timing, and content of information are all important behavior indicators to students as you express your feelings openly. These nonverbal signs of communication convey as much about your assertiveness as what you might be saying.

Disciplinary Counseling Model

Now that we have covered the types and reasons for regulations, the goals of disciplinary counseling and some assertive techniques, we can examine the process by which the goals of disciplinary counseling are accomplished. As in the counseling model, unless you have established yourself with your residents, your ability to confront students will be lessened. Students are more likely to respond cooperatively or to avoid a confrontation when they respect you and your position. It is difficult to confront people with their behavior and to refer them for possible disciplinary action, yet it is something that must be done if the environment and the goals of your program are to be ensured. The approach you take to accomplish this is important. We teach by the process we use in accomplishing our goals.

The model we use for a disciplinary encounter is similar to the one used in the helping-skills form of counseling discussed in the previous chapter. The major differences are in the dynamics of the disciplinary exchange and the student's perception of you. In most disciplinary encounters, there is a confrontation involving some alleged violation of regulations that may cause the student some form of punishment, whether actual or simply perceived. Chances are good that the student will view you as an adversary. The disciplinary model has five steps as follows: (1) collect the facts; (2) approach the student; (3) listen to the student; (4) take the necessary action; and (5) followup.

Step 1: Collect the Facts

Before you approach anyone with an allegation that he has violated a regulation, collect all the information you can. Often a student who relates information about the behavior of another student will not want it known that he provided this information. There is an interesting attitude in our culture that it is somehow more honorable to protect people who have violated regulations or the law than it is to hold these people accountable. Terms such as informer and stool pigeon are the labels our culture has attached to those who provide information on people who break the law. In any case, you will no doubt confront this problem regularly.

Obviously, the simplest way to resolve these situations is for the person who saw another person break a window to go to the culprit and tell him that he should pay for the damage and be accountable for his actions. What is more often the case is that you receive the information third-hand with the proviso that you not reveal your source. There are some circumstances in which you may wish to accept information under these conditions, but, in general, you should be reluctant. As a general rule, when a student tells you he wishes to share some information with you with the understanding that you will not pass it on to anyone else, you should tell him that you cannot offer this guarantee. After all, he may tell you that his roommate just robbed a bank or is selling hard drugs out of their room. Instead, tell the person that he will need to trust your judgment as to whether or not this information will need to be passed on to someone else.

Even though your informant has asked you not to tell the source of information, you can still approach the student who allegedly violated the regulation. It simply means that the credibility of your facts will be in question. It also means that you will have insufficient information to make a referral for disciplinary action to a college official. Neither of these points preclude you from approaching the alleged violator with the information you do have. This person may be very open about the situation and admit his involvement. If the person does not, you have still had the opportunity to discuss the behavior, a step that may have some long-range positive benefit.

You may at this point like to read ahead to the section on "How to Confront an Intoxicated Person" in the chapter on substance abuse. Note particularly the need to assess your own feelings about the person, and some suggestions on when to confront a person about his behavior.

Step 2: Approach the Student

Approach is a better word for this than *confront*. It is basically an attitudinal perception on your part. If you go to see the student with the attitude that this will be a "confrontation," you develop a mind-set that may be counterproductive to the accomplishment of your goals in contacting the student in the first place.

One of the key factors in a productive exchange is to engage the student in a meaningful dialogue concerning the alleged incident. If other people are present, the dialogue can become either a group discussion or an audience debate. Neither of these circumstances will be productive. It will be a losing situation for both you and the student. If you cannot isolate the student and must approach him while others are present, for whatever reason, deal only with the termination of existing behavior (*i.e.,* yelling, playing the stereo loud, or damaging property). Do not attempt to go beyond this point until you can find some future time to engage the student in a one-to-one discussion about his behavior.

Having said this, let us look at what you can expect from students when you approach them with an alleged violation.

One response students use is to deny that the event ever took place, to deny that they were involved, and to challenge you to prove in some legalistic framework that they are actually responsible. This we might call the "big lie" response. The student is often aggressive, hostile, and somewhat threatening. You can only relate the information you have and attempt to bring the issue to a level of common understanding. You may tell the student that you cannot resolve the situation at this point and that you will refer it to someone who can. This is probably the only course of action that may be available to you. It is unfortunate, because it really ends the opportunity for you to discuss his behavior with the student and to explain why you feel further action is necessary.

Students sometimes attempt to change the subject or minimize the consequences of their actions. This is a common response used to divert attention from the actual issue at hand to some other subject. The student may try to lead you into a discussion about the general correctness or incorrectness of a particular institutional policy. RAs who are expected to enforce prohibitions against marijuana are constantly confronted with these questions and should be prepared to respond to such challenges in a factual way that explains the policy and the institution's enforcement of it.

A version of the big lie is the third-degree questioning. In this response, the student challenges the information that you have received and your observations. Such questions as "How do you know that?" or "What makes you believe that?" or "Can you prove that?" are raised. Some students will want to examine every element of the information that you have and to place you on the defensive by demanding that you explain to them in detail every aspect of the information. They will attempt to refute and argue with you over every minor point. Bear in mind that it is the overview or larger picture that you must convey. Do not argue over "nit-picky" details that are probably irrelevant to what actually took place. You are only trying to determine the violator's view of what actually occurred.

Personal hostility and attacks on you as a person can be expected from some students. A student may become quite hostile and challenge your motives for questioning his behavior. He may suggest that you have singled him out because of some deep-seated personal hatred that you have for him. This is another defense technique intended to change the subject and to delay the issue at hand. Do not feel that you must justify your actions. Simply relate the behavior that you observed and question the person on why the behavior took place. Do not feel that you must defend yourself or your motives. It is enough to deny this accusation once, and it does little good to engage in a verbal exchange about past events or your perceptions of them.

Admission of guilt and a true act of contrition are yet another response technique. Some students will quite openly tell you that they were involved in some type of negative behavior and that they are sorry that they caused any problem—their goal being that you should, therefore, accept their true act of contrition and not make any further disciplinary referral. Though in minor situations, and based upon your perception of the individual, this might be appropriate, it can create a situation in which a student may feel that all that is necessary is to admit guilt and say he is sorry in order to evade accountability for his actions. Because a student says he regrets his actions does not necessarily mean that you should not make a referral. Admission of guilt is not necessarily the end goal. Remember, it is the process itself that is educational, and part of this process is an examination of values by the offending student. Sometimes going through the process of a disciplinary hearing or waiting to have a hearing is the most educational experience a student may have relative to this encounter. To avoid the process of disciplinary referral can leave the student with a less meaningful accountability for his action.

Often a student who admits guilt will then plead with you to not make a referral to higher authorities. This is an attempt to make you accept some guilt for doing your job and making a disciplinary referral. Remember, you are not doing anything to the student, he has brought the referral upon himself. If a student commits a violation serious enough to demand some type of disciplinary action, do not place yourself in the position of determining guilt or innocence or of giving dispensation to a person who has violated the regulations. It is important that students who attend your institution be treated fairly and consistently. Some of the realizations about the encounter can best be achieved through a session with a professional staff person, who will help the offending student examine the values that led him to make this inappropriate decision.

Establish a meaningful dialogue with the student. This is as much a goal as it is a technique. You want to reach a point where the student is willing to discuss the situation with you. Given the circumstances—a disciplinary encounter—establishing a meaningful dialogue can be difficult. You can do this, however, if you approach the student as an equal—an adult peer.

The student does not want to hear a lecture from you, nor does he want to be chastized or criticized. The approach that you should use is the same approach that you would use with a friend. You are not his parent and should not give him parental commands. The establishment of a meaningful dialogue means exactly that: dialogue, an exchange of ideas with a give-and-take response.

Disciplinary encounters may place you in a defensive position. Try to remain above the personal attacks that you may receive or the practical jokes that may follow a particular disciplinary referral. Chances are, if you accomplish your task well, the student will feel that your actions were justified and will respect you for taking the action. This can only be accomplished if you do not make the encounter a personal confrontation but rather deal with the situation objectively. The goal is not to see the student punished, but to help the student develop mature behavior.

Step 3: Listen to the Student

In this step, you listen to the student's explanation of what took place. You will use the same general listening techniques you learned in the previous chapter on counseling. You want the student to tell you what actually took place—the truth. This may not always be easy. The student may fear reprisal in the form of a disciplinary referral for the violation, or he/she might be afraid that you will lose respect for him/her. Either of these situations might cause the offending student to resort to some defense mechanism—that is, an attempt to explain behavior that cannot be excused in any other way. It is used by a person who feels threatened or insecure. Essentially, defense mechanisms help people protect their self-image or egos. Examples of defense mechanisms are: repression, anxiety, departmentalization, compensation, rationalization, and projection. The latter two, rationalization and projection, are probably the most common defenses used by students in a disciplinary encounter.

Rationalization is the attempt to justify one's behavior with excuses that offer a more acceptable motive for the behavior. The person denies accountability for the action, contending that it was justified because of special circumstances. For example, the student who is discovered to have stolen a book from another student may say that he was only borrowing the book for a short time to prepare for a test.

Projection is another way a person may reject responsibility for his actions. In projection, the person attempts to justify his behavior by attributing the same actions to everyone else. The all-too-common excuse of "everyone else does it" is offered as justification for the behavior. Apparently, if everyone else is violating a particular policy, it must be acceptable. The truth of the matter is probably that a few other people do violate the policy, but when their actions come to the attention of the staff, the offenders are held accountable.

Your objective is to help the student understand the faulty reasoning in offering these justifications. You wish to help the student understand that if his behavior was in violation of college regulations, he must accept responsibility for his actions. The willingness to accept responsibility is related directly to the student's maturity. As the student's values mature and as he develops a personal ethical standard of conduct, the willingness to accept responsibility for one's actions increases. The sole mitigating circumstance is what the person stands to lose by admitting responsibility. If this will mean that the student may be arrested, suspended from school, or subject to some removal of privilege or payment of fine, chances are less that the person will be willing to accept responsibility.

Remember, you are not talking with the student for the purpose of judging his guilt or innocence. If the student says he is not responsible for an alleged violation and you believe he is, you will probably need to refer him to a college official to review the situation and make the necessary determination. Your role is to help the student better accept responsibility for behavior that is for the most part known to both of you. Your objective is to assist him in sorting through what actually took place and to reach a common understanding without advocating any one particular point of view. You are the facilitator of the student's own review of the situation and an objective guide to help keep the student on a productive tract.

Step 4: Take Action

If it is clear that the student is in violation of a regulation of such a nature that it is necessary for you to make a disciplinary referral to a college official, inform the student of your decision. If you are not able to sort out the facts of the situation and there is a discrepency between what you believe to be true—based on the facts at hand—and what the student is willing to admit, make a disciplinary referral to resolve the disparity. It is generally not necessary to make a referral for a first-time violation of a minor college regulation, but it is important that you discuss the violation with the offending student and inform him that such conduct is not acceptable and if continued could lead to disciplinary action.

A disciplinary referral is regarded as punishment by most students. Realistically, it is the method that colleges use to educate students about their behavior. True, the student might be placed in some probationary status or perhaps suspended from school for a period of time. These actions, however, are educational. They state to the student that his conduct is not acceptable within the college community. If a student does not achieve academically, he "flunks out" of school. Similarly, if a student is unable to abide by the regulations set by the college community to guide student behavior, he has not fulfilled this aspect of his education.

By making a referral to the appropriate official of your institution, you are simply indicating that this particular student's conduct needs to be reviewed to determine if it is consistent with the expectations of the college community. If it is not, the college official, through whatever institutional process the school has adopted, will help the student bring his behavior within acceptable limits. If residence halls are truly part of the educational process and a student's conduct violates the reasonable standards agreed upon to guide conduct within this unique small group living situation, then there is every reason to believe that the student has failed this part of his education and should be held accountable.

Step 5: Follow-Up

If you make a disciplinary referral, chances are that your relationship with the student involved will be strained. You have two choices: you can continue to perpetuate the animosity between you and the other person, or you can make an effort to talk over the difficulty in the hope of reaching some common understanding. The only acceptable choice is the latter. After all, you will still probably be living in the same unit, and it is better to get feelings like these out in the open and then talk them over. The longer you wait to deal with the conflict, the more hostility will build up between the two of you.

Though it is easy to say that students should not take the referral as a personal affront, most students will. How you handle this follow-up can help ease the student's ego and help you remain above the immaturity and petty bickering that is likely to follow.

One of the more difficult aspects of a disciplinary referral is remaining objective. Your responsibilities are to bring the alleged violation to the attention of the appropriate staff person, to assist the student in understanding the reasons for the referral, and to help the student accept accountability for his behavior. This is where your involvement ends. If the student is found to be in violation of a regulation but very little action is taken, you should not feel betrayed. The student may believe he has beaten the system or beaten you, and you may feel that you lost and the student won. If you let yourself get caught up in this win-lose philosophy by becoming ego-involved in the outcome, you are defeating the purpose of the educational process. Remember, it is the *process* that is educational. The *outcome,* whether or not the student is punished in some way, is really less important to his education than the process of accepting accountability—even if his actions could not be clearly established by a college official.

After a student returns from a disciplinary hearing, he will probably need to reestablish himself within the peer group in the living unit. The student may allege that nothing happened to him, that he "beat" the system, or that in some other way he "won." There will probably be some attempt to minimize any action that may have been taken. You must maintain the confidentiality of any information you have about the hearing. This may be difficult, especially when you know that the student is not relating accurate information about his case. But you must remember that students have the right to disclose whatever facts about themselves they choose, and you do *not* have the right to disclose any such facts about them. Although you may feel that your personal credibility is at stake among your residents, in truth your credibility and personal integrity would be compromised more by sharing confidences and bringing yourself down to the level of engaging in petty bickering.

Tips on Disciplinary Counseling

1. Many students will want to discuss problems or information regarding a situation only if you promise not to tell anyone else. "I'll tell you if you promise not to tell anyone." What the student is really saying to you is, "I trust you, but not your judgment." What is more important is that this type of confidentiality can place you in a very awkward position. What if the student reveals a very dangerous situation? Or what if the student confesses his involvement in a crime? What do you do then? Do you withhold this information from the appropriate college officials and thereby become party to the violation, or do you breach the student's trust in you by promising to do one thing and then doing another? The only thing you can do is to tell the student that you will need to decide what you will be obligated to pass on and what you can retain as confidential after you have heard the information. To accept information under the promise of withholding it as confidential places you in a losing situation.

2. Be familiar with the college regulations and, most importantly, with the rationale behind them. This information can only be received by discussing the rationale for various policies with the people making those policies.

3. Never openly discuss your objections to policies or regulations with the people with whom you are expected to work in an enforcement capacity. You may have objections to certain policies; most people do. However, the appropriate forum for discussion is not in floor meetings or with residents of the floor, but in discussion with staff and the people who can affect changes. To share your personal concerns about policies with other students may make you seem hypocritical when you are obliged to enforce these policies.

4. Never tell your residents that as long as you do not see them violate a policy, it will be all right to do it. This often occurs in institutions where RAs

are expected to enforce marijuana and alcohol policies. RAs often say that it is all right for the residents to smoke or drink in their rooms as long as they, the RAs, do not know about it. This communicates to students that certain behavior is approved as long as they are not caught. You will find that this position will defeat your credibility in the unit very quickly when you are obliged to enforce the policy.

5. Do not withhold information from supervisory staff. If it is determined that you had information about certain events and made promises not to release it for personal reasons, this could be a justification for removing you from your position. Remember, you are not a student advocate whose function is to defend students against the college; you are an employee of the college whose function is to help implement its goals, policies, and philosophies. There is an appropriate place for dissension, but it does not include leading groups of your residents to disobey policies.

6. Enforce policies and regulations consistently throughout the year. Do not, however, earn the reputation of being a super-sleuth. Be flexible and understanding, but clearly outline the boundaries for acceptable and unacceptable behavior.

7. Always remember that the immediate goal of a disciplinary encounter is to terminate the violation. If the goal is to end a fight, deal with ending the fight and move on from there. Do not feel that every time you have an encounter with a student because of his behavior, you must make a referral. Referrals are made for situations in which, in your opinion, or by university policy, such a referral is called for.

8. Keep a personal log on students who continually seem to have minor problems of a disruptive and irritating nature but not sufficient to merit a referral. If you must talk with a student about specific behavior (*i.e.,* loud stereo, smearing shaving cream on the floor, or any number of other minor actions that do not merit a referral to a disciplinary officer), make a record of the time, date, event, and the fact that you spoke to him. If a referral at a later time becomes necessary, this information will help establish for others that you have been performing your duty and that you are not referring the student for a single small infraction. Too often, RAs become so fed up with a particular student that they make a referral in an "I finally got you, you SOB" mood. They expect a disciplinary officer or a hearing committee to come down hard on the student, but if the student has had no other violations and you are not able to establish that you have had continual problems with him, chances are that the disciplinary committee will view only the individual situation and will not consider past events or records. Some committees refuse to examine past events that are not substantiated by a hearing; however, most committees and disciplinary officers will listen to your statement of disciplinary encounters related to the student's behavior. The opportunity to introduce

such statements into a hearing depends on how legalistic your particular hearing group wants to become.

9. Do not become ego-involved in making referrals and in the outcomes of those referrals. A referral is not a win/lose situation. It is not important that the student be found guilty or that he receive a harsh punishment for a violation. There is no contest between you and the student. Your role is to provide information and to bring disruptive misconduct to the attention of officials who will help the student overcome his problem.

10. If you must make a referral in a threatening situation involving students who are intimidating or a situation in which you know there will probably be a disciplinary referral, make certain that you have the assistance of another staff member or at least someone else who is willing to support your statements. In a hearing, you will be given some degree of credibility; however, you too will need to substantiate or support your assessment of the situation and of how you conducted yourself.

CHAPTER 9
Conflict Resolution

Defining Conflict Situations

As an RA, you will be confronted by a number of different conflict situations. Most of them will involve conflicts between a person and a policy or conflicts between two individuals on a particular subject. A conflict may be said to exist when at least two parties perceive that they have mutually exclusive goals—that is, that the satisfaction of one goal is incompatible with the satisfaction of another.

Many people have misconceptions about conflicts. They often believe that conflict is bad, so it should be eliminated as soon as possible, or that a conflict disrupts the natural harmony of the state of man and thus should be eliminated. This is not true. It is also not true that conflicts frequently occur because individuals misunderstand each other or that all conflicts can or should be resolved.

A conflict can stimulate the examination and resolution of many problems. It stimulates curiosity, creativity, an exploration of personal values, and prevents stagnation. When conflict is viewed in a positive framework, it can be an enjoyable exchange of ideas; after all, it allows individuals to use their capabilities to the fullest extent to defend and augment their interests and to explore their own ideas. It is through conflict that people begin to shape their values by having their attitudes and beliefs challenged by others. A positive conflict situation can foster respect and can consolidate groups of individuals.

Conflict can be positive if all participants are satisfied with some part of the outcome. It is not positive if the participants leave with hostile attitudes or mistrust and defensiveness toward one another. Thus, a constructive conflict situation is characterized by: (1) constructive spirit and friendly attitude; (2) trust; (3) open, honest communication; (4) sensitivity to similarities; (5) a nonthreatening atmosphere; and (6) some satisfaction for all parties. (Cunningham and Berryman, 1976) A destructive conflict situation could be characterized by opposite types of behavior, such as distrust, defensiveness, hostility, lack of communication, maximized differences, and general competitiveness.

The causes of conflicts are (1) value differences, (2) life-style differences, and (3) inter-personal communication breakdowns. Of these, value differences probably create the greatest number of conflicts. One person may require a neat and orderly environment, whereas another person needs the freedom to be disorganized and sloppy; this difference can lay the foundation for a roommate conflict over the degree to which their room will be cluttered or kept clean. Some of the fiercest conflicts come in discussions of politics, religion, sex, and other heavily value-loaded subjects. Should America have a voluntary army or should it have a draft system for military service? This type of question is in an area in which conflict and the discussion revolving around it can be very positive. It gives all parties an opportunity to express and explore their values and to deal with other people's views. Such a conflict assumes the context of a potentially positive encounter. The conflict that arises, however, between a boyfriend and girlfriend in which one wishes to express his/her sexuality while the other wishes to protect his/her virginity is another form of value conflict. The discussion revolving around why each person believes the way he or she does can be a positive exchange.

There are many differences in life-style found among the residents of any living unit where people come from different cultural, economic, and educational backgrounds. People are usually most comfortable with other people who are most like themselves and least comfortable with people who are most unlike themselves. When a number of people from different backgrounds are placed together in a living unit, the foundation is laid for conflicts based on differences in life-styles. For example, if a roommate who likes classical music is placed with a roommate who likes hard rock, the result could be some real conflicts based upon life-style. Such a situation, however, also provides the opportunity for each to learn something about the other's background and life-style and, perhaps, to alter, change, or at least reevaluate her own. It all depends upon how the people involved perceive it. If they understand that differences exist based upon life-style differences and talk about the differences in their backgrounds and life-styles, why they believe what they do, and how they were raised, chances are that many negative conflict exchanges could be avoided.

Lack of appreciation or understanding of other people's human needs lays the groundwork for a number of other conflict situations. If a person feels that she is not being treated openly or fairly, or if she believes that her ideas are discounted or devalued, she comes to feel rejected and may lash out in some form of defensive revenge. Such conflicts are created by poor interpersonal communication and the inability of one person to accept the other without being judgmental or evaluative. Conflicts of this type are common, but they often require the attention of a skilled observer to discover the reason why one person may react negatively to another.

Management Model for Roommate Conflicts

As an RA, you will deal with two general categories of conflict: conflicts between people and conflicts between a person and university policy. In the first conflict situation, conflicts between individuals, you will serve as mediator or moderator (facilitator). In the second conflict situation, you may find that you become an agent in the conflict itself. Let us deal with the second type of conflict, that between an individual and a policy, first. As an RA, you are often called on to confront a student with a violation of policy. Your role in this encounter is that of arbitrator. After all, you are not the one who developed the policy nor do you, as an individual have a vested interest in its enforcement, other than as it applies to your position as an RA. In these situations, it is important to remember that the conflict is not between you and the other person, but between the university policy and the student's behavior. Should you become involved in such a situation, you may wish to review the chapter on disciplinary counseling.

Roommate conflicts are probably the most common kind of conflict with which you will come in contact. Most of the time the individuals involved will be able to work through their problems without outside intervention. This is usually the best way to have these conflicts resolved. Roommate conflicts can be a little bit like family feuds, where outsiders are not always welcome. Occasionally, however, a roommate conflict may spill over to affect other residents in the unit. When this happens, you will be compelled to intervene in some manner. On other occasions, both or one of the roommates will come to you for advice, suggestions, or mediation in the conflict between them. When entering into this type of situation, bear in mind that they are not coming to you for a judgment on whose behavior is correct and whose is incorrect, but for assistance in working through their conflict.

Grant E. Miller and Steven D. Zoradi (1975) have developed a simple behavioral approach for roommate conflict resolution. It is based on a seven-point model often used for resolving marital conflicts. The roommate model is as follows:

1. *Problem recognition.* RA calls roommates X and Y into their room for a conference to urge a discussion of the conflicts.
2. *Problem definition.* RA listens alternately to both roommates' stories, using frequent paraphrasing to achieve full understanding.
3. *Commitment.* RA asks both X and Y if they are willing to solve the problem.
4. *Highlighting pleasing and displeasing behaviors.* If both roommates agree to attempt to resolve their conflict, specific pleasing and dis-

pleasing behavioral data are obtained about each roommate from the other in each other's presence. Pleasing and displeasing data must be observable. They must not be judgmental statements such as "X is sloppy," but rather "X never washes his/her jeans."

5. *Negotiation.* Roommates trade and negotiate specific behavior to satisfy the needs of each. For example, X will allow Y to smoke in the room if the window is open.

6. *Contracting.* A contract is made using the specific likes and dislikes of each roommate. After X and Y come to an agreement, they cosign a contract that will be posted conspicuously in their room.

7. *Follow-up.* New contracts are made weekly. Intervention by the RA is terminated as soon as possible.

Using this model, Miller and Zoradi conducted an experiment in two residence halls with approximately six hundred students. In the experiment, half of the RAs were trained in the conflict-resolution model and half were not. In most of the conflicts in living units where the RAs were trained to use this model, the RAs used it to resolve conflicts. In the living units where the RAs had not been trained in the use of the model, conflicts were handled by using whatever other resources were available to the RA, along with her individual skills. At the end of the semester, the number of roommate changes in the living units where the conflict resolution model was used was compared with changes in the other living units where the conflict-resolution model was not used. Almost twice as many roommate changes occurred in living units where the conflict-resolution model was not used.

It is important to know that in using this model, the RA serves solely as a mediator. She does not sit in judgment over who is right and who is wrong. The goal of the model is to help the students work through their own problem. No attempt is made by the RA to resolve the conflict by a determination of right or wrong.

Analyzing Conflict Situations

The negative elements of conflicts, such as competition, mistrust, defensiveness, impaired communication, maximized differences, reduced alternative courses of action, and threats, coercion, and deception, seem to be identified closely with nonconstructive conflicts between individuals. It is possible to analyze the conflict interaction between two individuals. If you happen to be an agent in the exchange, it is still important that you stop and analyze the conflict situation.

The first thing to look for is defensive communication. People become defensive when they feel threatened and attempt to dominate, impress, or assert they are correct. Characteristics of such defensive communication are an almost total lack of listening or understanding, and attacking, aggressive, and hostile behavior. Defensive communication is typical in some exchanges and is not conducive to the resolution of the problem.

Hostile communication is another form of conflict behavior characterized by direct verbal assaults. The opposing individual or her ideas are criticized, ridiculed, or made fun of by the other person. Hostile communication is often a prelude to some type of overt action such as a physical encounter or threat.

Manipulative communication often takes place in conflict situations. One of the opponents tries to manipulate the situation or make things turn out in her favor. Often she tries to get the other person to do a particular thing or to manipulate the other person into doing something against her will.

Avoidance is a way of changing the subject to avoid dealing with a topic that is threatening. An opponent in a conflict situation may use this ploy to escape the responsibility of dealing with the conflict.

Evaluative responses of the other person's message or communication are another approach that some people use when they attempt to discuss conflicts they are having. One person makes a statement, and the other person, instead of responding directly to the statement, evaluates or judges it.

People in a conflict situation often hear only what they wish to hear. This is called selective perception. They hear either what they want to hear or what they are expecting to hear; that is, they fail to listen and truly understand what the other person is saying.

All of these communication exchanges are typical in a hostile conflict encounter. They are characterized by conflict confrontation and by each person trying to win the support of the other person or of third party nonparticipants. As a mediator or facilitator in the resolution of the conflict, you can employ two communication approaches to intervene in helping the disputing individuals resolve their differences.

The first communication technique is called metacommunication. It means talking about what has been communicated. For example, you can make such statements as, "What I hear both of you saying is . . ." or, "I don't believe you are actually hearing what student X was saying," or "Could you paraphrase for us what you just heard student X say?" In this way you are establishing a common understanding of what is actually being transmitted. The real difficulty in communication is conveying one's thoughts and feelings through the abstract symbols of words. Words do not always accurately convey what people are trying to say; after all, as we said earlier, words and phrases have different meanings for different people. As you might imagine when lifestyles are in conflict, different words and phrases frequently carry different cultural meanings. It is important, when discussing the differences between disputants, that you emphasize an understanding of what each person is saying.

Empathy is the second skill that you can employ as a mediator. That is, you should not take the side of one person against the other, but rather you should empathize with each person's situation. You must be careful, however, that each individual does not address you as a way of trying to win your support for her particular point of view. Your goal is to have them exchange ideas about how they feel about one another, not to try to convince you that one is right and the other is wrong. So, while you show empathy for each person's problem, at the same time you must remain objective. And this means that you must be able to empathize to some degree with each one of the individual situations and show compassion and caring for the resolution of the particular problem. You should try to feel what each person is feeling, but most important, you need to help each of the parties understand what the other party is feeling. Help each of the parties to empathize with the other person's view or perception of the situation.

To prevent threats, coercion, deceptions, and hostile types of conflicts, attempt to maximize the similarities between the differing points of view. Concentrate not on their differences, but their similarities. Define the differences and help each of the participants understand why the differences exist. It is not productive to the conversation for one person to condemn or judge the other person's behavior; rather she should express how she feels about that person's behavior. It is important that one party does not devalue or discount the other person's views and that they each listen actively and asks questions for clarification and meaning.

Six Rules for Conflict Mediation

1. Never take sides. This means that you should never become the decision-maker. Never side with one individual against the other. Never defend one person's point of view. When necessary, you may ask questions for clarification or feed back your perceptions, not to devalue one person's position but to bring to her attention how other people perceive what she is saying.
2. When possible, employ a strategy of win-win to resolve conflicts. It is almost always possible that each person can walk away feeling that she has made her feelings understood and has won at least part of the conflict.
3. Help to assure that each person's personal integrity is maintained. It is never acceptable to have one person feel debased or humiliated. This simply lays a foundation for greater hostility and is not an adequate resolution to any conflict.
4. Get conflicts into the open. If people are arguing back and forth about a particular situation, as mediator you may be able to assist them in defining their conflicts. It is better to get a conflict out in the open where it

can be confronted rather than to keep the hostility bottled up inside and react negatively to each other without adequate explanation.

5. Be aware of barriers to conflict resolution. Defensiveness, put-downs, judgmental reactions, gamesmanship, manipulation, discounting, aggressive attacks, and similar types of behavior are barriers to communication and play a counterproductive role in the resolution of conflicts.

6. Do not escalate conflicts by involving more people than necessary. Resolve conflicts at the lowest possible level between the individuals who are directly involved. When too many people are involved, some individuals become too concerned with maintaining loyalties and are hence less interested in resolving the conflict.

CHAPTER 10
Suicide Intervention

Suicide is the third leading cause of death among college students. More than 5,600 young people under the age of 25 took their own life in 1981 alone; the last year for which these statistics are available (Kraft, 1983). In the decade of the 70s, there was a 66% increase in suicide for this same age group (National Center for Health Statistics, 1983). One recent study (Kraft, 1983) showed that 70% of some 100,000 college freshmen surveyed had recently thought about suicide, however, fewer than 1% had made an attempt.

These statistics may represent only a portion of the actual number of people who kill themselves. Because of the religious and social stigma attached to the act, families are quick to cover it up. Many deaths attributed to automobile accidents, as one example, may actually be suicides. In 1963 Dublin estimated that 15% of the automobile accidents were actually suicides. Given the recent rise in suicides, it is likely that this percentage has increased. Because of the poor reporting of suicides, it is estimated that the actual number of suicides in the United States may be three to four times higher than reported. Klageburn (1976) estimates that there may be as many as 200,000 to 400,000 suicides annually.

Few if any campuses have been spared the tragic occurrence of a student committing suicide. The pressures of college life and the difficult transition from adolescence to adult roles while balancing the pressures of academic work, parental demands, financial problems, and competition for grades all too frequently culminate in suicide. At institutions where academic pressure and competition for grades are rigorous, there is increased potential for suicide. Students at some of these schools have coined terms for the act of suicide, such as "gorging out" used at Cornell University which refers to a student committing suicide by jumping into one of the gorges or ravines that run through the campus.

Causes of Suicide

The causes of suicide are many. Binstock (1974) attributes many suicides to cultural pressures placed on individuals that prohibit them from freely expressing their aggressive feelings. In child-rearing practices and other forms of interaction in our society, she feels that we repress natural feelings of aggression through an emphasis on guilt as a source of control. In support of her contention, she points out that suicides are highest among people with better educations, artistic and professional people, and generally people who fall into the upper-middle class. Repressed feelings of anger among these individuals, she explains, encourage some of them to escape from this inner anger and pressure by suicide.

Cantor (1972) suggests that the combination of sex, sibling position, and family composition during the developmental years in early life make certain individuals more prone to attempting suicide. In studies by Balser and Masterson (1959) first-born females with younger brothers were found to have the most difficulty with the sibling relationship and tended to be more competitive, anxious, submissive, and dependent. These things, they hypothesize, provide a way of viewing the world that may permit the individual, at some point, seriously to consider taking her own life.

Pretzel (1972) attributes suicide to the combination of increased stress beyond what an individual considers tolerable and the recognition of an inability to cope with this stress. Coleman (1972) attributes the cause of suicide to an interplay of (1) interpersonal crisis, (2) failure in self-evaluation, and (3) loss of meaning and hope. These three factors bring about a sense of despair and stress beyond the individual's tolerance. Suicide then becomes a means of escape, a final solution to the problem.

Symptoms of Suicide

People who are suicidal share some common characteristics. Shneidman (1969) identifies four characteristics of a suicidal person as follows:

1. Depression. The person's feelings shift from external to internal sources, and he becomes increasingly concerned with his own emotional well-being and exhibits different sleeping and eating patterns, and a general withdrawal from other individuals and ordinary activities.
2. Disorientation. A person may experience a misperception of reality and a difficulty in developing a frame of reference in which he can function.
3. Defiance. In an attempt to reestablish control over his environment, a potentially suicidal person will react negatively to other people and be particularly defiant of authority, rules, regulations, and other constraints placed upon him.

4. Dependence/Dissatisfaction. A person who feels dependent upon somebody else and is very unhappy about this condition may also feel despair over his inability to change things.

Ingal (1968) identifies five other characteristics often associated with suicidal persons:

1. Giving up—feelings of helplessness or hopelessness.
2. A depreciated picture of oneself.
3. A loss of satisfaction from personal relationships or from one's role in life.
4. A break in one's sense of continuity between the past, present, and future.
5. A reactivation of memories of earlier periods of giving up on life.

These are common characteristics of an individual undergoing severe emotional strain that may culminate in suicide. They are recognizable in a counseling situation or in discussions with the individual. They are not, however, readily observable without some type of interaction with the individual. A trained observer, such as a psychologist, may identify the composite of these characteristics as silhouetting a suicidal person; however, a casual observer or an RA may not recognize the same characteristics as indicative of a person who is suicidal.

Some of the more obvious symptoms are such things as giving away prize possessions, living alone, a radical change in the person's life-style, or the loss of something very important (home, money, parent, etc.) (Benensohn 1976). Continual loss of sleep, general stress, anxiety, a feeling of depression, and the loss of a sense of identity are also indicators of a person's dissatisfaction with the current state of affairs.

Lee (1978) divides the signs and symptoms into three general categories, which she identifies as (1) emotional, (2) behavioral, and (3) physical. The symptoms or signs that can be observed, according to Lee, by people in contact with a potential suicide are as follows:

1. The emotional signs include a dull, tired, empty, sad, numb feeling, with little or no pleasure derived from ordinary enjoyable activities and people.
2. The behavioral signs are expressed as irritability, excessive complaining about small annoyances, inability to concentrate, difficulty in making decisions, crying, and excessive guilt feelings.
3. The physical signs are described as loss of appetite, insomnia or restless sleep, weight loss, headache, and indigestion.

These are signs you should be able to observe through your daily interaction with the students in your living unit. Reports by a roommate or other people in the unit can also be indications that a person is experiencing some problem. Most people indicate that they plan to take their own life prior to the actual commission of the act. In essence, the person is asking for somebody to help. Through nonverbal signs, such as severe depression and anxiety, or by talking about the act of suicide itself, the person may be signaling for assistance.

One may summarize the symptoms of suicide into two major categories: (1) those that relate to depression, and (2) those that relate to ambivalence. These are the two major components or characteristics of the suicidal person. Though not all persons who are depressed are suicidal, almost all people who are suicidal are depressed. Weiner (1975) states that depression is the psychopathology found most often in the deaths of adolescents fifteen to nineteen years old. As Lee (1978) points out, "unrecognized and unrelated depressive illness all too often leads to suicide or at least attempted suicide. Anxiety, agitation, apprehensions, and a pervasive feeling of worthlessness are the components of a depressive state that could lead to suicide." (p. 201)

The feeling of ambivalence is analogous to a feeling of hopelessness and a loss of caring about the future. It is characterized by no longer thinking in terms of the future. Once a person has reached the decision to end his life, the person will often exhibit a feeling of elation. This occurrence of "good spirits" is often interpreted as an improvement in the person's psychopathology. In reality, this improved sense of well-being may be a signal that the person has made the decision and is now relieved that finally the pressure and stress are lifted and that there is a resolution to the problem. The ambivalent attitude of not caring what happens is also a typical sign that summarizes many of the symptoms previously discussed.

Suicide Myths

One of the main difficulties in understanding the suicidal person is the amount of misinformation and myth that surrounds the subject. Below are listed a series of common myths about suicide.

Myth 1. Suicide is an inherited characteristic that passes from generation to generation. Children who have parents who commit suicide are more likely to commit suicide themselves.—Actually, there is no correlation to suggest this.

Myth 2. People who talk about suicide do not follow through.—This is not true. Stengel (1964) has shown that 70 percent of all people who commit suicide clearly announce their intenions within three months prior to the act.

Myth 3. Once a person has tried to commit suicide, he will not try again.—Not true. Approximately 12 percent of those who fail an attempted suicide try again within three years (Schochet 1970).

Myth 4. People who commit suicide have an intrinsic death wish.—Not true. Most suicidal people are actually gambling with suicide. Generally, suicidal people will leave themselves a way out. On the one hand, they want to take their own lives; on the other hand, they are still not sure that they really want to die.

Myth 5. Women are more likely to commit suicide than men.—Not true. Though more women attempt suicide, approximately twice as many men actually succeed in killing themselves. This is due to the fact that most men choose a method of suicide that is more lethal than the methods women often choose (Davis 1968).

Myth 6. The decision to take one's own life is a sudden decision generally triggered by some traumatic or immediate crisis.—Actually most suicides are the result of a long period of stress, crisis, depression, and poor self-image.

Myth 7. Only mentally ill people commit suicide.—Though many who commit suicide are unhappy and emotionally upset, most people are not mentally ill when they commit suicide.

Counseling Potentially Suicidal Students

Whatever the causes of suicide—and there are many who speculate on them—the key problems for you as an RA are how to deal with the crisis when it occurs and, most importantly, how to recognize a potentially suicidal student. The possibility of a suicide occurring within your living unit is very real. As a counselor/helper, you need to develop a compassionate, sensitive, and informed approach to recognizing the signs of stress and the appropriate responses to facilitate constructive assistance to the would-be suicidal person. Because of your close contact with students in your living unit, you are the person with the greatest likelihood of recognizing the symptoms of a potential suicide.

Before you consider working with a potentially suicidal student, it is important that you understand your own feelings about the subject. If you have strong religious beliefs about suicide and view the taking of one's own life as a violation of moral law, as Emmanual Kant did, or if you view life as a form of vital existance, as William James did, you must be sensitive to how this will affect your ability to help a student accept the intervention of a trained professional. The opposite is also true. You may believe, as David Hume did, that an individual has the right to commit suicide or that suicide is only an abandonment or denial of the will to live, as Schopenhuer believed. Whatever your personal view, consider it carefully and weigh your feelings about it.

You must also be prepared to work with the student who has attempted suicide and has returned to live in your unit once again. This person may continue to be a potential suicide for some time after the occurrence. Your ability to recognize and understand your own feelings about the subject and to help the individual work through the problems will be a key factor in your ability to intervene effectively and constructively in working with the potentially suicidal student.

Kennedy, (1977) in his book for the nonprofessional counselor explains the importance of maintaining a psychological distance when working with a potentially suicidal person. He explains it as follows:

> It is hard for counselors to realize that they are not God and that although they approach their task with sensitivity and dedication, they neither prevent, nor postpone suicide or any other unhappiness in life. It is a sad but true axiom for psychology that a person who wants to commit suicide will eventually be able to do so no matter how we may try to prevent it. Counselors need a sensible approach to their own mental health in these circumstances. They cannot make demands on themselves that they cannot possibly meet. They cannot take responsibility for all the things that their clients do. We say yes to life for our clients, but we must be prepared for the fact that some of them will say no.
>
> The capacity to be realistic in the dangerously unpredictable circumstances connected with suicide actually frees a counselor to be more sensitive and responsive to troubled individuals and their families. There are many good things counselors can do, but there are things they cannot achieve in the way of controlling the decisions of others. The counselor's ability to balance these considerations determines their success in managing their own stress. (p. 247)

Counseling suicidal people is a difficult and complex task. No RA can be asked to master the necessary skills. Professional counselors spend years learning to understand and help people through the personal crises that precipitate suicide. Your responsibility as an RA is to be a supportive guide to the individual in crisis and your goal is to have the student seek professional assistance with his problems.

Do's and Don'ts for Working with the Suicidal Student

The first rule in approaching a situation in which the student may be suicidal is to recognize your own skills and limitations. Remember, you are not in this alone. You have the support of a professional staff and the guidance of other people at your institution. It is imperative that these people be kept informed and involved in the on-going discussions with the individual student through this time of crisis and stress. Your assistance in bringing about a realization on the part of the troubled student that he may need additional help will be the greatest service that you can render. If you are confronted with a student who is discussing suicide or perhaps a student who is attempting suicide, there are some things that you should and should not do.

Don'ts for Counseling the Suicidal Person

1. Don't dismiss or discount any suicide threat.
2. Don't argue with the individual about whether or not he should live or die. This is not the time for a philosophical discussion about the pros and cons of living. The only discussion should center around the person living.
3. Don't make statements like, "Oh, go ahead and do it, I dare you." Such challenge and shock statements may be all the impetus the student needs to commit the act.
4. Don't be afraid to ask the person if he is considering suicide. This may be the opportunity the student is seeking to discuss the subject. Most people do not really want to commit suicide and are looking for people to help them find reasons to live.
5. Don't overreact or panic when a person begins to talk about suicide.
6. Don't argue with the person by making such statements as "This isn't going to make things better. Suicide is a mortal sin, and you will go to hell."
7. Don't try to cajole a person out of suicide by changing the subject and trying to make light of a situation by being overly humorous. The person intends you to take this situation seriously and does not need you to be overly cheerful and happy-go-lucky.
8. Don't be overly cool about the crisis. Show concern and care, not ambivalence, about the person's crisis and stress.
9. Don't try to analyze and interpret the person's behavior. He does not need a psychoanalytic session with you. He needs you to listen and to be supportive.

Do's in Counseling

1. Do take every suicide threat seriously. Sometimes a person who is only making a suicidal gesture to get attention may accidentally injure himself seriously enough to cause death.
2. Do be aware of information regarding drugs and how it may be lethal. Kiev (1975) found drugs have been found to be involved in over one-third of all reported suicides.
3. Do use questions that force the student to concentrate on his positive resources and on contributions that he has made. Such questions as "I know that there have been many things that you have enjoyed about life, what are they?" Or "You must have considered the reasons for living as well as dying. What reasons did you consider for living?"
4. Do seek support and help in a crisis situation by sending others for assistance.
5. Do stay with the person if he has attempted suicide.
6. Do be willing to listen. Do be sensitive, empathetic, and attentive.
7. Do be supportive and offer your continued help to the student in the future.

Model for Suicide Intervention

One course of action for working with a potentially suicidal person is outlined here. This model is intended to apply to a student who is contemplating suicide. It is not designed to be used with a person who may be in the process of attempting suicide. This is, obviously, an emergency situation that calls for the involvement of professional staff and medical personnel. Should it happen that someone has taken an overdose of drugs or is in some way threatening to kill himself, send for help and continue talking with the individual, in a calm, soothing voice about reasons he may have considered for living.

This model is designed to help you in counseling a student who may be contemplating suicide. If you panic and immediately run for the telephone to get a professional staff member to handle the situation whenever there is a mention of suicide, you may be overreacting to the student's comments. Many people contemplate suicide at some point in their lives, and it is all right to think and talk about it. This model is designed to help you assess the seriousness of the potential suicide, as well as to help you in your discussions with the individual. Any attempt or discussion with a student about suicide should be taken seriously. Although the person may be asking only for support, or attention, you are not in a position to second-guess the motives. If a student is unable to get attention in this manner, he may take additional steps to see that you do care and are concerned.

Kennedy (1978) reports on a **lethality scale** used by the Los Angeles Suicide Prevention Center to assess the immediacy and severity of a person's crisis by assessing the potentiality of suicide. A modification of this scale appears below for you to use in assessing the suicide potential of a student in crisis.

1. *Sex*—The potential is higher if the person is male or a first-year female student.
2. *Symptoms*—The potential is greater if the person cannot sleep, expresses feelings of despair, or has dramatically altered sleeping or eating patterns within the past few weeks.
3. *Stress*—The potential is greater if the person is under stress from exams, pressure from parents, or pressure to be admitted into grad school, etc.
4. *Suicidal plan*—The potential is greater when the plan is more detailed, where the victim has access to a means (guns, drugs) and where the method is highly lethal.
5. *Family and friends*—The potential is greater if the person is a loner in the living unit, and has no family or close friends.
6. *Past history*—The potential is greater if the person has attempted suicide previously. It is particularly high if this attempt has occurred within the past year.

7. *Communication*—The potential is greater if the person has few outlets for communicating with others about his problems. If the person tends to internalize their problems, and seldom shares them with others, the potential is greater.
8. *Medical problems*—The person suffering from a terminal illness has a greater likelihood of taking his own life.

You make these assessments by asking fairly direct questions, such as, "How are you planning to take your own life?" or "Have you ever attempted suicide before?" Once having gotten some basic information about background, and how serious the person is about it, the next step is to assess the availability of others who can assist. These would include the student's roommate, any friends that he or she may have, and members of the professional staff at your institution. Discuss these options with the individual, expressing your availability and the availability of the professional staff to assist. Whenever you have a discussion like this with a student, it is advisable to discuss your observations with your hall director, and to follow up with the student on a regular basis.

In your discussion with the student, you should focus on coping mechanisms the student has available to deal with his problem. One method of doing this is to begin by helping the student focus on what he sees as a problem. By doing that, you are helping the student clarify the problem. Ask the student the causes of the problem, what he has done about it, and what can be done about it. Together with the student, brainstorm some alternatives and possible solutions. It is important that most of these solutions come from the student. Examine the consequences of these alternatives, and identify specific steps the student can take. Do this within the framework of a timetable so that the student will have goals to accomplish, and something to look forward to tomorrow and the day after. Schedule a followup meeting to check on the student's emotional well-being.

In various discussions, where the student claims that he is seriously thinking about suicide, it may be possible for you to get the student to agree to make a contract with you. In a contract of this type, a student agrees not to harm himself for a specified period of time. This might be an hour, a day or a week. In making such a contract, it is necessary that the student clearly understand that you are concerned about him/her, and that you expect the student to honor the contract. Ask the student directly if he/she intends to honor the contract and to repeat in detail the agreed upon commitment, such as, "I agree not to harm myself in the next 48 hours, to talk with you at the end of the 48 hours, and not to break the contract for any reason." This gives you some time to get the professional staff involved, and to give the student time to rethink alternatives. This permits the student to retain the power that he needs and a reason to continue living—that of a personal commitment to you.

Suicide contracts do work, but, not always. If a person seriously wants to take his life, there is very little you can do about it. Your responsibility is to help the student through the immediate crises, help analyse the severity of potential suicides, to keep senior staff members at your institution informed, to recognize the signs of a person who is potentially suicidal, and to lend emergency crisis intervention whenever and wherever possible. If you can do these things and do them well, you increase the likelihood of a student making a positive decision to continue living.

In summary, this counseling model can be stated as follows:

1. Assess the immediacy or severity of a student's potential for committing suicide.
2. Assess the availability of others to help.
3. Discuss with the student coping mechanisms he has available to deal with the problem.
4. Help the student determine a course of positive action by helping him assess the problem, brainstorm alternatives, consider consequences of each, identify a specific alternative, determine a time table, and schedule a second session.
5. Get the student to agree not to kill himself for a stated period of time as a suicide contract. If the student refuses, immediate help is necessary.
6. Inform your hall director or senior resident staff member of your observations, your discussion about suicide with the person, your observations and your discussions about suicide with any student.

SECTION 4

Information on Contemporary Social Issues Confronting College Students

CHAPTER 11
Substance Abuse

Substance abuse is a serious problem in America. It is not a problem that is isolated just to college students. It affects all of us in some form whether it be through personal experience, the experience of friends, or the effect it has on society.

In this chapter we will discuss three commonly abused substances. In the first section we shall discuss food abuse, perhaps the most commonly abused substance. We will not be discussing diet and health care, but, two relatively contemporary problems of bulemia and anorexia nervosa. These two forms of food abuse primarily affect women and are most often seen in the college years. The next segment of the chapter will be devoted to the topic of alcohol abuse. It will discuss a number of issues from the behavior surrounding alcohol misuse with residents to educational programming about alcohol, to the issue of alcoholism itself. Finally, the last segment of the chapter will be devoted to pharmacological substances or what is commonly referred to as drugs other than alcohol.

Food Abuse

Bulimarexia

Bulimarexia is an eating disorder characterized by a cycle of binging by consuming mass quantities of food and then purging oneself of the food usually by vomiting and/or the use of strong laxatives followed by fasting. It is a form of obsessive, compulsive behavior that is estimated to occur in somewhere between 5% to 25% of all college aged women.

A person with this form of eating disorder has usually come to associate eating with emotions so that not only hunger, but also emotions trigger the desire to consume food. The food is used to satisfy the emotion. It usually involves consuming large quantities of food, often those foods used as desserts like cookies, ice cream, etc. The person feels guilty about the binging, usually for weight control reasons, and purges the food to alleviate the guilt.

As mentioned earlier, bulimarexia occurs primarily in women. It is estimated that approximately 90% to 95% of all bulimarexics are women. Most of these women are from white, middle and upper middle class families, with parents who are generally achievement oriented. Bulimarexic female students usually express fears of not pleasing their parents. This is coupled with low self-esteem and the high need for achievement. They often feel that they are being dominated by others, and that they have lost control of their lives.

Many of these young women place an emphasis on an idealized romantic relationship and in doing so place an emphasis upon their physical attractiveness and sexuality. American women have been socialized by magazines, movies, and television to believe that thin and slim is beautiful and seductive. To enter this idealized romantic relationship, in other words to be loved, these women believe they must emulate this American sexualized fantasy. They translate their self-worth and self-esteem into the physical desire to be thin. Bulimarexic behavior is usually associated with low self-esteem resulting from unrealized love from parents and/or significant others.

Harms Associated with Bulimarexia

The binging and purging of bulimia sets up a cycle triggered by emotions. As these women purge their systems of food, usually by vomiting, it causes physical changes in the body. Vomiting reduces the potassium in the body system. It disrupts blood sugar and insulin levels, and impacts the body's fluid and electrolyte balance. Continual vomiting removes the mucous membrane of the esophagus which acts as a protective layer in the throat and leaves it open to infections and the body open to illness. In some extreme cases, the person may develop a conditioned response to the consumption of food such that whenever they eat food their body has a conditioned response to regurgitate the food. The nutritional problems inherent in this constant disruption of the system are evident. In extreme cases, people have died as a result of this disorder.

Coping Mechanisms

One of the difficulties in confronting this problem is the embarrassment that is associated with the behavior. It is not something about which a person usually talks. Usually, the purging is done in private and the person experiences guilt. Sometimes in the residence hall, female RAs are made aware of this behavior as a result of discussions with residents, by observing a particular resident in the restroom, or by reports from the janitorial staff.

This substance abuse problem should be treated like any other substance problem. The primary goal in working with students with this problem is to get them in touch with a counselor who can begin a process of therapy that will assist them with their problem. As an RA, you are faced not only with the problem of identifying a bulimarexic person, but also with the problem of confronting her with this behavior. Because these women are dealing with issues of low self-esteem, confronting them with the idea that there is something wrong with them and that they need assistance will not be easy. Your primary goal in helping these students is to get them into a counseling situation. Many college counseling centers and health centers have recently developed brochures about bulimarexia. The realization of the physical problems associated with this disorder and the desire to regain control of one's life may help a student make the decision to seek assistance.

Therapy for bulimic students will focus on increasing personal self-esteem. It is usually done in a group counseling situation to help them gain positive feedback from peers and to help them understand that their problem is not unique. In addition to the therapy, sometimes they are referred to a nutritionist who will help them design a weight management program as one step in beginning to regain control of their lives.

RAs in the residence halls may wish to consider doing some educational programming in this area if they have not already done so. Pamphlets and other materials should be made available some place that is inconspicuous and easily accessible to students. If you have suspicions about a person who may be exhibiting this behavior, talk it over with your hall director. Together the two of you may be able to design a strategy for helping this resident.

Anorexia Nervosa

Anorexia nervosa is an eating disorder that may include bulimic behavior. Again, it is a problem that almost exclusively affects women. Like bulimarexia, it stems from a need for love and a belief that being thin—sexually attractive—will result in being loved. Low self-esteem issues, with an emphasis on approval from others as the determinant of selfworth is characteristic. One of the primary ways it differs from bulimarexia is that anorexia nervosa is a self-destructive suicidal form of behavior. It shares with the disease of alcoholism the desire to die, the rejection of love, and a distorted sense of reality.

Anorexics actually develop a fear of food. They come to believe that if they eat any food at all they will put on weight. If they do eat anything, they are likely to force themselves to regurgitate. Anorexia nervosa is sometimes seen in women who have lost a considerable amount of weight through crash dieting, prolonged fasting, and other hazardous weight reduction methods. Even when they become so thin that they become emaciated, their perceptions of themselves are that they are still too heavy. Anorexics are never thin enough. They believe that once they reach the ideal thinness they will suddenly be loved by everyone. If this illness is left unattended they will die from malnutrition. Anorexics sometimes require hospitalization and force-feeding. Even this is not always in time to save their lives.

Again, the anorexic shares many of the same characteristics as the bulimarexic. They are usually from a middle to upper class family background with affluent parents. They have low self-esteem, high need for approval from others, an idealized concept of romance, and an intense desire to be loved which they believe can be realized by becoming thin.

You can identify the anorexic in some of the same ways that you can identify the bulimarexic. In addition, you can also watch for fainting spells, nutritional disease problems, and continual illnesses. The person will usually be extremely thin, will have an unhealthy look about her, will usually say that she believes she is still overweight, and will usually turn down food or consume minute portions of selected foods.

Anorexics require psychotherapy, and medical health care. Because they want to die, and because their judgment is blurred, they are difficult. In psychotherapy, they are often described as unwilling, obstinate, uncooperative, and disbelieving. They reject help and by doing so force increased concern in others. Some anorexics require involuntary mental health commitments and court-ordered medical treatment. For these reasons, it is often not until the advanced stages of the disease that the person gets treatment. Sometimes the person has to be in such a life-threatening situation, such as unconsciousness, for them to begin to get health care. A person who is anorexic should be viewed as a person who is suicidal and in immediate need of psychological care. It is possible, however, that a psychotherapist may have little or no effect upon the person until the person is in an immediate life threatening situation or is in a situation in which therapy is offered as her only alternative, as might be found in a court ordered commitment.

Alcohol

The consumption of alcohol has become as much a part of college life as the football game. It is part of the collegiate experience that dates back to the early colonial period. Robert Straus and Sheldon Bacon (1953), reviewing the history of drinking in America, note that the consumption of alcohol in the early days of the republic recorded imports of spirits in the 1790's of approximately a gallon a year for every man, woman, and child. In 1807, it is recorded that Boston had forty distilleries on the average of one for every 625 persons—but it had only two breweries.

It was really not until after 1840 that the consumption of beer increased in the United States, generally reflecting the immigration of large numbers of southern, eastern, and northern Europeans during the early 1800s. Beer was not the beverage of choice among all college students at that time. Whiskey and ale played an important part in collegiate life in the 1800s with some institutions, such as Yale University, appointing a full-time faculty member as an ale tester.

Colleges and universities found themselves at the forefront of the temperance movement in the early 1900s. During prohibition, however, a sizable number of college students patronized the speakeasys. Drinking continued at most colleges and universities through World War II, even though most institutions had policies prohibiting its consumption on campus. After World War II, colleges and universities saw an influx in the number of older students, due to the benefits extended by the GI Bill. Although most institutions still prohibited drinking on campus—which for all practical purposes meant in the residence halls or at football games—some extended approval for students who were over twenty-one or granted some form of tacit approval for students who had seen military service. This approval, it should be noted, usually came more as a result of policy enforcement than as a result of any change in written regulations.

Throughout the 1960s, alcohol was still the drug of choice among most students. However, was not really until after the eighteen-year-old age of majority was accepted by most states that colleges and universities began to permit the authorized or controlled use of alcohol on campus.

Today, somewhere between 76 and 92 percent of all college students drink alcohol, if only occasionally. It is the drug of choice among college students as well as the rest of the American population. In fact, it is the most heavily used drug in America today—even more so than aspirin. Alcohol has a prominent place in higher education, and it is here to stay.

Problems Associated with Irresponsible Use of Alcohol in College

Nearly 33 percent of all college students will experience some difficulty as a result of drinking during the academic year (Jessor and Jessor 1975). One out of three students will fail an exam, destroy a friendship, commit some infraction of college policy, or violate the law as a direct result of drinking behavior. The more serious criminal acts take the form of assault against another person, damage to public or private property, driving while intoxicated, or attempted suicide. The University of Massachusetts/Amhurst Student Health Services reported that as many as 17 percent of their weekend contacts with students, for selected periods in the spring, were alcohol-related (Kraft 1979).

One study (Engs 1977) sampling thirteen colleges in four geographic regions found that the majority of the 1,128 students sampled had experienced some problem as a result of drinking behavior. Approximately 9 percent of these students admitted to damaging university property, approximately 4 percent had trouble with the law, and another 4 percent had trouble with the school administration. A startling 1.8 percent of the students had been arrested for driving while intoxicated. Considering that only a small fraction of intoxicated drivers are ever apprehended, this is a significant number.

Nationally, approximately 27 percent of people between eighteen and twenty have experienced some problem (frequent intoxication, psychological dependence, physical dependence, or problems with friends, relatives, employers, etc.) as a result of drinking (Harris and Assoc. 1974). The next highest frequency of problems related to drinking was for people twenty-one to twenty-four years of age, among whom approximately 18 percent experienced some problem related to drinking.

Perhaps the most serious and frightening abuse of alcohol occurs when a person ingests enough alcohol to kill himself. This has happened at a number of colleges. The University of Nevada (November, 1976), Alfred University (April, 1978), the University of Wisconsin-Stevens Point (November, 1976), Loras College (October, 1978), and Georgetown University (January, 1975), among others, have had students die as a direct result of the irresponsible use of alcohol (C.H.U.C.K., 1979). Many other colleges have had students come near to death from ingesting too much alcohol and who have developed acute alcohol toxicity. An untold number of injuries and near-fatal accidents have occurred that were directly attributable to the misuse of alcohol.

Most of these deaths or near-deaths occurred when alcohol was irresponsibly used by the students, usually through the encouragement of their friends.

Drinking games that require a participant to consume large quantities of alcohol in a short period of time were the cause of most of these incidents. In these games, the body does not have time to expel the alcohol from the system before it reaches a critical level. If a person consumes a large quantity of alcohol in a concentrated period of time, but not all at once as might occur in a chug-a-lug contest, he will usually pass out when the concentration of alcohol in his blood reaches approximately .3 percent. This is the body's natural way of ensuring that the person will not continue to drink. Vomiting is another way the body attempts to expel alcohol after the person begins to reach the critical level of alcohol poisoning, which is usually a blood-alcohol level of about .4 percent.

Causes of Alcohol Abuse in College

The age of eighteen to twenty years old is the period in which there is the heaviest consumption of alcohol among men. The heaviest drinking among women occurs between twenty-one and twenty-nine years of age. (DHEW 1974) The obvious question is why, during this particular age period, is there such widespread abuse of alcohol?

There are many reasons why a person may abuse alcohol. Depression, celebrations, and alcoholism are only a few of many explanations. College, however, presents a special set of demands during a period in which the individual is struggling with the transition to adulthood. There are four major explanations, other than chronic alcoholism, why so many students abuse alcohol in college.

Sex-Roles

The heavy use of alcohol is part of the traditional sex-role assigned to men (Zucker 1968). Men use alcohol more often than women and in greater quantities (DHEW 1974) though in recent years drinking among women has increased sharply (Rachal *et al.* 1975).

In the college years, when most students are struggling with the transition to adulthood, it seems important to emulate behavior that confirms the appropriate sex-role to themselves and to others. Wilsnack and Wilsnack (1982) explain it this way: "masculine roles may encourage boys to drink: by selectively exposing them to situations in which unrestricted drinking is normally expected, by making it useful to drink as a means of showing adult manliness, and by creating internal needs and conflicts which drinking can assuage. . . . It is important to note also that traditional masculinity not only encourages drinking, but in contrast to traditional femininity, apparently does not impose any specific *inhibitions* on drinking behavior." (p. 11). The traditional drinking role for women has been one of moderation or abstinence, but, as mentioned previously, this role appears to be changing. Park (1975), in a study of the drinking behavior of college women, found that the heavier use of alcohol was related to a rejection of the traditional feminine role in favor of the more contemporary role of a "liberated woman." As Wilsnack and Wilsnack (1982) summarize: "traditional masculine and feminine roles may influence drinking behavior in four ways: by creating opportunities to drink, by creating normative obligations to drink (or not to drink), by creating needs and desires to drink, and by creating symbolic uses for drinking" (p. 4).

Peer-Group Influences

Closely associated with the fulfillment of the perceived appropriate sex-role is the influence of one's peers. Take, for example, the new freshman who comes to live in the residence hall. Like most students, he wants to be accepted by the other members of the living unit. To do this, he emulates the behavior that he believes will gain him the acceptance of others or that he believes is expected of him.

Taking the traditional male sex-role as a model, a young man may consume a large quantity of alcohol to demonstrate to his peers that he is manly. The probable response from his peers, depending on the student's behavior, will, in some manner reinforce the excessive use of alcohol. As the student's peers continue this reinforcement through laughter, joking, and often nicknames that reflect a past drinking episode, the student may continue or even increase his abuse of alcohol. Once a certain kind of drinking behavior becomes tied to the student's position among his peers, his recognition within the group can be dependent on that behavior.

As a person matures, he becomes less dependent on outside approval, and the importance of peer-group recognition is diminished. Interests broaden and role expectations change as the student grows older. The behavior that was once socially acceptable eventually draws social disapproval and is usually curtailed.

Unfortunately for the RA, this need for peer approval is strongest during the first year or two of college, the years when the average student is most likely to be drinking the heaviest and most likely to be living in a residence hall.

The Search for the College Experience

Movies, books, television, and stories from friends and relatives about the wild and crazy things they did in college all go into building a new student's expectation about what his college experience will be like. Much of the behavior that is exhibited as a result of drinking and also the excessive use of alcohol are built upon myths about the college experience. A student enters college with the expectation that college is one of those unique experiences where freedom abounds, and students often involve themselves in dangerous or irresponsible acts for the assumed benefit of such experiences or their story-telling value. Sit with a group of students who are telling stories about their experiences in college and count how many times the stories include the phrases, "I was so drunk that. . . ." or "I was so high that . . ." The experiences that many students relate fulfill their preconceived ideas about college life and help to perpetuate the myths about it.

Most contemporary students have been taught to demand the right and freedom to experience, try, experiment with, and possess as much as possible *now*. This orientation is different from past generations who were taught that some experiences were morally unacceptable or that certain experiences came only after a lifetime of hard work and perseverance. The current philosophy is not to be faulted. College is certainly a time to discover new things, but it is also a time to learn the responsibility that comes with the freedom acquired in adulthood.

Maturity

Freudian psychology hypothesizes that there are three basic spheres that govern the psychological composition of the individual: the id which is the base of the primitive instincts of every individual; the ego, which constitutes the reasoning abilities of the individual; and the superego, which is comprized of the ethical and moral principles of man in his society (Kendler 1963). When a person consumes alcohol, the higher-order nerve centers in the brain are anesthetized. In the Freudian model, this means that the superego and the ego are suppressed and the more primitive instincts of the id begin to emerge. The longer a person has lived with social mores, expectations, and standards, the longer it takes to suppress these entrenched patterns of behavior. In short, a person's experience in life makes him somewhat more inhibited. Students who are eighteen to twenty-four simply have not lived with these expectations as long as people who are older. Thus, alcohol permits younger persons to act out their feelings or desires more freely.

Summary

There are undoubtedly many other reasons beyond the four just described why a college student may choose to drink in excess. When asking students why they consumed more alcohol than they probably should have, the response most often is, "I didn't realize I was drinking that much." Other common reasons that students give for drinking too much are simply that they like the taste, like the effect that it gives them, or like to get high occassionally. Whatever the case, the person who drinks bears the obligation to drink responsibly.

Responsible Drinking

Responsible drinking does not harm the individual, other persons, or their property, is appropriate to the social situation, and is used to enhance the social experience. You can encourage the responsible use of alcohol by taking the following steps recommended by the Department of Health, Education, and Welfare (DHEW 1974, p. 164):

1. Respect the person who wishes to abstain.
2. Respect the person who chooses to drink in moderation; do not be insistent about "refreshing" his drinks or refilling his glass.
3. Provide food with alcohol at all times, especially proteins such as dairy products, fish, and meats.
4. Provide transportation or overnight accommodations for those unable to drive safely, recognizing that the host is just as responsible for preventing drunken driving as his guests.

One of the best ways to encourage sensible drinking habits is to provide guidelines for responsible drinking behavior:

1. Use alcohol as an adjunct to other activities and not as the primary focus of any particular activity.
2. View alcohol as a beverage and not as a means to achieve a desired mood state.
3. Avoid drinking games and other contests involving the rapid consumption of alcohol.
4. Pace drinks to approximately one per hour.
5. Do not use alcohol to impair social relationships or to degrade or humiliate a person.
6. Never use alcohol in conjunction with other drugs.

Tips for Responsible Drinking

Below are listed a few easy tips that you and your residents should know when drinking:

1. Know your limit.
2. Plan ahead of time how many drinks you intend to have.
3. Try not to consume more than four drinks in any one evening.
4. Have a drink only when you truly want one.
5. Eat something while you are drinking.
6. Be careful about consuming unfamiliar drinks.
7. Use mixers with your drinks.

8. Do not participate in drinking games or encourage others to do so.
9. Try to pace your drinks to approximately one per hour.
10. While drinking, occasionally switch to a nonalcoholic beverage, like plain soda or tonic water.

Party-Planning Suggestions for Responsible Drinking

Floor parties and similar gatherings are important socializing functions. New students coming to the university need to share some common experiences, and planning and attending a party together can be one of these experiences. These gatherings will aid students in developing social and organizational skills and in gaining a better understanding of themselves in social situations. Of course, it also provides an acceptable vehicle for meeting new people and establishing social relationships with the opposite sex.

Sometime during the academic year, you will probably be involved in planning a social event with your residents that will include the consumption of alcohol. There are ways to plan a party that will encourage responsible drinking and thus eliminate some of the problems often associated with the abuse of alcohol. Here is a list of suggestions for planning a party:

1. *Have an alternative beverage available.* Approximately one in five college students does not drink alcohol. They, too, should be made to feel comfortable at the gathering. An alternative beverage, if not required by your college or university policies, gives everyone a choice. If you choose to make a nonalcoholic punch, make certain that you keep it in a closed container. Sometimes inconsiderate people "spike" the nonalcoholic punch, thinking such a trick is funny or cute. Remember that there are some people who choose not to drink because they have a problem with alcohol, either medical or personal. Their rights must be protected. Alcohol added to a supposedly nonalcoholic punch may produce an unforeseen drug reaction that could result in convulsions or shock. Giving alcohol to someone who doesn't want it should be viewed with the same disdain as slipping somebody any other drug without his knowing it.
2. *Have snacks available.* A party is more than drinking. Small amounts of alcohol stimulate the appetite, and people will be hungry when they first begin drinking. Simple, inexpensive snacks, such as popcorn or potato chips, will satisfy this hunger and slow the absorption rate of alcohol. This should keep people more sober.
3. *Use a bartender at the party.* A bartender, if it is not a bring-your-own-bottle party, can control the flow of alcohol. He will also help prevent drinking contests and other disruptions that may occur at the party.

4. *Set a cut-off time for the party.* Make sure that you actually stop the party at that time. This will allow people to plan ahead and will discourage people from staying around drinking into the early hours of the morning.

5. *Use a moderate size glass or paper cup when serving from a beer keg.* An eight-ounce or a ten-ounce cup is sufficient and will tend to limit individual consumption. It will cause guests to go to the bartender each time they want more and may have a subtle inhibiting effect.

6. *Purchase fewer beer kegs, not more.* Take a rough estimate of how many people will be attending the party and divide this into the number of gallons of beer that the keg will hold. Be conservative in this estimate. If you are afraid of not having enough beer on hand, it is better to purchase additional alcohol in cans or bottles. Use these only if all the beer in the keg is consumed. Too often people feel that they must empty an entire keg once it is tapped, claiming that they hate to see the beer go to waste. In some ways, it becomes a contest to empty the flowing fountain of beer. Anything you can do to discourage this will lead to the more reasonable consumption of alcohol at the gathering. The best way to avoid this whole situation is to not use kegs or have people bring their own beverage.

7. *Discourage people from pushing drinks.* Talk to the residents on your floor and try to convince them that this practice is both immature and often obnoxious.

8. *Try to provide some form of entertainment.* If the party is small, the conversation may be sufficient entertainment. If, however, it is to be a large gathering—such as the residents from an entire residence-hall floor—dancing or some other form of party entertainment should be planned. If the main focus of the party is on dancing or some form of party game, people will be less inclined to focus on the consumption of alcohol. People at discotheques seldom get drunk because the main focus in these encounters, outside of the socializing function, is the dancing. When people are active, alcohol becomes an adjunct to the activity and not the activity itself.

9. *Appoint one or two people to monitor the flow of guests into the party.* Appoint people who are capable of making sensible decisions. These persons should inform uninvited guests that they are not welcome at the party. As an RA, you can exert control over situations arising between residents of your living unit, but outsiders whom you do not know and with which you have no personal relationship can present additional difficulties. If the party becomes an open public gathering, you put yourself in the difficult position of dealing with irresponsible behavior by people whom you do not know, in what might

be a very negative and embarrassing confrontation in front of your residents. It is easier to prevent such problems than to try to deal with them. A sign at the door saying something like "Invited Guests Only" will help to discourage roving bands of social marauders who often search out floor parties in residence halls—sometimes for the sole purpose of creating trouble.

Short-Term Effects of Alcohol

Alcohol is such an integral part of our society that it is difficult to realize that it is a drug, that its misuse can kill, and that it is the cause of one of the most serious diseases in America today. Many people believe that alcohol is a stimulant because its moderate use increases the heart rate, slightly dilates blood vessels, increases appetite, stimulates the output of urine, slightly lowers blood temperature, anesthetizes higher-order nerve centers in the brain, and provides energy (DHEW 1972). Part of this energy surge results from the fact that alcohol is a food containing approximately one hundred calories per ounce—a similar surge of energy is achieved by ingesting a candy bar or some refined sugar.

Though the moderate use of alcohol appears to have a stimulating effect upon the body, it is actually a depressant that affects some of the functions of the central nervous system. The degree of depression is related to the concentration of alcohol in the blood. Because the liver continually oxidizes the alcohol, and because some alcohol is lost through perspiration, the actual concentration of alcohol in the body varies. The rate and type of alcohol ingested also affects the percentage of alcohol in the blood.

Alcohol is absorbed directly into the bloodstream through the stomach walls and the small intestine, so its effects are felt rapidly. If there are other substances in the stomach, the rate of absorption is slowed. Some alcoholic beverages, such as beer and wine, contain nonalcoholic substances that also slow the absorption rate. As the concentration of alcohol increases, more of the central nervous system is anesthetized. In the brain, alcohol first depresses the higher-order functions and gradually moves down, depressing lower-order functions. The stages that the alcohol follows in depressing brain functions are as follows: (NIAAA-DHEW, 1972)

1. When the concentration of alcohol in the blood is less than .1 percent, a person feels relaxed, has some difficulty solving complex problems, and may become talkative, very active, or aggressive.
2. When the blood-alcohol level is between .1 and .2 percent, the person begins to lose motor-skill coordination. Reaction time is impaired, and judgment and coordination are lessened. Driving in this state of intoxication is very dangerous and in most states illegal.

3. When the blood-alcohol level is between .2 and .3 percent, there is severe impairment of motor skills, as well as general confusion and disorientation. Equilibrium is also affected.

This is the stage in which a person may accidentally injure himself by falling down or stumbling about. At .3 percent and above, the person will usually pass out. If someone is able to consume enough alcohol to reach a blood-alcohol level of .4 percent without passing out, coma or death is possible. This .4 percent level can be achieved by consuming a large quantity of alcohol in a short period of time. Such drinking games as "chug-a-lugging" or downing shots of alcohol one after another in a short period of time can produce this state.

Of course, individuals vary on how they react to exact concentrations of alcohol in their systems. The concentration of alcohol in the blood depends on body size and weight; for example, a person who weighs 200 pounds and consumes two drinks in one hour will not be affected as much as a person weighing 90 pounds who consumes the same quantity of alcohol in the same period of time. This assumes the same ratio of muscle mass—muscle and not weight alone affects drinking capacity. The following chart shows the general relation between blood-alcohol levels and behavior for a 155-pound moderate drinker who rapidly consumes 90-proof whiskey on an empty stomach.

Quantity	*Percent blood-alcohol level*	*Resulting behavior*
3 oz. whiskey (2 "shots")	0.05	sedation and tranquillity
6 oz. ''	0.1	lack of coordination
12 oz. ''	0.2	obvious intoxication
15 oz. ''	0.3	unconsciousness
30 oz. ''	0.5+	possible death may result

A number of things affect a person's reactions after using alcohol. These can be divided into two major categories—psychological and physiological. Physiologically, the following factors affect the body's reaction to alcohol: (NIAAA-DHEW, 1974)

1. *The speed with which alcohol is consumed.* Normally a person can consume one-half ounce of pure alcohol, or what might be considered one shot of whiskey, per hour with very little effect. The liver can oxidize approximately this much alcohol per hour. Lingering over a

drink or sipping a drink is a good way to prolong the drink and to minimize the concentration of alcohol in the bloodstream.

2. *Body weight.* The greater a person's weight (muscle tissue, not fat), the greater the quantity of alcohol he can consume with fewer effects. Women physiologically—because their bodies have a higher percentage of fat—are not generally able to consume the same quantity of alcohol as men of equal weight. This, however, is a relative comparison and must be viewed in connection with other physical and psychological factors affecting the consumption of alcohol.

3. *Type of beverage consumed.* Pure-grain alcohol has the most immediate and dramatic effect. Practically 20 percent of the alcohol is absorbed immediately by the stomach and the other 80 percent by the time it reaches the small intestine. Other beverages such as beer and wine have the same effects; however, the rate at which the person becomes intoxicated is lessened because of other substances contained in the beverages.

4. *Whether the stomach is full or empty.* If you are eating and drinking or have recently eaten a large meal, the absorption of alcohol into the system is slowed. Drinking after a meal or drinking in conjunction with any type of food are ways to slow the absorption of alcohol into the system—and thus to stay more sober.

Psychological factors also affect a person's reaction to alcohol. Some of these factors include: (NIAAA-DHEW, 1974)

1. *Why a person is drinking.* If a person is drinking for the purpose of getting drunk, because he is depressed, or because he wants to celebrate, these psychological states will help determine how alcohol will affect him.

2. *Drinking history.* A person who drinks regularly develops a certain tolerance to alcohol. An experienced drinker will react differently to the same amount of alcohol when compared to an inexperienced drinker of the same weight and similar physiological condition. This tolerance means that an increased amount of alcohol must be used to produce the same effect that a lesser dosage did when the person began drinking.

3. *Body chemistry.* Each person has a unique body chemistry that in part determines how alcohol affects him. Body chemistry is related to the psychological mood or state of the individual. This is most apparent in what is clinically referred to as the "Dumping Syndrome." This refers to how rapidly the stomach empties into the small intestine. The rate at which the stomach empties can be slowed or in-

creased by psychological conditions such as anger, fear, stress, euphoria, state of relaxation, and other factors. This is why a tired or upset person is more susceptible to effects of alcohol.

4. *Drinking Environment.* Certain social situations encourage misuse of alcohol. If, for example, you are comfortably sitting with a friend and alcohol is used as an adjunct to this activity, the impact of the alcohol will probably be less than if you were drinking in a singles bar, at a cocktail party, or during a "happy hour" in what might be a stress situation. Other people's expectations of how much you have drunk, or should drink, or how you are acting will also affect your behavior.

Sobering-up

Once you have ingested alcohol, the body must metabolize it in order for you to sober up. This process takes place primarily in the liver, though approximately 2 to 5 percent of the alcohol ingested will be excreted through the urine, breath, and perspiration. The liver turns the alcohol into acetaldehyde, then into acetate, into a variety of other compounds, and finally oxidizes it completely into carbon dioxide and water. The rate of metabolization may be affected by a variety of factors, including body chemistry, but generally the liver can oxidize approximately seven grams of pure alcohol per hour.

At this rate, it will take approximately one hour to sober up for every one alcoholic drink ingested. Coffee, oxygen, cold showers, and other home remedies have little or no effect upon the rate at which a person will sober up. A moderate amount of exercise, however, increases the metabolic rate and thus aids the sobering-up process, although, it will have a minimal effect upon behavior and can be dangerous if the person is quite intoxicated.

Hang-overs

Often the result of consuming too much alcohol is a hang-over the next morning. Scientists are not certain what causes a hang-over. Some researchers have hypothesized that it is caused by vitamin deficiencies or by oils that remain in the alcoholic beverage after fermentation; however, there are no conclusive findings to support either of these or other theories. The only known way to cure a hang-over is time, bed rest, and solid food when possible. Aspirin can be used to ease the pain, but will not prevent or cure a hang-over. Other home remedies, such as drinking a foul-tasting concoction of tomato juice, raw eggs, and hot peppers, does not work, nor does consuming "a hair of the dog that bit you" (some of the same type of liquor that got you intoxicated in the first place), vitamins, tranquilizers, oxygen, exercise, or any of the other traditional remedies to cure a hang-over.

Alcohol and Other Drugs

Alcohol reacts with other drugs. One of the most dangerous effects of alcohol is when it is mixed with depressants or "downers." This combination causes a synergistic effect; in other words, if a person mixes one beer with one downer, the combined effect will be greater than the individual effects of either drug when consumed alone. The effect could be the same as having consumed three or four beers. Combining alcohol with downers can so rapidly intoxicate a person or shock his system so badly that a person can go into a coma and die.

The second way that alcohol reacts with other drugs is that it potentiates them. This means that it can accelerate or change the effect of some other drugs. Such drugs as antihistamines, antihypertensive agents, anticoagulants, anticonvulsants, antidepressants, diuretics, sedatives, and tranquilizers, among others will be changed when ingested with alcohol. Mixing alcohol with these drugs can cause negative side-effects.

How to Confront an Intoxicated Person

Almost every RA will be confronted at some point with a resident who is intoxicated. It happens with predictable regularity on weekends on many campuses. With equal regularity, the intoxicated student returns to the residence hall and starts trouble. The manner in which you confront an intoxicated person can make the difference between a quiet agreement and a physical brawl.

First, let us consider the intoxicated person. His judgment is somewhat impaired, his physical coordination is diminished, he is more unpredictable, possibly more aggressive, and generally less inhibited. He will probably resent interference and will question the authority or motive of any person who confronts him. If he is with friends, he will undoubtedly be concerned that his friends view him in the most favorable light, which may mean that he will be defiant. If your past relationship with the student has been strained, the alcohol could bring to the surface any hostility that he may harbor against you.

Confronting anyone is not easy. Confronting a person who is drunk is simply more difficult. So, when possible, avoid confrontations with people who are intoxicated. If a student returns to the residence hall after drinking at one of the local bars, is a bit loud but presents no real problem, do not confront him about the behavior. It is only necessary to confront an intoxicated resident if: (1) he disrupts the living environment; (2) he is damaging or destroying property; or (3) he physically injures or threatens to injure himself or another person.

When one of these situations presents itself, intervene. Start by assessing your present emotional state. Are you angry, upset, frightened of the other person? If you are any of these things, that is all right. You just need to be aware of it before you make the confrontation. If you are angry, it is acceptable to express your feelings to the other person, but it is not acceptable to demonstrate your anger through inflammatory remarks.

Once having assessed your feelings, immediately gather all the necessary information on what took place. If the person's stereo is too loud and other residents have asked him to turn it down, get the facts from these people before confronting the resident. If another student saw him damage property, make certain you have the details of what the witness did and did not see.

If the gravity of the situation, your past relationship with the student, or your assessment of your feelings suggest that you should not handle the situation alone, do not hesitate to ask for assistance from your hall director, another RA, or possibly the campus police. If possible, however, these situations should not be escalated unless, in your judgment, failure to involve other people would be worse.

The last step before actual confrontation is to stop and consider exactly what specific behavior you wish the person to stop, change, or alter. What is it you want the person to do at this particular time? Can the confrontation wait until a time when the person is not intoxicated? If the person is disrupting the environment, the goal of your encounter is obvious—to return the environment to its previous state. If the person is fighting with another person or is about to initiate a fight, again the goal is obvious. If, however, the person has damaged property or left beer bottles strewn throughout the corridors of the residence hall, there may be very little you can do by initiating a confrontation at this particular time. There is no question that the person will need to be held accountable for the behavior, but the question is, when is the best time to do it? The following day, after the person has sobered up, he will probably be much more reasonable than when intoxicated.

At this point, you have assessed your own feelings, have the necessary facts about the situation, have made a decision as to whether or not to involve another staff person, know what behavior you wish the person to modify, and have decided whether or not to initiate the confrontation of this behavior now or wait until the person is sober. Assuming that you feel a confrontation is needed immediately and that you will handle it yourself, you must now actually confront the person.

Your first task in the confrontation is to make sure the person knows who you are. If he is not one of your residents, it will be necessary for you to identify yourself as a resident assistant. Once this is accomplished, try to isolate him from any of his friends or any spectators. Ask the person to step into your room, if it is convenient, or into his own room, if that is the most isolated place you can find. If at all possible, avoid attempting to discuss the situation in front of other people.

In approaching the person, do so in as nonthreatening a way as possible. Remember, your goal is to return the environment to its previous state or to prevent some injury; it is not to moralize, lecture, condemn, evaluate, or in some other manner demean the person's behavior. Be sincere in your emotions and in what you are saying. Avoid accusations or inflammatory remarks. Use an approach that will elicit a feeling on the student's part that he is cooperating. Ask for his cooperation, do not demand it. Use techniques and skills of assertiveness that you learned in the chapter on disciplinary counseling.

Never become physical, unless it is to protect yourself—and then *only* to protect yourself—not to retaliate or demonstrate your force or anger. Grabbing, pushing, or in some manner attempting to restrain the person may lead to unnecessary problems.

If the student chooses to escalate the situation by failing to cooperate or if you are threatened in some manner, do not hesitate to involve other members of the residence hall staff or the campus police if it is appropriate. Whatever your college pays you, it is not enough for you to place yourself in a position of imminent physical harm. Though physical altercations between students and staff are rare, they do happen. Even most of these could be avoided if people would exercise more discretion.

Confront only specific behavior that the person has exhibited. Do not make value judgments about behavior. It is enough to say that the disturbance is creating difficulty for others or that it is presenting some other problem. If you are disturbed by the situation or if you were awakened because of the disturbance, express your feelings. Tell the person that you are angry. It is not necessary, however, to lecture. Use questions to clarify the particular situation that require more than a simple yes or no answer. Such questions as "Why are you yelling?" or, "Why is your stereo that loud?" or, "Why are you acting this way? How do you feel about your current behavior?" In any case, communicate clearly. Ask the person to explain or clarify behavior. Do not threaten; instead, clearly and calmly tell him the ramifications of his actions.

Remember always that your goal is to get the person to cease the behavior that is causing the disturbance. If you can do this by asking him in a friendly and cooperative tone to change the behavior, you may have a better chance of accomplishing the goal. Depending upon your personal judgment, the degree to which the student has disrupted the environment, the student's history of similar past behavior and what your institutional policy considers customary in these situations, it may be necessary for the student's behavior to be reviewed by an administrator to determine if the behavior is of such a nature as to violate college or residence hall disciplinary policies. If, in your judgment, such a referral is necessary, it is appropriate that you indicate during your confrontation that this referral will be made. It should in no case be used as a threat. Rather, you should present your decision in such a way as to inform the student without it appearing as a punishment in and of itself. You might say something like, "David, I will be discussing this incident with the hall director for possible disciplinary action. I would like to talk with you about it again tomorrow."

Things to Look for in Identifying the Problem Drinker

It is difficult in this age category to distinguish a problem drinker from other drinkers. Students from eighteen to twenty are among the heaviest drinkers in the United States. During this period, they will probably drink more than at any other time in their lives. In time, most of these people become moderate and reasonable drinkers. A percentage, however, will be problem drinkers or alcoholics.

National statistics show that approximately 20 percent of all people who graduate from college eventually become alcoholics. This rate is higher than the rate among noncollege graduates. Interestingly, if you ask a group of college students if they know anyone who has a drinking problem who is currently in college, the overwhelming majority will admit to knowing such a person.

There is a good chance that during your time as an RA you will encounter one or more students who have a definite problem with alcohol. Some of these students may be alcoholics, meaning that they suffer from alcoholism. Alcoholism can be defined as follows: "Alcoholism is a chronic disease, or disorder of behavior, characterized by the repeated drinking of alcoholic beverages to an extent that exceeds customary dietary use or ordinary compliance with the social drinking customs of the community, and which interferes with the drinker's health, inter-personal relations, or economic functions" (Keller 1958).

Another way of defining alcoholism is through the behavior of the alcoholic. Generally the alcoholic will: (1) lose control of the amounts of alcohol he has consumed; (2) in some way damage himself psychologically, emotionally, physically, economically, or in other ways; (3) come to rely on alcohol as a panacea for all ills, turning to it during any time of stress or discomfort.

As an RA, you can watch for:

1. Blackouts. This is distinguished from passing out. A blackout occurs when the person experiences a temporary loss of memory and cannot remember what happened during an interim while he was drinking. Some alcoholics experience blackouts for several days. A person in the first stages of alcoholism may experience these blackouts for shorter periods of time—like one evening.
2. A change in drinking behavior. The person begins drinking more often or continually, drinking in the mornings or early afternoons, or on a regular basis. He may also find that each time he begins drinking, he

drinks until he passes out. Either an increased frequency in the consumption of alcohol or the increased usage of alcohol in a drinking episode is an indicator of possible alcoholism.

3. Avoidance. The person who avoids talking about his drinking behavior or is ashamed of discussing it probably has a problem with his drinking. Hiding liquor in the room, carrying liquor to classes, and drinking before or between classes are other good signs of a person with a drinking problem.

4. Chronic hang-overs. A person who finds that he is sick almost every morning because of drinking has a drinking problem. (Adapted from NIAAA-DHEW, 1976)

If you believe someone has a drinking problem or is a possible alcoholic, confront him with the behavior that you have seen him exhibit. Do not accuse him of having a drinking problem or of being an alcoholic. He will undoubtedly be defensive, deny your evaluation, and possibly react quite negatively. You, after all, are not in a position to make this type of diagnosis. What you can do and what you should do is discuss what you have observed with the person in a one-to-one dialogue.

If you have noticed the person not attending classes but instead staying in his room and drinking, this behavior could be pointed out. You might say something like, "John, I have noticed that for the past few days you have not been attending class and have been drinking all day. How do you feel your classes are going? Do you find this is possibly infringing upon your studying? What kinds of things are bothering you? I have noticed you have just started doing this. Do you find this is creating a problem for you?"

Questions like this can aid in the helping relationship. It is very possible that the first time you bring this behavior to the person's attention, he will not respond. Do not give up. When you notice other or similar behavior in the future, bring it to the person's attention again. Do this only if you are sincere and willing to help. If you are not interested or willing to help, then you may need to discuss alternatives with your hall director.

In this type of encounter with a student who has a drinking problem, your goal is to refer the person for professional guidance. If a person is an alcoholic and is experiencing problems because of drinking, he needs help. The most effective help is often Alcoholics Anonymous; its success ratio is higher than almost any other form of therapy available. Many college campuses have their own AA chapters. If there is not an AA chapter at your institution, you might try the local community, since almost every community has at least one chapter.

It should be noted that heavy drinking does not necessarily mean alcoholism. There are other indicators, both psychological and physiological, that must be evaluated before any decision of this sort can be reached.

Alcohol Education Programming

In the past few years, many colleges and universities have begun programs to help students drink more responsibly. These programs have grown out of an increased concern for the behavior of irresponsible drinkers, the increased awareness of alcoholism, and the more blatant abuses visible on college campuses since the drinking age in many states was lowered. The focus of the programs has not been on preventing students from drinking. Most students have made this decision prior to coming to college. It has also not been on the prevention of alcoholism; students seldom view themselves as potential problem drinkers or potential alcoholics. The most successful programs have focused on helping those students who choose to drink to do so in a manner that does not harm themselves, other people, or public or private property.

How this concept is taught and whether it can be instilled as a popular attitude among students depends on many factors. Researchers found that simply providing students with information about drinking does little to change attitudes about drinking or drinking behavior itself (Engs 1977). This was also true during the 1960s with the drug-education programs. Researchers found that students who participated in drug-education programs had more knowledge about drugs but that the increased knowledge did not change their drug-taking behavior. In fact, in some instances, it actually increased experimentation with different drugs (DeHaes & Schuurman 1975).

A variety of approaches are required to change the drinking attitudes of students. Although having only one alcohol education program is better than not having any program at all, it alone will not change the drinking behavior of students. It will take a continuing program of information, value-oriented discussions, role-modeling, and opportunities for students to experience the moderate use of alcohol to achieve the desired goal.

The potent peer environment in the residence hall will play a critical role in determining the standards of drinking behavior expected by students. If that standard encourages the overconsumption of alcohol on a regular basis, chances are, as the RA, you will spend a disproportionate amount of your time confronting behavioral problems created by alcohol abuse. However, if the acceptable standard of drinking is defined early in the academic year as moderate, and students are reinforced for this behavior, excessive drinking behavior then can come to be viewed as a sign of immaturity. If you can accomplish this, chances are that you will have the opportunity to spend more time in the pursuit of other more productive endeavors.

Below are listed a few program ideas that you can plan for early in the academic year. Additional program options are no doubt available through your residence life office or your counseling center.

1. Posters and pamphlets on alcohol abuse.
2. Symposium on alcohol.
3. Films on alcohol.
4. Speakers.
5. Have a breathalyzer brought to your floor.
6. Have a nonalcoholic dance.
7. Have a wine-tasting course.
8. Distribute an alcohol use and abuse survey.
9. Have a bartending course.
10. Have a speaker talk about liquor laws in your state.
11. Print a newsletter with information about alcohol in it.
12. Take a field trip to a distillery or brewery.
13. Visit an alcohol detoxification center.
14. Have a poster contest on responsible drinking.
15. Have an essay contest offering a prize for the best essay on responsible drinking.
16. Organize students in your unit to do a service project for your local alcohol abuse center.
17. Have a trivia contest about alcohol.
18. Provide other programs in such areas as value-clarification, assertiveness training, human sexuality, and interpersonal skills to help student's mature and broaden their awareness.

Resource Information

Below is a list of resources provided by the National Institute of Alcohol Abuse and Awareness, to whom you can write for posters and more information about alcohol.

1. The National Institute on Alcohol Abuse and Alcoholism maintains a state-by-state listing of most private and public treatment facilities currently available. For the appropriate list, write to:

   National Clearinghouse for Alcohol Information
   P.O. Box 2345
   Rockville, Maryland 20852
   (301) 948–4450

2. Local Alcoholics Anonymous chapters and Al-Anon Family Groups are also listed in virtually every telephone book. For further information, you may wish to contact the national headquarters:

> Al-Anon Family Groups Headquarters, Inc.
> P.O. Box 182, Madison Square Station
> New York, New York 10010
> (212) 475–6110
>
> Alcoholics Anonymous
> P.O. Box 459
> Grand Central Station
> New York, New York 10017

3. This organization can provide a list of member groups that are the major state agencies concerned with alcoholism:

> Alcohol and Drug Problems Association of North America (formerly the North American Association of Alcoholism Programs)
> 1130 Seventeenth Street, N.W.
> Washington, D.C. 20036

4. This organization has a list of major nonprofit organizations in many cities that can refer clients to private physicians, as well as public and private agencies providing treatment for alcoholism. Some of these referral organizations not only provide generalized information service, but also have individualized counseling and treatment services.

> National Council on Alcoholism, Inc.
> 2 Park Avenue
> New York, New York 10016

5. Any veteran who is eligible for VA medical benefits can receive alcoholism treatment at no charge. Treatment of acute intoxication for alcohol related problems is available at any VA hospital in the country. A number of VA hospitals now also offer special comprehensive treatment programs for the disorder:

> Veterans Administration
> Alcohol and Drug Dependent Service
> 810 Vermont Avenue, N.W.
> Washington, D.C. 20420

6. Most facilities sponsored by this organization provide food, shelter, or rehabilitation and take the form of halfway houses. In some areas, the Salvation Army provides a broad range of other services:

> The Salvation Army
> 120 West 14 Street
> New York, New York 10011

Alcohol Information Quiz

Questions

T or F   1. A cold shower and a cup of black coffee will help a person sober up faster.

T or F   2. One beer contains as much alcohol as a jigger (1½ oz.) of 80-proof whiskey.

T or F   3. The use of alcohol increases sexual ability.

T or F   4. A person will get intoxicated faster by switching drinks rather than by taking the same amount of alcohol in only one form, such as scotch.

T or F   5. Over 80 percent of college students use alcohol regularly.

T or F   6. There is a higher percentage of students using alcohol today than there was ten years ago.

T or F   7. The best way to handle someone who is drunk is to be assertive and understanding.

T or F   8. The greatest majority of serious behavioral infractions in residence halls are related to behavior resulting from an excessive use of alcohol.

T or F   9. A student with a drinking problem should be held accountable for his actions and made to suffer any consequences.

T or F   10. Most students, by the time they reach college, have already made a decision about whether or not to drink.

T or F   11. Eating some butter or drinking a glass of milk will coat your stomach and enable you to drink more.

T or F   12. Having several good drinks before you go to sleep will insure a deep restful sleep.

T or F   13. Vitamins, and/or "the hair of the dog" (small quantity of the alcoholic beverage that was used to become intoxicated) will help a hang-over.

T or F   14. Drinking alcohol will kill brain cells.

T or F   15. Approximately one-third of the students on your floor will have some problem associated with drinking during the coming academic year.

T or F   16. You can die from drinking too much alcohol.

T or F   17. Drinking alcohol in moderate amounts does the body little permanent harm.

T or F   18. Blackouts are common after a few drinks.

Answers

1. FALSE   Nothing will really help except time. The body needs approximately one hour to metabolize each drink consumed.
2. *True*   A large five- or six-ounce glass of wine is equivalent to one beer or one jigger of alcohol.
3. FALSE   It takes away inhibitions and provokes the desire, but reduces the physical performance.
4. FALSE   It will only make you sick. It is the alcohol content that counts, not the type of drink.
5. *True*   Even at schools where the drinking age is twenty-one, studies have shown that as much as 81 percent of freshman and 88 percent of sophomores drank regularly.
6. *True*   Studies show that the percentage of students who drink regularly has grown steadily from 76 percent in 1968 to 92 percent in 1974.
7. *True*   Drunk people cannot be reasoned with. When putting them to bed, place them on their sides in a fetal position with pillows behind their backs to prevent them from rolling over on their backs and gagging should they throw up.
8. *True*   Alcohol depresses inhibitions and allows one to act out anxiety and frustration.
9. *True*   Alcoholics Anonymous proposes this. It seems to be the most common excuse for behavioral infractions.
10. *True*   They have made the decision to drink or not to, but not how much to drink, where, and how often. That is determined by peer-group pressures.
11. FALSE   The stomach does not get coated. Eating while drinking does slow down absorption, however.
12. FALSE   In fact, it inhibits good sleep by not allowing you to get into the deepest Rapid-Eye-Movement phase of rest.
13. FALSE   There is no real treatment.
14. *True*   Excessive drinking will do noticeable damage. Normal social drinking will not do determinable damage but does kill a very few brain cells.
15. *True*   These problems will probably be related to school work, social complications, trouble with the law, or driving.
16. *True*   If the blood alcohol level reaches .4 percent, death is likely.
17. *True*   The body can handle moderate drinking.
18. FALSE   Blackouts are not common. They are one of the first signs of a serious drinking problem.

Drug Abuse

Drugs have a long history in the United States dating back to morphine addiction among soldiers in the Civil War, the use of codeine in patent medicines throughout the 1800s, and the use of amphetamines "speed" by American and Japanese pilots during World War II. Opium and heroin addiction in the United States was not uncommon in the early 1900s. It is the decade of the 1960s, however, that is most often identified with the abuse of drugs in the United States. During this period of social change that gave rise to a counter-cultural youth movement, experimentation with drugs was a way of expanding one's mind and enhancing one's abilities. Drugs became identified with a process of self-discovery and as a way of making a statement in opposition to the established social/governmental system that supported the war in Viet Nam. A Harvard professor, Timothy Leary, is frequently identified as a forerunner of experimentation with mind-altering drugs. As a way to expand consciousness, he experimented with LSD.

As more people began experimenting with drugs in the hope of expanding their minds or to identify with the counter-cultural movement of that decade, the federal government moved to restrict the use of these new substances through increased drug enforcement and more stringent laws. When popular drugs became more difficult to obtain, street varieties or substitutes were developed to take their place. The result of this has been a variety of different substances sold on the streets as something that they are not. Suppliers of these drugs unscrupulously cut or dilute the original drug with other substances, creating street varieties that in many cases are very dangerous. As the drug supply increased to meet the demand, possession and use of certain drugs in the college age community became socially acceptable and within certain groups a status symbol. It was "cool" to be able to supply your friends with certain drugs. It became acceptable to use certain drugs at parties with almost the same freedom that one has customarily used alcoholic beverages. Drugs became readily available among college students, and soon thereafter, in the high schools and grade schools as well. The alarm that people felt over the visible sign of change within the American culture helped foster the emphasis on more closely monitored distribution of drugs, enforcement of drug laws and on research into drugs.

By the late–1970s, the predominant use of drugs among college students fell into three major categories: cannabis, stimulants, and depressants. Though some psychodelics such as LSD were also used, they became less popular.

Narcotics, such as heroin and morphine, though experimentally used by some college students in the '60s, never gained any degree of popularity in the general college population. The greatest change that has been seen in the 1980s has been the increase of cocaine among college students. Marijuana, amphetamines, and barbiturates are still in use by college students, with increasing evidence suggesting that they are becoming less popular and being replaced by increased consumption of alcohol.

The National Institution for Drug Abuse regularly surveys high school seniors on their use of drugs. In 1980, the institute found that approximately 46% of high school seniors indicated that they had used marijuana in the past year and that 26% admitted to using stimulants during that same period. Cocaine use also increased while the use of barbituates has remained fairly constant. Out of that group of high school seniors, those that went to college actually used drugs more frequently. Approximately 68% of incoming college students admitted to using marijuana.

Snodgrass and Wright (1983) did a study of the use of drugs among college students attending a large state university in the southwest. They sampled 770 students and found that out of this group 16% of the males and 9.4% of the females used marijuana on a regular basis; 10.4% of the males and 9.2% of the females used cocaine on a monthly basis; 11.9% of the males and 9.8% of the females used uppers on a monthly basis; and 6.5% of the males and 5.8% of the females used barbiturates on a monthly basis. In terms of popularity, alcohol was still the most popular drug followed by marijuana, amphetamines, and cocaine in that order. Men who lived off campus were more than twice as likely to use marijuana daily than those males who lived on campus. Among females, there was little difference between on- and off-campus use, however, those who lived off campus were almost four times as likely to use marijuana daily as to use alcohol.

The first part of this segment of the chapter contains information about drugs that are being or have been used among college students. It includes a brief discussion about each, however, it is not intended to be a definitive statement about each of these drugs nor to include all drugs that may be available. Pharmacological desk reference guides are available to give more in-depth discussions than are provided here.

The next segment of this section concentrates on ways to recognize individuals who are using drugs and most importantly, those who may be having difficulty with the use of those drugs. The third section outlines appropriate emergency procedures in cases of drug overdose, and the final section discusses the philosophy of helping students make positive self-directed choices about the use of these drugs.

Before going any further in this chapter, the authors wish to express their personal point of view about the use of drugs. From a purely physiological perspective, it is inadvisable for a person to ingest substances that alter the body chemistry without a clear understanding of the ramifications of using such substances. There is clear evidence that the introduction of any drug, unless prescribed for a specific medical purpose by a qualified medical expert, creates an effect that may not be beneficial to the body. It is the authors' view that drugs are not only physically harmful to the individual, but also may present major social adjustment problems. It is our opinion that students who are experimenting with drugs, or uses drugs for recreational purposes, inhibit their ability to perform at their optimum personal and academic level. Having said this, that all drugs have negative side effects, we shall devote the next section to discussing the major drugs in use by college students.

Reference Section on Drugs

Cannabis

Marijuana

Marijuana is generally classified as a mind-altering drug with a low potential for overdose. Although it is generally believed there is no physical addictive potential in the use of marijuana, it is clear that the drug may be habitual—meaning that it becomes emotionally or psychologically addictive. Marijuana is consumed by either smoking it or ingesting it, usually through some food substance. A person under the influence of marijuana will generally have dilated pupils, impaired coordination, be given to laughter and rambling speech, have increased appetite, and distortion of time or space. If the drug is used heavily over a prolonged period of time, fatigue and psychosis may result.

Marijuana has been written about probably more than any other drug in the past twenty years. The country has moved from extremes of placing people in prison for prolonged periods of time for possession of marijuana during the early 1960s, to laws in the late 1970s in some areas that simply assessed a small monetary fine of $5 for possession of small amounts of the drug. Most of the marijuana sold in the United States is of relatively low potency containing 1% to 3% of THC (tetrahydrocannabol), the active drug agent, although some reports suggest that the potency of marijuana sold in the United States in the past few years has increased.

Marijuana is used primarily among the age group of 18 to 25 with a clear trend toward earier use. In the 18 to 25 year age group approximately 60% of college students report having used marijuana at least once. There is no significant evidence of any mental injuries from the moderate use of this drug, and there is no correlation between the use of marijuana and the need to advance to drugs of stronger potency.

The two principal dangers associated with the use of marijuana are that it is illegal in all states, and that its frequent use may impair normal social developmental experiences needed for growth to maturity. One of the interesting findings of research with adolescents and college students who use marijuana frequently is that they often do not have the same type, frequency, or intensity of normal socializing experiences that help a person grow and mature as those who do not regularly use the drug. If much of one's life centers upon the use of a particular drug which clouds perception and distorts reality, it is difficult for that person to internalize socially learned developmental skills that prepare one psychologically and emotionally for adulthood. In the authors' opinion, it is this deprivation of social learning that is the greatest threat to the individual in the use of marijuana.

Some of the marijuana available "on the streets" today is sometimes treated with PCP (sernyl or phencyclidine) also known as angel dust. This animal tranquilizer is a strictly controlled substance and is no longer available on the streets in any quantity. Derivatives of this, or imitations, are sometimes used to "enhance" the marijuana. Marijuana that has been mixed with these or other substances will taste and smell like a strong chemical.

Hashish

Hashish is generally regarded as an hallucinogen with low overdose potential and no physical addiction properties, although again, it may be habitual. It is generally either smoked or ingested in some food substance. Hashish is generally sold in grams or by the ounce. It is cut or broken into small bits and smoked. Like marijuana, it is sometimes mixed with liquid PCP or other fillers. Hashish is made from the resin of cannabis plants. Its effects are different from that of marijuana. It is more hallucinogenic and less calming. A person using this drug will act very much the same as someone who has been smoking marijuana, however, the person will be more irritable and more agitated. Historically this drug was used as an anesthetic for pain, but because it was slower than some modern anesthetics it was eventually abandoned.

THC

THC is the active chemical of marijuana, pharmacologically known as tetrahydrocannabinol. At one time, drug dealers were claiming to be selling THC, and occasionally today people will claim that a substance they are distributing is actually the chemical derivative of marijuana, thus giving the same effects without having to smoke the drug. Though dealers often claim to be selling THC, in actuality this drug has never been available except to clinical government researchers. The synthetic processing is time consuming, very costly, and requires that the substance be kept at a very low temperature. Because of its highly unstable condition and its high cost, it has never been available on the street. Usually, the substance they are selling is PCP or some other substance that is represented as THC.

Psychodelic Drugs

LSD

LSD is probably the best known of the psychodelic drugs. It has a high potential for overdose, although no physically addicting properties. It is consumed in a variety of ways including tablets, capsules, or in liquid form that has been put on sugar cubes or pieces of blotter paper. People under the influence of LSD have an array of wide and varied mood swings ranging from excitement and hyperactivity to lethargy. They can become anxious, panicky, confused, and out of control. Constricted pupils, glazed eyes, and a complete disorientation of space and time are some of the physical signs. The long term effects of the use of this drug involve convulsions, unconsciousness, psychotic episodes, increased delusions, and panic psychosis.

LSD is also known as "acid" and pharmacologically as lysergic acid diethylamide. An LSD experience varies with the individual, the environment, and the amount of drug that has been ingested. Generally, however, the person will begin to hallucinate and have erratic changes in emotions. LSD was popular in the late sixties as a consciousness expanding drug that promised to increase activity and intelligence. The drug was originally developed by the defense department to create disorientation and confusion in an enemy. LSD is by far the most potent of all psychodelic drugs with which students experiment. A small amount can produce dramatic changes in the brain and its function.

Most of the LSD available today is produced in illegal laboratories. Because it is odorless and tasteless, it is difficult to detect. Like other illegally produced street drugs, LSD is often diluted with other substances such as speed to produce a "high." Two of the greatest harms associated with the use of this drug are having what is called a "bum trip" which is a bad emotional hallucinogenic experience while taking the drug, and having flashback experiences later on when not taking the drug. While having a "bum trip," people have been known to attempt to destroy themselves or to remove themselves from an hallucination. Some who are psychologically unable to deal with it remain in a permanent psychotic state. Flashbacks occur at unpredictable times—for some users, several weeks to several months after the ingestion of the drug. These flashbacks are spontaneous hallucinations or series of hallucinations produced without warning or additional ingestion of LSD.

There is evidence to suggest that the use of LSD produces chromosome damage, the effect of which may be genetic defects in offspring. It is not known if this chromosome damage is permanent or temporary. It is clear, however, that if a person is currently experimenting with the drug, or has taken it some time during the past 6 to 12 months, there is an increased probability of genetic damage in children conceived during this period.

PCP or Angel Dust

PCP is a tranquilizer-hallucinogen that has a high risk for overdose and a potential for physical addiction. A person who is under the influence of this drug will act drowsy, euphoric, panicky, confused, and will have impaired coordination and dizziness. This substance was originally developed as a horse tranquilizer, and pharmacologically is known as sernyl or phencyclidine. This substance is often sprayed on marijuana or parsley and either smoked or ingested. The repeated use of this drug causes severe paranoia and damage to the central nervous system. The drug causes hallucinations, and the person usually has a bad experience while hallucinating. One of the side effects of the drug is that it can cause either temporary or permanent paralysis in the individual. The person may also become very panicky and violent when using the drug. This panic reaction may have lingering psychological effects, even when the chemical effects of the drug have worn off. PCP is distinguishable if used in marijuana or other substances by its heavy chemical odor and heavy chemical taste. This substance should be avoided as it presents a serious risk to the person's life and other people's safety. This drug is becoming more difficult to obtain, and in some cases, is being removed from the commercial drug market.

STP (DOM)

STP is a synthetic acid originally developed for military use to instill terror in enemies. It has a high potential for overdosing and creates a negative experience. STP (which stands for serenity, tranquility, and peace), also sometimes referred to as DOM is virtually unavailable today. This drug creates long-lasting hallucinations that may last as long as 8 to 10 hours. Like other psychodelic drugs, it is not physically addicting. Again, like other psychodelics, behavioral signs associated with someone using this drug include wide and varied mood swings, hallucinations, depressions, rambling speech, tremors, etc. Long term effects of this drug include psychosis and possible psychological dependency. The drug is generally distributed in tablet form which is usually pink and cone shaped, but sometimes white or blue or peach colored.

DMT

DMT stands for dimethylteryptamine. The effects of this drug are similar to those of LSD. It is generally distributed in the form of liquid or colorless crystal and has a high potential for overdose. It is most commonly consumed by spraying it on marijuana and then smoking it. One of the dangers associated with the use of this drug is that it causes a sudden rise in the blood pressure that can cause hemorrhages in the small blood vessels of the brain resulting in death.

Psilocybine and Mescaline

Psilocybine is the chemical found in the stropharia cubensis mushroom. This drug is sometimes acquired by boiling the mushrooms and making a type of mushroom tea. In laboratories it is possible to extract the chemical from the mushroom. The substance is ingested orally. A person under the influence of this drug will act excited, restless, anxious, and will begin to hallucinate. The person may become irrational at times, have rambling speech, increased perspiration, dilated pupils, and periods of insomnia. The effects of the drug, depending upon the amount taken, will last for approximately 6 hours. If the drug is taken over a prolonged period of time, the person may begin to have increased delusions, and eventually a type of panic psychosis. Mescaline, a drug developed by western plains Indians for use in ritual ceremonies, has similar effects.

MDA and MMDA

MDA is a synthetic chemical called methylenioxyampatepamine. This is a chemically based amphetamine drug which is classified here as a psychodelic because of its ability to cause hallucinations in the person consuming it. Other behavioral signs of somebody under the influence include increased energy, panic, perceptual changes, anxiety, exhaustion, vomiting, and often psychosis. Continued use of it will increase hallucinations, flashbacks, and may again develop a panic psychosis. This chemical was originally developed by the government as a weapon to tranquilize an enemy into submission. MMDA is a similar organic substance with the same general behavioral signs. It is derived from myristic oil, a substance found in nutmeg. Both of these substances are difficult to obtain on the street, but often a combination of LSD and PCP is combined and sold as MDA or MMDA.

Stimulants

Amphetamines (Speed)

Amphetamines, commonly referred to as speed, are stimulants with a very high potential for overdose and high potential for physical addiction. They are usually distributed in capsule or tablet form and marketed among college students by such names as "black beauties," "white cross," "reds," and "uppers." Because of their ability to reduce the appetite in someone taking the drug, amphetamines were commonly used as diet aids. The use of amphetamines as "diet pills" to decrease the appetite is no longer an acceptable medical practice. Other effects of this drug include hyperactivity, irritability and restlessness, anxiousness, euphoria, and irrationality. The person taking it also tends to be much more talkative, somewhat paranoid, will have impaired coordination, spells of dizziness, depressed reflexes, and constricted pupils. The long term effects of this drug include insomnia, skin disorders, excitability, and malnutrition. One of the real dangers to the users of this drug is that it increases the heart rate and blood pressure, increasing the possibility of a stroke.

Speed is very popular on college campuses during exam times. It has the effect of creating a state of total stimulation. Wide awake alertness is characteristic of this drug, and it was this property that caused it to be used during World War II and the Korean War by pilots on long bombing missions. Prolonged use of the drug creates significant damage to the body. Because of the increased acceleration, the liver and kidneys cannot filter the impurities fast enough and are forced to overwork. In a short time, they begin to disintegrate. The accelerated blood pressure, coupled with decreased food intake and erratic sleep, push the effects of many years of living into a short period of time. Irreparable brain damage, speech impairment, and other negative side effects have accompanied the prolonged use of this drug. A person who has been using the drug regularly for a period of time may have difficulty withdrawing from it. Though the withdrawal itself does not generally require hospitalization, the immediate "come down" after withdrawing from the drug can create significant psychological disturbance.

Imitation Drugs

Within recent years, imitation or "legal drugs" have been produced and marketed to college students. These are usually capsules which use many of the traditional names assigned to actual amphetamines, such as black beauties, yellow jackets, white cross, etc., but usually containing caffeine or some other legal substance. One of the dangers associated with the use of these imitation drugs is that they are sometimes confused with the real drug, and they set the precedent for the use of substances to meet certain demands of the individual. Although the use of caffeine or other moderately stimulating substances in low amounts may not in and of itself present a serious risk, concentrated or excessive dosages of the substances may. A person needing to study may decide to take a handful of the imitation speed drug and physiological create some of the short term effects.

Cocaine

Within the past few years, cocaine has enjoyed a new popularity among the more affluent college students. It has come to be known as the rich man's drug. Cocaine is a narcotic stimulant. Although it has a low potential for overdose, it does have the potential for addiction similar to the type of addiction found in those who use amphetamines. It is most often consumed by sniffing or snorting it, however, it can be injected. When using this drug, a person will be hyperactive, somewhat irritable, a little anxious, generally euphoric, talkative, and will have a distorted sense of time and space. If this drug is used for a prolonged period of time by snorting or sniffing it, it will begin to destroy the mucous membrane tissues of the nose. Some of the signs of someone who has been using the drug for a period of time are a red and runny nose, dilated pupils, and a rather hyperactive an anxious state of being.

Cocaine is an odorless, white fluffy powder. It is a stimulant that activates the central nervous system, which produces constriction of blood vessels and other physiological effects similar to that of amphetamines. Although the potential for overdose of cocaine is limited, it is possible—particularly if the substance is injected. The excess consumption of this drug may cause convulsions and death. The drug, originally developed as an anesthetic, causes an effect similar to that found in speed but for a shorter duration. It is very costly, and its regular use can amount to thousands of dollars per week. Even though this drug is expensive, the National Institute of Drug Abuse found that between 1978 and 1981 the use of cocaine jumped from the seventh most popular to the third most popular illicit drug in use with the number of students reporting its use doubling from 6% in 1975 to 12% in 1980.

Depressants

Barbiturates is a category of depressant drugs commonly referred to as downers. They have a high potential for overdose, particularly when mixed with alcohol. Physical addiction is possible with the use of this drug as has been seen particularly with the rather liberal prescription of tranquilizers by physicians until just several years ago. Barbiturates may be injected, however, the most common form of consumption is by ingestion in tablet or capsule form. People under the influence of this drug are drowsy, belligerent, depressed, irrational, often confused and frequently slur their speech. They may begin laughing for no reason at all and they have impaired coordination, dizziness, increased sweating, and constricted or dilated pupils. People who continue to take barbiturates over a prolonged period of time will become excessively sleepy, confused, irrational, and will experience severe withdrawal symptoms when they cease taking this drug. These symptoms include vomiting, tremors, hallucinations, hypertension, and grand mal seizures. Barbiturates are particularly dangerous for people who suffer from low blood pressure, heart defects, or depression.

The overdose of barbiturates in the form of tranquilizers and sleeping pills is often seen in suicide attempts. The overdose produces respiratory failure and cardiac arrest. If a person survives an overdose of barbiturates, she often experiences permanent brain damage.

One of the more foolish methods of consuming barbiturates is to consume them in combination with alcohol. This combination accelerates the effect of the alcohol and the drug beyond the effect that each would reach independently. This combination of taking barbiturates and alcohol is sometimes referred to as "loading." The combination of these two chemicals results in a multiplier effect. The total effect of this combined drug is greater than the sum of the two original components. This effect is known as a synergistic effect. It causes increased risk of overdose, brain damage, psychological damage and related physical problems.

Narcotics

Heroine and Other Opiate Drugs

Heroin and other opiate derivatives, such as morphine, codeine, and opium, have a high potential for overdose and a high probability of physical addiction. Although these drugs are sometimes taken by inhaling them through the nostrils, or by sprinkling them on marijuana and then smoking it, the most common method of consumption is through injection. A person under the influence of heroin or other opiate derivatives will appear drowsy, euphoric, have impaired coordination, have depressed reflexes, constrictive pupils, and loss of appetite. If used over a prolonged period of time, the person will show dramatic weight loss, lethargy, temporary sterility and impotency, and demonstrate withdrawal symptoms to cramps, sickness and vomiting. Because a person develops a tolerance to the drug, increased dosages are required to maintain the euphoric effect.

Much has been written about opiate drugs. They are highly addictive, very dangerous, and are not usually found on college campuses. Though there is sporadic experimentation with these drugs on college campuses, their daily use almost permanently impairs an individual's ability to cope with college life. They are difficult to obtain on most college campuses, although like most other drugs, a person searching hard enough can probably find them. This category of drugs is generally considered to be so dangerous that most college students consider its use to be a serious problem. Even the students who experiment with some of the other drugs that have been discussed thus far, draw the line when it comes to heroine and opiate derivatives.

It is expensive to obtain these drugs, and often dangerous. The sale of this drug is scrutinized carefully by federal and state police agencies. Although police officers may be willing to overlook the use of some other drugs, they seldom overlook students who use and deal in narcotics. Narcotics are not considered recreational drugs. Possessing even small amounts of these drugs can result in serious legal repercussions.

Counseling about Drugs

It is the opinion of the authors that the use or possession of drugs in a residential environment is inconsistent with the goals of an educational environment and cannot be permitted to exist unchecked by the educational institution. The use of drugs in the residence hall presents major problems for the university. Where drugs exist unchecked in the residence halls, it encourages the sale and distribution of these drugs in the residence halls. There is no one more vulnerable to violence than somebody who is dealing in drugs. Through personal experiences, both of the authors can recount stories of students dealing in drugs who were beaten, robbed, and in several situations killed for their money and their drug supply. This kind of violence does not belong in any community whether it be a residence hall of the college, or a city. University administrators have an obligation to create a safe living environment in residence halls. No environment, where drug use is open and drug selling continues, is a safe environment.

As we have said many times throughout this book, the college years of late adolescence and early adulthood are a period of time in which men and women are subject to considerable peer pressure. The desire to conform, is enhanced by a living environment such as a residence hall. In this environment where peer groups play such an important role in the development of students, the widespread use of drugs sets a peer standard that encourages the use of drugs. Students, who under other circumstances, may not consider trying drugs, may be encouraged to do so when there is strong peer pressure. In an effort to gain the approval of their peers, students can easily be caught in a cycle of drug abuse that will inhibit them from attaining their educational goals.

The use of the drugs clouds a person's perception and retards the ability to obtain important socially learned skills for maturation. The college years are comprised of a multitude of experiences, both in and out of the classroom. One of the advantages residence halls provide is the opportunity to grow and mature in an enriched educational environment with other intelligent people pursuing academic goals. Students learn from interacting with their environment, their peers, by handling crises, understanding their emotions, and by learning new social skills. If a person is under the influence of drugs, her perception is clouded and her emotions are artificially controlled. This important social development is never fully realized and the person will not be able to obtain the full benefits of the educational experience the university has to offer. Because one of the goals of higher education is to help people realize their full academic and personal potential, students who have made the decision not to pursue this goal by choosing to impair their development through the use of drugs, probably do not belong in college. Students who attend the university for the purpose of developing their character and their intellect are wasting their time and money, and the resources, and interest of the university when they make the decision to inhibit this development through the use of drugs.

Universities have a broad constituency. Their reputations affect not only students enrolled, but also the faculty, the Alumni, the community, and future students. Because these educational institutions enjoy the benefit of the laws of the communities in which they thrive, they have an obligation to uphold these laws. Universities also have a social responsibility to develop an educated and law-abiding citizenry in students who graduate from their institutions. No state institution of higher education can, in all good conscience, refuse to uphold the laws of the state which supports it.

Having said that universities should prohibit drug use in residence halls, the issue of how a university goes about dealing with the problem of drugs on campus through enforcement by RAs, the campus police department, or through drug counseling is a separate issue. The educators at some institutions see the role of the RA as strictly a counselor. They hold the belief that enforcement of policies related to drugs and similar violations of the law interferes with the primary counseling role of the student and is the responsibility of law enforcement agencies. They see the role of the RA as a friend, confidant, and counselor, believing that drug enforcement inhibits students from sharing their concerns about drugs or other issues.

At the other extreme are a few institutions who require their RAs to call the campus police whenever they suspect a violation of drug policies has occurred or is occurring. The role of the RAs in this case is clearly one of enforcement, which the residents of the floor understand to be an expectation of that RA at that institution.

Most institutions fall somewhere in the middle of these two extremes. The issue of enforcement of drug policies is usually handled internally within the university disciplinary system. At this point we need to draw a distinction for the purposes of enforcement between detectable drugs such as marijuana and hashish that would be detectable outside the room by the odor and what we shall classify as the undectectable variety of drugs which the RA would need to physically observe in the room, or have contact with the student while the student is experiencing the effects of the drug. Most institutions have established procedures for handling detectable drugs in the residence halls. It often results in a first warning and explanation that any future violation may result in referral to university disciplinary authorities. Any second violation of this policy regarding detectable drugs usually involves some type of confrontation between the RA and the student. Each institution establishes its own set of policies for handling these confrontations. One that is commonly used is that, the RA accompanied by another staff member knocks on the door and identifies herself to the resident of the room asking permission to enter. If the person does not respond within a reasonable period of time (usually 3 minutes) the RA is usually authorized to use a pass key to enter the room to determine the cause of the smoke odor for fire safety purposes. Upon entering the room the RA is able to stand and observe but not conduct a search. Things that are observable include towels stuck under the door, the odor of marijuana or hashish, smoking pipes and related paraphernalia, fans exiting smoke from an open window, and any drugs that are in plain view. Depending upon the institutional policies, sometimes drugs are confiscated by the RA or a senior staff member (usually if there is a large quantity, the room is secured by the staff until the police can arrive). The students are generally informed that they are going to be referred to university disciplinary authorities. To reiterate, each institution has its own set of policies. Some have selected a less confrontive method, which may or may to involve entering a student's room. The RA is nevertheless expected to discuss the issue with the students at some point.

The discovery of students using other drugs such as speed, LSD, cocaine, etc., happens less often. Occasionally an RA may be informed that a resident is using drugs, the RA may observe a resident who may be using drugs, or an RA may enter a student's room and accidently see certain drugs in plain view. RAs are really not in a position to be detectives, or supersleuths in the discovery of drugs. This is not their primary function.

Although it is the authors' belief that there is a need to address this topic with residents and to confront the problem when it becomes apparent, RAs are not in the residence hall for the primary purpose of enforcing drug policies. It is realistically an element of their job and it should be performed with the same efficiency as other elements of their job. When you as an RA believe there is a problem with the use of drugs by one or a group of your residents, particularly such substances as amphetamines, barbiturates, and narcotics, you should discuss it with your hall director or senior residence hall staff person. These individuals have training, experience, and skills in handling these situations. They may have information about the student that has not been shared with you, or there may be special ways of treating these situations within your institution.

From time to time students may address the topic of drug use with you. Sometimes it will be in the context of what they did in high school, some experimentation they are currently doing or the discussion may be in the context of what friends of theirs have done with drugs. These discussions on the legitimacy of drug laws and the effects of certain substances can be as informative to a student as a college lecture. It is helpful if you have some facts about drugs, and can relate them to students. It is also helpful if you can provide students with referrals to campus counseling services if they are interested. If such a discussion materializes, and it is likely that at some point it will, it should provide a good opportunity to invite a speaker on the topic of drugs, their legality, and their effects. Many city or state run detoxification programs, which have come to be involved with not only alcohol but other drugs, will often have a public service program available on the topic.

It is possible that you will learn of someone who is experiencing a problem with the use of drugs in your living unit. This information may come from another resident or the person with the problem may come to discuss it with you. Your role in these counseling situations is to support the person's desire to get assistance with the problem and put the issue of drug enforcement and policies aside for the more important goal of assisting the student with her personal crisis. People who have been abusing drugs for a period of time will need the assistance of a professionally trained counselor. They need to attend a detoxification program to handle some of the psychological and physical withdrawals. These individuals also need to build their own concepts of self-worth and discover new ways of coping with the stress of everyday life in college. This therapeutic change can be accomplished by working with a trained professional over a period of time in the right environment. You can be of greatest assistance in helping students to locate a professional person to help with their problem and then reassuring them that these matters will be handled confidentially, without involvement of the police, extensive University disciplinary records, or any breach of confidence to parents, employers, or others outside the University. Only in rare circumstances would it ever be necessary to include the parents of a student, and this decision would be made by members of the professional staff in consultation with the student whenever possible.

Drug Overdoses

Drug overdose occurs whenever the body is called upon to react to a substance beyond the body's ability to do so. The body will react to substances up to a particular point, and then will either damage itself, or will begin shutting off systems in the body. This may be life-threatening. If a person ingests too many amphetamines, the body will begin pumping blood, and increase respiration to the point that the body begins breaking down by causing hemorrhages in small blood vessels in the body which may in turn cause death. Sometimes the body will attempt to expel certain substances that have been ingested by vomiting, or at other times the body may simply shut down or become only limitedly functional as when a person becomes unconscious. Many substances in excess can be toxic to the body. Too much alcohol, too many aspirins, or a handful or two of salt can have a toxic or fatal effect upon a person. The overdose potential is particularly high among the drugs that we have discussed in this chapter. As a staff member you need to be familiar with the emergency procedures at your institution.

Generally, if you confront a situation in which someone is unconscious and you find it difficult to arouse them, your first responsibility is to stay with the person and send someone else for assistance. Have the person call for an ambulance, the campus police, or the health infirmary, whichever is the procedure at your institution. Your hall director should also be notified at this time. If the person is unconscious, check for breathing. If she is not breathing, first check to see if there is an obstruction in the throat. If there is, clear the obstruction and administer mouth-to-mouth resuscitation. Check to see if there is any evidence of an accident, such as falling from a chair or being shocked by an electrical appliance. If the person has fallen, do not move him/her. If the person has received an electrical shock, immediately attempt to initiate breathing by use of mouth-to-mouth resuscitation. Check the pulse by locating the carotid artery in the neck directly to the right of the larynx (adams-apple). In the absence of any evidence of injury, convulsion, accident of any kind, and the appearance of such things as drugs lying around or any evidence that the person may have injected something, try to arouse the person. You may try by calling the person by name, placing a cold washcloth on the person's face or shaking the person to awaken her.

If the person is not unconscious, but has taken a lethal dose of some drug, not a caustic or corrosive poisonous substance in the past half-hour, attempt to have the person vomit by having her put her fingers down the back of the throat or having the person drink a glass of warm salt water or a mixture of mustard and water.

Look around the room to see if you can locate any drugs in plain view. If there are, make sure they are handed over to the medical personnel when they arrive. This will assist in determining an antidote for the drug. If you are unable to find any drug in the room, question the person's associates to determine what the victim may have taken.

In cases in which a person has ingested some psychodelic drug and is not unconscious, but is simply experiencing the drug and is in a trance-like state, one of two options exist. You or someone else may stay with the person to help assure that the person does not injure herself or others. It is important to keep a calm tranquil atmosphere in the room and at least two people in the room besides the person who is "tripping." The second option is to contact medical personnel, who can take custody of the person and assist the person should he/she become violent or experience a negative physical reaction. It is the opinion of the authors that the latter option is a preferable method of handling students who are "tripping." Unless you, as an RA, are highly skilled in dealing with people who are on drugs, and familiar with the behavioral effects associated with drugs, you run the risk of being injured by a student or bearing some responsibility for a student possibly being injured. This is particularly true if a student has taken PCP or what is commonly referred to as angel dust. This animal tranquilizer is very dangerous. It can cause paralysis, brain damage, and in many cases excessive violence. The adrenaline surge is so strong in people using the drug that they may become disproportionately strong for their size. Because they are reacting to the drug and not thinking, they may seriously injure themselves or someone else unintentionally. LSD can create fear, panic, and hallucinations from which the person will try to escape. Any person standing in her way may be injured. The excitement or need to escape may cause the person to smash through a window, or jump from the top of a building. It is preferable to get early assistance from medical personnel trained in handling these situations rather than to find yourself in the midst of a crisis and have to send for medical assistance at the last minute.

CHAPTER 12
Sexuality

by Jan Miltenberger*

The purpose of this chapter is to discuss several important aspects of human sexuality as they relate to the resident assistant's responsibilities. A basic understanding of male and female anatomy and physiology is important, and it is assumed that the reader has access to this information from other sources.

Before beginning the discussion, it is necessary to define some basic terms. Sexuality may best be described as involving all that one is in regards to being male or female. It involves attitudes, emotions and behaviors which include issues related to the biological-physiological perspective, the psychological perspective and the sociological perspective. *Sex* is defined here as anything connected with genital stimulation, sexual gratification, and involvement. Thus, kissing, petting, coitus, and masturbation constitute forms of sexual behavior and are referred to here by the term *sex*. Sexual feelings are manifestations of our emotional, physical, and spiritual selves.

As an RA, you will be confronted with a variety of situations related directly or indirectly to aspects of sexuality. Before you can assist others, however, it is important that you be aware of your own sexual self. From the moment of birth, your gender helps to determine who you are, what you are like, what you do, and how you live your life. Your family, friends, teachers, and others play a role in forging your identity as a man or woman. Even the television shows you watched as a child shaped to some extent the way you behave today. What you are as an individual is the result of the cultural and social environment in which you have lived. Sexual values, gender identity, and appropriate sex-role behavior have been learned as you have developed as an individual, physically, emotionally, socially, and sexually.

Sexuality on the College Campus

Today's college students reflect society's more open attitude toward sexuality. Many students have taken or plan to take classes in human sexuality,

*Jan Miltenberger, R.N., M.S. is an Instructor in the School of Nursing, Indiana State University.

and many have attended lectures or programs involving frank discussions of such topics as virginity, intimacy, birth control, abortion, premarital sex, and homosexuality. Students show an increasing willingness to know and sometimes talk about sex and their own sexuality.

Going away to college is often a student's first experience of living with persons outside the nuclear family. As an RA, you are acutely aware of the vast number of adjustments that must be made as one encounters the experience of going to college and living in a resident hall. Consider for a moment the various regulations and university policies regarding living situations and their possible effects on the sexual behavior of students. Many residence halls allow open visitation with coed wings and floors. This permits more freedom, particularly for females, to initiate informal heterosexual social contacts. Consider also the adjustments that are required with respect to the increased use of alcohol and other drugs in our society. The use of alcohol and other drugs in connection with situations possibly involving aspects of sexuality calls for some difficult decisions that must be made by the student who is new to the college.

Birth Control

Among the concerns regarding sexuality that face college students and you as an RA, one of the most important involves the use of various birth control methods. Birth control has become exceedingly important in an era of changing life-styles and attitudes. Most young people today have attitudes which permit greater sexual freedom and thus there is an increase in awareness and knowledge of birth control methods. Almost everyone has the ability and certainly the right to use their bodies as they choose. Full control of your life means being responsible and knowledgeable about the various methods of birth control. Decisions concerning birth control are crucial for anyone but especially the person who is sexually active.

There are four methods of birth control—abstention, abortion, contraception, and sterilization. The first three are primarily used by college students. In the past more emphasis was placed upon abstinence and the moral standard that sex was solely for procreation. Some college students choose abstinence for a variety of reasons which may or may not be related to religion or morals. The important point is to accept and respect an individual's choice. This part of the chapter will deal with the issues of abortion and contraception as they might concern the RA. Contraception is discussed first.

The Psychology of Contraception

There is much more involved in contraception than knowledge and information. Certainly being informed about all of the various methods is the foundation of preventing an unwanted or unplanned pregnancy, but there is a whole psychology involved with the contraceptive issue.

Even though most college students are aware of contraception, many women students still have unplanned pregnancies. The key to effective contraception is to use it regularly and knowledgeably. Intentions may be good but condoms are not effective in the wallet, diaphragms do not provide a barrier in the purse and the pill is ineffective if it is not taken. Some of the topics raised in a discussion of the psychology of contraceptive use are the following:

1. It is often underestimated how easy it is to get pregnant. The more frequently one has unprotected intercourse the greater the chances of doing it again and getting pregnant.
2. Both the man and the woman share responsibility for birth control.
3. Some persons feel that contraception may interfere with the feeling of spontaneity, yet what feelings emerge with finding out about an unplanned pregnancy?
4. Some persons feel guilty or embarrassed about buying condoms or foam or going to a health facility for an exam to get the pill or a diaphragm.
5. No birth control method, including the pill, is 100% effective against pregnancy.
6. Using or not using contraceptives may involve rebelling against God, parents and religion.
7. The Catholic Church opposes the use of any contraceptive device. How effective is the rhythm method?
8. It is important for sexually active people who do not want an unplanned pregnancy to make responsible decisions regarding contraceptive practices.

A study by Kathryn Rindskopf shows that a significant proportion of college women are poor contraceptors, are using unreliable methods or none and have surprisingly high pregnancy and abortion rates (Rindskopf 1981, p. 113). Several patterns of behavior were noted in her study.

1. Poor use of contraception at the first intercourse.
2. Poor use of contraception involving a casual encounter.
3. A shift to the female being almost totally responsible for contraception.
4. A reliance on medically prescribed methods such as the pill and diaphragm.

It is interesting to note from Rindskopf's study the paradox that exists in this era where college students have unprecedented sexual freedom, widespread sexual activity, relatively easy access to contraceptives, highly effective contraceptive techniques and yet are not effective contraceptive users.

Contraception

It is important for a person to be aware of the available options, to understand reliability, advantages and disadvantages. An informed choice greatly increases the effectiveness of any method. Most unintended pregnancies are a result of improper or inconsistent use of contraceptives or failure to use any birth control measure. "More than half of all pregnancies are reported to be unplanned; about one-quarter are terminated by abortion" (*Making Choices* 1983, p. 3).

According to a report issued by the Alan Guttmacher Institute (1983), an organization devoted to birth control policy and research, a major reason for ineffective use of contraceptives is fear of health risks associated with modern methods. The Institute's report was issued to help people evaluate the risks and benefits of contraceptive methods, compare them with the risks of not using contraceptives and to decide upon a safe and sensible contraceptive course for the three decades of life during which women are most fertile. The best contraceptive choice is likely to change several times during a woman's sexually active years. What is best at 18 may be inappropriate at 28 and potentially dangerous at 38.

Currently, 36 million American women are faced with the problem of avoiding pregnancy and more than 90% of them are using some form of birth control (*Making Choices* 1983, p. 10).

Contraceptive sterilization is now the leading method relied upon by 11.6 million American women. The pill is the second most popular method, used by 10 million women especially for those under 30. The condom is in third place, depended on by 4.5 million women, followed by the IUD, the diaphragm, spermicides, withdrawal and the various "rhythm" or fertility awareness methods. More than 3 million women risk having an unplanned pregnancy because they use no contraceptive method (*Making Choices* 1983, p. 10).

In evaluating the health risks of contraceptives there are three clear facts:

1. There is no such thing as risk—free contraception.
2. In almost all cases, every method of contraception is safer than getting pregnant and having a child.
3. There is no one method that is best for everyone.

Oral Contraception

Since many college students seem to have questions about "the pill", some additional information will be presented about birth control pills or oral contraceptives. It is important to know that oral contraceptives collectively known as "the pill", are not a single drug or a single formula. There are approximately 50 different "pills" that have been marketed in the U.S. since 1960 and most usually involve the synthetic female hormones estrogen and progesterone.

For women under 25 who do not smoke, the pill is the safest method of contraception. For sexually active teenagers, the pill is most effective and in most cases the safest method.

Because of pre-existing health problems, some women students should never take birth control pills. Among them are a history of phlebitis, stroke, heart disease, liver tumors or liver disease, cancer of breast or reproductive tract, hypertension, diabetes and unexplained abnormal vaginal bleeding (*Making Choices* 1983, p. 46). In the United States the number of monthly packets sold in 1975 was 103 million which dropped to 32 million in 1981 and has remained relatively stable since then. The pill costs $7–$10 for a month's supply (Ross November 1983, p. 220).

Most of the problems related to the pill were due to increased amounts of estrogen. Now most pills contain less than 50 mcg. of estrogen and 1 mg. of progestin.

Potential health benefits should also be considered. These include a reduced risk of developing cancers of the ovary and uterus, benign breast disease, pelvic inflammation, iron deficiency, anemia and a variety of menstrual disorders.

There is no demonstrated health benefit associated with periodically stopping use of the pill, nor should use be discontinued after 5 years unless there are other risk factors making a cessation medically adviseable (*Making Choices* 1983, p. 57).

Statistical data about contraceptives can be obtained from the booklet, *Making Choices—Evaluating the Health Risks and Benefits of Birth Control Methods,* which can be purchased for $6 from the Alan Guttmacher Institute, 360 Park Avenue South, New York, New York 10010.

New Contraceptives

The RA might want to be aware of some recent contraceptive developments. After more than 7 years of research and development, the vaginal contraceptive sponge can be purchased for about $1 each. It is a barrier contraceptive that can be bought over-the-counter in a one-size-fits-all. It is a small (less than 2 inches in diameter) pillow-shaped sponge with a concave dimple on one side which fits against the cervix and a woven polyester loop on the other for easy removal. A spermicide is incorporated into the sponge during the manufacturing process. The spermicide is nonoxynol-9 which has been used in vaginal contraceptives for over 20 years with no apparent health risks.

The sponge is moistened with water, and placed high in the vagina against the cervix providing 24 hours of continuous contraception. It is not necessary to use each sponge the full 24 hours as long as it is left in place at least 6 hours after the last act of intercourse. Some of the advantages and disadvantages are as follows:

1. It is available in 1 universal size so no need for a prescription or fitting.
2. It is suitable for multiple-coital use for 24 hours unlike the single-coital condom.
3. It is both a spermicide and a barrier.
4. It is easy to use, inexpensive and generally unobtrusive when in place.
5. It is considered to be about 85% effective so it is not as effective as some other methods.
6. There have been complaints of odor if left in over 18 hours. It must be left in 6 hours after intercourse.
7. Some have had difficulty in removing and being able to distinguish the loop from their own body.
8. About 2% of men and women are allergic to the spermicide and develop a local rash.

In August, 1982, the FDA approved a new type of condom that is lubricated with nonoxynol-9 spermicide. This can be bought over-the-counter and may provide additional safeguards against pregnancy and some sexually transmitted diseases (STDs).

You will need to read the literature and keep informed by your health practitioner about future use and research regarding the sponge and other methods currently being studied such as the tailless IUD's, a 6–10 year progestin IUD and contraceptive vaccines.

Contraceptive Summary

Students who have infrequent or unexpected sexual relations may prefer using a non-prescription method. The most effective is the condom plus a spermicidal agent preferably the foam which is more evenly distributed in the vagina. If used properly the effectiveness of condom plus spermicidal is slightly less than the pill, about 99 percent.

There are many excellent references about the specific aspects of various contraceptives. All students who wish to avoid an unwanted pregnancy should know all that they can about the various methods. The more you know, the greater your personal choices. The RA might want to have a floor program with a question and answer session regarding various contraceptives. Be selective in choosing a knowledgeable person who feels comfortable in a casual, spontaneous discussion situation. Some possible guest speakers are professors who teach human sexuality classes, nurses from the student health center or personnel from a family planning agency. It is often a good idea to have students write down questions prior to the guest speaker's appearance.

Abortion

Abortion is another method of birth control. Some people prefer to say termination of pregnancy rather than abortion since the latter has negative connotations for some people. However, in this chapter the term abortion will be used. The moral issue of abortion has been argued elsewhere, and it is not the purpose of this chapter to condemn or condone. The purpose is to present the medical facts.

An abortion is the removal of the tissue of pregnancy from the womb or uterus before the time of "viability"; the time when a fetus might be able to live outside the womb (presently thought to be about twenty-six weeks). The word *abortion* means to miscarry. In fact, when an abortion results from natural causes, it is called a spontaneous abortion or miscarriage.

"On January 22, 1973, the United States Supreme Court ruled that the performance of an abortion before three months of gestation was strictly the decision of a woman and her doctor. After three months, the same holds true except that the states are allowed to more stringently regulate the medical practices of facilities where abortions are performed.

A 1981 Gallup poll found the public fairly evenly divided in supporting the 1973 Supreme Court decision permitting a woman unrestricted choice in obtaining an abortion her first 3 months of pregnancy. Forty-five percent favored the decision while 46% opposed it. A key component in people's attitude toward abortion is when they believe life begins. In 1981, the National Academy of Sciences unanimously adopted a statement declaring: "Defining the time at which the developing embryo becomes a 'person' much remains a matter of moral or religious values." (Strong 1982, p. 499).

Since 1977 there have been a number of restrictions related to federal and state funding of abortions. As of 1981, the federal government provides funding for abortions only in the case of a threat of death to the mother should she carry the pregnancy. Some states have chosen to provide funding for selected abortion service. (Hatcher 1982, pp. 166–167).

Henshaw's 1981 study of abortion showed that the majority of women obtaining abortions were young, white, unmarried and childless; generally these were first abortions. Nine-tenths of the abortions were performed by vacuum aspiration and rarely dilation and curettage. Seventy-five percent of the women who received abortions in 1978 were unmarried. (Strong 1982, p. 499).

Abortion is a decision that a woman must make for herself. It should not be thought of as a primary birth control method. It should only be used as a last resort by a woman who is definitely convinced that it is the right decision for her.

There are many articles and books which describe in detail the recommended methods, procedures, risks, and possible complications of abortion. The RA should familiarize herself with basic information as to how and when abortions are performed. However, actual counseling and assistance in decision-making should be done by a professional counselor, nurse or physician.

Most women in the first trimester of pregnancy (through twelve elapsed weeks from the last menstrual period) who choose abortion can get one fairly close to where they live, although for a woman in the second trimester of pregnancy (over twelve and up to twenty-four weeks), it is often very difficult to find abortion services. Many clinics have opened to perform abortions for women less than twelve weeks pregnant. Some, such as Planned Parenthood clinics, are non-profit, but too many are profit-oriented and most are not truly patient-oriented.

Without going into great detail, there are two strong challenges to the legalized abortion issue. First, there is a strong antiabortion movement, known by such names as Birthright, the National Right to Life Committee, the Celebrate Life Committee, Life Lobby and other similar titles. Second, the quality and availability of abortion services vary tremendously throughout the country. Legalization does not guarantee decent abortion services, which ideally should provide concerned safe care, counseling, good health education and birth control services in an atmosphere that is accepting of the individual's sexuality. With such health care, freely provided, there would be fewer unwanted pregnancies and consequently less need for women to have to choose abortion at all.

For all women, abortion involves health issues of vital importance; abortion is an operation involving the risks of blood loss and infection. Like other surgical procedures, it should be avoided if possible.

Because the decision to abort or complete a pregnancy is so great many women feel isolated and alone. Often only she and her partner are aware of her pregnancy. They may both have feelings of guilt and prior confusion and fear. They may both need emotional support.

Women continue to feel anxious and depressed even after they have made the decision to have an abortion. In Freeman's study (1978) she writes, "The most trying time for most of them was the period after their pregnancies had been confirmed but before termination. Clearly, their abortions resolved a distressing event in their lives which they could not and did not accept casually." (Strong 1982, p. 150).

The RA must be especially careful not to be judgmental of the pregnant student's final decision. A woman who has chosen to undergo an abortion needs emotional support and acceptance during this difficult time. In addition to expressing her concern and availability, the RA should be aware of the support services available on campus and in the local community to help a woman deal with any emotional problems resulting from the abortion.

After an abortion, a patient is given a few basic instructions that an RA should also know:

1. Bleeding and cramps vary from woman to woman; some have none but most have both during the first 2 weeks after an abortion. Some may have spotting for 4 weeks after surgery.
2. The next normal period should begin in 4–6 weeks. If she is taking birth control pills, the period will probably start after the first packet.
3. It is important to rest for one or two days after the operation and to avoid strenuous exercise.
4. Be aware of possible complications: excessive bleeding, vomiting, fever, severe cramping, or a foul-smelling vaginal odor or discharge.
5. Avoid possibilities for infection: no douching, tampons, tub baths, or sexual intercourse for at least 1 week or whatever I recommend.
6. Have a postabortion check-up two or three weeks after the operation and receive instruction in contraception.

Usually, it is a great relief for a woman to end an unwanted pregnancy. However, there may be mixed or confused feelings after the operation. The RA needs to understand that some sadness and a sense of loss may occur.

The RA may be involved with students who have repeat abortions. The woman is more likely to receive censure from other students because they may now view her as careless and irresponsible. Anyone can make one mistake, but two is viewed with much more concern since the emotional feelings and reactions to a second abortion may be quite different from a first one. The RA may be quite challenged to not only work with the pregnant student but with others on the floor who are aware of the situation. Freeman's research (1978) showed that the most effective users of contraceptives are women who have had abortions. They have learned not to take chances because sooner or later their luck runs out and they don't want to go through the emotional upheaval again. (Strong 1982, p. 138).

The person who has almost been left out of the abortion scene is the man. If the man is thought of, it is usually with hostility and blame. Linda Frenke (1978) describes the men in an abortion clinic. "Abortion is very hard on the men who wait in clinics. By the very fact of being their while there wives and girlfriends are having pregnancies terminated, they are showing support and commitment. But they have nothing to do but wait." (Strong 1982, p. 152).

The RA might lend a sympathetic ear to the male student who wants to talk about what a personal experience with abortion has meant to him. Research by Frenke (1978) shows that abortion may be more a dilemma for men than previously recognized.

Pregnancy

The most common sign of pregnancy is a missed menstrual period. Nausea and vomiting, breast tenderness, frequent urination, and tiredness can all be early signs of pregnancy. However, none of these signs *always* means pregnancy. Uncertainty and wondering are so agonizing that any woman who suspects she may be pregnant should go to a clinic, health center, or physician to have a pregnancy test done. Confirming a pregnancy as soon as possible not only relieves a woman of uncertainty but allows the physician to discover any health problems that may endanger the life of the mother or the unborn child. The RA can serve a vital function if she understands the importance of having the pregnancy test done and can properly advise the possibly pregnant student or her boyfriend.

Women miss menstrual periods for all sorts of reasons, and a missed period does not necessarily indicate a pregnancy. Verifying pregnancy involves two procedures: a laboratory test that checks the urine for human chorionic gonadotrophin, a hormone produced by the developing embryo; and a pelvic examination by a trained person to check for relevant changes in the cervix and uterus. The most common urine test is the two-minute "slide" test, which starts to be effective forty-two days from the day of the last normal menstrual period and becomes more accurate a week or so later. Another urine test is the two-hour "tube test," which is quite accurate by thirty-five days after the last normal menstrual period. These tests are 95–98 percent accurate.

Pregnancy tests are available today which can give accurate results as early as 6–8 days after ovulation and before the first missed period. The benefits of early diagnosis may outweigh the cost difference between the routine urine-slide pregnancy test and a more sensitive blood test. (*Contraceptive Technology* 1982–83, p. 158).

A pregnancy test can be either "positive" or "negative." A positive means that the woman is most certainly pregnant and should be seen by a physician to verify the pregnancy with a pelvic examination. False positives are fairly rare. A negative usually means that the woman is not pregnant, but false negatives are fairly common. In other words the woman is pregnant, but the test results do not confirm the pregnancy at that time. A false negative could be a result of urine that got too warm on its way to the lab; urine that was not concentrated enough; or contamination of the urine by soap, aspirin, or whatever was in the specimen bottle. If the specimen is taken too early in the pregnancy, there may be an insufficient amount of the hormone. If it is too late in the pregnancy, after about three months, the test may also be falsely negative.

If the woman had a negative test and her period does not start, she should return for another test in a week and continue using contraception because if she is not pregnant and continues to be sexually active, she could get pregnant. After two or three negative tests, she should be advised to schedule a pelvic examination, as some pregnancies never give positive test results.

There are presently available "in-home" tests kits that claim accuracy as early as nine days after missed menstrual bleeding. As one might expect, however, the accuracy of the test varies from person to person, depending both on skill and individual hormone variations. Experts on pregnancy caution that women should be careful in depending on the "in-home" tests which may delay seeking professional medical care during the crucial early weeks of pregnancy. The usual cost of "in-home" tests is about the amount one would pay to have the test done by a clinic.

If a student is pregnant, it is important to determine how far along she is in the pregnancy. Medical people calculate the weeks of pregnancy from the first day of the last normal menstrual period and not from the day conception may have occurred.

Early in the pregnancy the student has some time—not a lot—to make her choice about what to do. She can (1) continue the pregnancy and keep the baby; (2) continue the pregnancy and give the baby up for adoption; or (3) terminate the pregnancy by having a legal abortion at a medical facility. Usually this is a very difficult and personal decision for a woman to make. The important point is that she should be aware of all of the options available and not be pressured by parents, friends, or sexual partner to do something she does not want to do, whether it be to have an abortion or to continue the pregnancy. The RA should be aware of agencies where the woman can receive proper counseling. Some of these agencies are the college health center, the college counseling center, the community mental health center, a local women's center, Planned Parenthood clinics, child and family services, or a religiously affiliated person or group. Antiabortion groups such as Birthright, will give her information but will also probably try to persuade her not to terminate the pregnancy.

The decision of whether to share the information with the sexual partner is sometimes difficult. If the woman does not share the hassle and pain of the unplanned pregnancy, then she either allows her partner to avoid his responsibility or else prevents him from assuming it.

If the student is single and considers keeping the child, it would be advisable for her to talk with other single mothers about their experiences. Some of the groups mentioned above would help her realistically prepare for single parenthood. If the student is considering terminating the pregnancy, then it is important for her to know that the earlier an abortion is done, the safer it is.

Abortion is one of the most controversial political, religious, and ethical issues of our time. Women choose abortion for various reasons. Proper usage of contraceptive methods cannot absolutely prevent unwanted pregnancies. Whether or not a woman feels she has the right to terminate a pregnancy, she definitely has the right to know what is involved in an abortion procedure.

Homosexuality

Americans seem to pride themselves on their freedom of expression. However, the homosexual's freedom to express himself or herself is often nonexistent. The majority of college students have never had a frank and open encounter with someone who prefers sexual relations with partners of the same sex. Many of their prejudices are based on patterns of thinking and responding that are learned from the "straight world." Many students have been taught that homosexual behavior is perverted, unnatural, and socially unacceptable. But each person is an individual, and each person should have the right to decide on his or her own sexual life-style as long as it is not harmful to others. Although homosexuality is one aspect of an individual's personality, our perception of such people is distorted if we label them solely in terms of their sexual preferences. We do not refer to people whose preferences are heterosexual as "heterosexuals," because this is not the only aspect of their humanness that is of interest or significance to us.

Homosexuality is no longer considered a mental illness or a deviance by the American Psychiatric Association (APA). In 1974, the APA Board of Trustees stated that "homosexuality shall no longer be listed as a mental disorder if the individual is not dissatisfied with homosexuality and if it does not regularly impair his or her social functioning." A study cited in the *American Journal of Psychiatry* found that homosexuals are no more subject to conflicts or psychological disturbances than any other members of society. This finding is backed up by a new Kinsey Institute study published under the title *Homosexualities: A Study of Diversity Among Men & Women,* which shows that many homosexuals, especially lesbians, lead lives of quiet, unhurried domesticity. (Read 1979, p. 134)

Very few people are exclusively homosexual in their relationships. Kinsey (1953) estimated that among those between the ages of twenty and thirty-five, only 1 to 3 percent of the women and 2 to 16 percent of the men were exclusively homosexual at any one time. Many individuals engage in brief homosexual encounters, either during adolescence or later in life. This does not mean that these individuals are homosexual, and it makes no sense to label such persons as "latent homosexuals." The danger in labeling a person as homosexual, heterosexual, or bisexual is that the label may become a self-fulfilling prophecy, and the person may act in ways different from his or her desired or natural behavior. True homosexuality means that the individual's sexual relations or emotional attachments are exclusively with persons of the same sex.

American college students seem to be particularly hostile toward homosexual men, possibly because our culture considers sexual relations with females a measure of masculinity. Most psychotherapists believe that many of the men who are especially hostile toward homosexual men are fearful of their own homosexual impulses. This hostility may be a means of denying homosexual responses and of helping to affirm one's own heterosexuality. Men who are secure in their own heterosexuality tend to be more tolerant of homosexuality.

College students appear to be very concerned about homosexuality. Unfortunately, they are quick to stereotype male homosexuals as effeminate, swaggering sissies or faggots and lesbians as aggressive, gruff, masculine "dykes." Fewer than 15 percent of male homosexuals and even fewer women resemble these stereotypes. "As more homosexuals—in government, the military, sports, business—'come out of the closet,' such stereotypes are wearing down." (Combs 1980, p. 162)

There are as many different kinds of homosexual people as there are heterosexual people. Those who are homosexual do not necessarily talk or act differently and are certainly not always identifiable by their appearance. Some have emotional problems, others do not. Homosexuality is not necessarily a cause for unhappiness or emotional disturbance any more than heterosexuality is.

The Kinsey Report estimated that as much as 10 percent of the U.S. population, or 21.5 million persons, may be homosexually inclined (Read 1979, p. 135). For fear of ostracism, persecution, and disgrace, many men and women who prefer homosexual relationships try to "pass as straights." Some homosexuals do engage in heterosexual marriage.

Lesbians may experience similar difficulties, but their homosexuality can be more easily disguised. Women are not expected to be as sexually active as men in our culture, and failure to respond to a man does not necessarily imply that a woman is homosexual. Two women can live together without undue suspicion more easily than two single men can.

There is much information available today about homosexuality, and the RA should be well informed on this topic. There are situations involving homosexuals that will confront the RA as she deals with various individuals and their chosen life-styles. Some may wish to share information with you about their sexual preference. Some may face discrimination by the "straights"— especially the males. A heterosexual individual may have had an encounter with a homosexual and may want to discuss it with you. A student may want a single room because she is homosexual.

Often, because our own personal experiences and life seem so "right," it is difficult to understand, let alone accept, the ways of another person without making an effort. It is especially difficult when his or her sexual life-style seems contrary to our own. Then we are fearful that we may be "wrong." The development of understanding is very important in these situations, because we all need to accept the reality of other sexual life-styles besides our own.

A tremendous amount of human misery is caused by lack of understanding. People do not attempt to understand other people, and often they do not understand themselves. We need to learn to accept rather than reject. College students seem to pride themselves on being tolerant, accepting of differences, willing to try new and different experiences, yet, when it comes to understanding the sex preferences of homosexuals, they often have great difficulty listening to the other point of view. The key to understanding seems to be in realizing that people who choose to live alternative life-styles are not asking that we live with or even like them; what they are asking is that we understand them and allow them to live their own lives with dignity.

The RA can promote an attitude of understanding on the floor in relation to homosexuality. There are so many myths and misconceptions regarding homosexuality that the RA could devise a quiz with facts and fallacies and then discuss the quiz and major issues. You could show the film entitled "The Pink Triangle" which could aid in discussion and awareness of this delicate topic. The pink triangle was the Nazi insignia for gay men and was worn by gays in concentration camps during World War II. Possibly a member of a gay rights group or a gay faculty member would be willing to discuss various aspects of this lifestyle. This type of floor program involves preplanning to create an atmosphere of learning and behaving in an adult, mature manner.

What are some practical points on how an RA can deal with a homosexual who lives on the floor? First, you can be a role model by accepting the person as he/she is. If you have strong biases or negative feelings you may wish to discuss your feelings with your hall director or a campus counselor. Examine your own beliefs and feelings and try to decide why you feel or react the way you do. Can you change these feelings and reactions? If you have analyzed yourself and feel that you cannot objectively deal with the person, then at least be aware of other resources—the hall director, the counseling center, etc.

Some of the problems that homosexual college students must confront include:

1. Should they come out of the closet? Should they tell their roommate? Their parents? Their friends?
2. Can they acknowledge and accept their homosexual feelings? Do they need or want counseling?
3. Do they join a college or community gay group?
4. Do they enter the homosexual subculture and become involved with social and sexual activities? The subculture provides approval, acceptance and support.
5. How do they cope with their first homosexual love affair? Bell and Weinstein (1978) found that "virtually every homosexual and lesbian they interviewed had at least one long-term relationship. The first love affair usually took place between the ages of 20–23." (Strong 1982, p. 459).

Intimate Relationships

We have all been involved in many different kinds of relationships prior to arriving on the college campus. We had to learn to relate to parents, siblings, and friends. We realize that human relationships are a necessity. All of us need people; all of us need each other.

The variations of relationships are countless. There are superficial contacts that involve minimal commitment, and close relationships that demand a deeper emotional investment. Then there is the all-important intimate relationship—the special relationship that should involve mutual caring, commitment and trust. College students frequently become involved in intimate or serious relationships. Intimate relationships involve a lot of time and communication.

Probably one of the most important aspects of an intimate relationship is the ability to communicate. No one can read another person's mind. A couple must verbalize their desires and expectations. As intimacy grows, people must be willing to discuss difficult issues such as sex, contraception, marriage, children, money, careers, and values. They must also learn to communicate feelings of anger and frustration, as well as of pleasure and satisfaction. Communication involves talking, listening, and feedback. If and when love grows, we find ourselves as concerned with the other person as we are with ourselves.

Intimacy is a very involved emotional relationship. Intimacy needs time to grow and develop. It is a process of evolving, of self-revelation, of exposing, of expressing, and of getting to know someone as fully as possible while he or she is getting to know you. Intimacy is by no means synonymous with sex, but it is often involved in a sexual relationship.

We all know that love and sex do not necessarily go together. Sex is not an emotion. It is one of the animal drives. Emotions are the ways we are taught to feel about our drives. College students seem to have a lot of drive for some things. Generally men seem to be more concerned with the sex drive: how did you do? did you score? And generally women seem to be more concerned with the emotion: what's he like? how did you feel about him?

As dating continues, the relationship may or may not progress. If the relationship is to progress and become intimate, then enjoying, sharing, and caring are natural outcomes of being with someone you like.

The longer and more intimate a relationship, the harder it is to readjust or change when the realtionship ends. The RA must be aware that no person is ever quite the same after a relationship of real intimacy has dissolved. Men may forget "one-night stands," but they do not forget intimate friends or the women they have loved. And if women have loved and been loved, they do not forgive and forget, and their characters may be permanently affected. In extreme cases, the RA may want to refer a troubled individual to the counseling center or the residence hall director.

There is an excellent college student workbook of self-tests entitled, *Wellness RSVP*, 2nd edition by Kammerman, Doyle, Valois and Cox, 1983. It is published by The Benjamin/Cummings Publishing Co., 2727 Sand Hill Road, Menlo, CA 94025. It would be a convenient way for RA's to have interesting participatory floor programs that would help students examine their attitudes and behaviors related to many current topics.

Rape

The 1980 FBI Uniform Crime Report states that there is a 20–30% probability that a girl now entering her teens will be sexually assaulted sometime in her life. Rape or the threat of rape is a fact of life for most women. The fear of rape causes many women to limit their activities. Women have to be cautious in going places alone such as the library, concerts, laundromats, hiking, walking and using buses or subways. You should know that,

1. Over 50% of rape victims are under 21 years of age.
2. Over half of the reported rapes are committed by non-strangers.
3. Rape by someone a woman knows can cause the greatest psychological harm.
4. Rape poses a crisis in a woman's life and her future relationships.

Rape is not primarily sexual, but is an act of violence involving male aggression against women. In addition to aggression, it can occur because of frustration, power, or punishment, but seldom if ever is rape provoked by sexual needs. The rapist forces the victim into an intimate physical relationship primarily as a means of degrading the person.

Rape has been a theme in history since the earliest times. It is an integral part of warfare, inspiring terror in civilians and a sense of power in soldiers. Rape is an everyday occurrence in prisons, where it generally occurs between persons of the same sex. Children as young as six months and women as old as ninety-three years have been raped.

The prevalent belief about rape in this and other countries is that women cannot be raped unless they want to be. This is nonsensical. Many men have fantasized about raping women: however, most men have never acted on these fantasies. Some people blame the victims of rape by saying that they asked for it. It is no easier for a woman to resist an armed rapist than for a bank teller to resist an armed robber.

Early in the school year, you may wish to schedule a hall program dealing with various aspects of rape. Topics may deal with rape fantasies, characteristics of a rapist, what to do if you have been raped, the medical examination after rape, physical and psychological aftereffects of rape, and the legal aspects of rape. You may want to include guest speakers from the campus police, the psychology department, the health sciences department, the campus health center, the counseling department or the counseling center, and possibly community groups that deal with rape. Obviously, it is most important to discuss preventive measures that the women in the hall can take to protect themselves. You should also become familiar with the reporting procedures on your campus for dealing with a possible rape victim.

When the RA is confronted by a person who says he/she has been raped, probably the most important response is to be sympathetic and understanding. You should contact the hall director as soon as possible. A rape is traumatic, and it is important that the victim have supportive friends and/or counselors to share his or her feelings. Sometimes rape victims feel too embarrassed or humiliated to speak about their experience. However, it is known that women who have been raped and who have talked about it afterward are apt to feel less guilty and ashamed, because they were able to express their anger and to discuss the crime as something that happens to many women.

The hall director will usually notify the campus police. In many areas, there are officers who are specially trained in working with rape victims. If possible, you can ask the victim if he/she would prefer to work with a male or female officer.

It is also important to get immediate medical attention. The victim should not wash or change clothes, shower, or douche until he/she has been examined. An extra change of clothes should be taken along to the hospital emergency room, since the original clothes may be needed for evidence. Rape crisis centers have people who are enormously helpful to the rape victim. This is a time when the victim needs support, since he or she will need to make several important decisions during this time of crisis.

At the hospital there are two basic concerns: (1) medical care, and (2) gathering evidence for a possible prosecution. The victim does not need to prosecute, but in most situations it is a good idea to encourage prosecution. Prosecution of the rapist is important both to protect others from future attacks and to let the community know the frequency of rape. There is no question, however, that prosecuting is difficult and often humiliating.

The rape victim should be examined by a doctor as soon as possible, certainly within the first twelve hours after the attack. Most hospitals have special rape kits and forms to help them obtain the necessary samples and information to aid in prosecution. Many rape prevention groups have pressured hospitals to create twenty-four rape units and to provide better, more sensitive medical care to rape victims.

The medical examination should consist of general inspection involving description of bruises, lacerations, redness, and pain. A pelvic examination should be performed to look for evidence of trauma. This may be very upsetting to the victim, but it is necessary to look for damage. "Approximately 25–50% of women have some physical trauma from the rape incident, so the general examination and pelvic examination are very important" (Cooke and Dworkin 1979, p. 399). Other tests and/or treatment may be done for sexually transmitted diseases or possible pregnancy, depending on the time and circumstances. It is usually a good idea to get the name, address, and telephone number of the examining physician before you leave, in case further problems arise.

A rape victim, and often his or her family, will need follow-up counseling to cope with difficult feelings. On college campuses, the victim may receive counseling from the counseling center, the psychology department, or the health center. Other sources of help might include the community mental health center or a rape crisis center. Humiliation, embarrassment, disgust, horror, and anxiety are all possible reactions to rape.

Avoiding Rape

The National Center for Prevention and Control of Rape indicates that early, aggressive action taken by women is a primary determinant for women escaping rape. Research done by Pauline Bart (1980) showed that the five most frequently used forms of resistance were:

1. Escaping or trying to escape (The least frequently used approach but the most successful).
2. Screaming (Those who screamed were less likely to be raped than those who did not).
3. Physical resistance (Sixty-eight percent of the women who avoided rape physically resisted).
4. Cognitive-verbal techniques of reasoning, conning or flattering (It was the most frequently used method but not particularly effective).
5. Pleading (Those women who pleaded were more likely to be raped than those who did not plead). (Strong 1983, p. 511).

McIntyre (1980) also found that if a woman fights, screams, or tries to escape, she is more likely to escape being raped. The media and other resources have implied that if you tried to resist you would be more seriously injured. However, complying with the rapist does not guarantee that you won't be seriously injured. McIntyre also found that women who resisted usually did not receive injuries that required hospitalization. They often avoided rape but received minor injuries as they battled their assailants. An important determining factor was whether the woman feared murder and/or mutilation more than rape. There are also situational variables such as a weapon, the time (rape is more likely if the attack is between 12 midnight and 6 a.m.), and the place (it is easier to flee if outside). (Strong 1983, pp. 511–512).

Date Rape

Sexual aggression on a college campus is surprisingly common. Kanin and Parcell (1977) in a survey of 282 university women found that 143 (51 percent) had experienced some form of sexual assault during the past year (Rathus 1983, p. 443). Some men believe that taking a woman out to dinner or a show should be rewarded with sexual activity. Kanin's study (1969) of some 300 male university students showed that about 25% of the sample had tried to force at least one dating partner into intercourse. These assaults occurred among couples who were going steady as well as casual dates.

RAs may wish to discuss this problem with women students especially freshmen or transfer students. They may discuss ways to prevent these potential date rape situations. They need to be aware that some men see sex as a contest that one wins by "scoring" or having coitus. They need to realize that some men see sex as domination and exploitation. Unfortunately, our culture encourages men to be aggressive, and women to be passive and cooperative.

Emotional Responses to Rape

Through emergency room interviews with 92 women at Boston City Hospital, Burgess and Homstrom (1974) identified the common response patterns as a result of rape as the "rape trauma syndrome".

1. The Acute Phase—Disorganization: shock, disbelief, anger, fear, anxiety, crying, agitation, shakiness. Some tried to mask their feelings. Many reported increased insomnia, eating problems, cystitis, headaches, mood changes, depression, loss of temper and menstrual irregularities.
2. The Long-Term Process: Reorganization. They often change addresses and phone numbers. They often have bad dreams and intense fears. A study by Judith Becker (1979) of 137 rape victims found that a year following their rapes, 25 women feared the indoors, 30 the outdoors, 80 feared being alone, 55 apprehensive of people behind them and 50 continued to have sexual problems.

Preventing Rape

1. Tell someone else your schedule or plans, where you are going and when you plan to return.
2. Try not to go out across campus at night by yourself. Try to walk in groups and in well lighted areas.
3. Never allow a strange man into your room.
4. Do not hitchhike on or near the campus. Do not pick-up hitchhikers.
5. Have your keys ready if you are going to your car late at night.

6. Park your car in well lighted areas.
7. Drive at night with your car windows up and doors locked.
8. Check the rear seat of the car before entering.
9. Do not accept a ride from one or more male acquaintances who have been drinking at a party.
10. Do not talk to strange men on the street.

Sexually Transmitted Diseases

Initially, it may appear that the RA would not need to know about sexually transmitted diseases. However, these diseases do involve the college population, so it is important for the RA to be knowledgeable and informed.

"Venereal disease" and "V.D." are value-laden and troublesome terms. It is more appropriate and accepted to use "Sexually Transmitted Diseases" or "STDs".

The STD problem is truly epidemic. Despite the seriousness and increased incidence, the majority of sexually active people have little awareness of the risks and dangers involved in STDs. This section will present facts on the common STDs and a special section on herpes.

STDs always involve at least two people; and any person who has a STD should assume the responsibility for informing those with whom he/she has had sexual contact. Obviously, some may feel embarrassed to discuss it or fear the effects on a particular relationship. However, the consequences of undetected infection are so potentially harmful that there is no legitimate excuse for not telling one's partners. If some persons are afraid to tell their partners directly, the local public health services or college student health centers will do it for them, preserving anonymity.

Free diagnosis and treatment for STDs are available at public health centers throughout the country. However, the infected persons must take the initiative by reporting the earliest symptoms. Ignoring the symptoms, hoping that they will disappear, is very risky. Sometimes symptoms will disappear or seem to subside, but this does not mean that the disease is gone. With some infections, such as syphilis, it means that the infection may be entering a new stage.

At either the college health center or a public health center, the individual will be asked to describe the symptoms and to recall if he or she has had sexual contact with someone who may have had a STD. Patients will then be examined and laboratory tests done to determine if a disease is actually present.

Once the specific disease has been diagnosed, the recommended treatment will be instituted. Sometimes antibiotics are effective, and other times specific medications or treatments will be prescribed. The examinations, tests, and treatments vary with the disease. However, reexamination is important to make sure the disease has been arrested.

Following diagnosis and treatment in a clinic, the patient will be asked who may have infected him/her and whom he/she may have infected. This information is confidential, and contacts will not be informed of the source of identification unless permission is given to do so. Usually the contacts are notified by means of a letter informing them that they have been exposed to STD and that they are required to go to a doctor or clinic within forty-eight hours. These people must be examined and possibly treated so they will not spread the disease to others.

Reference Section on STDs

Bacterial Vaginitis (Nonspecific vaginitis, Hemaphilis vaginalis, Gardenerella vaginitis)

1. Symptoms
   greyish or whitish watery vaginal discharge
   pain on urination·
   vaginal itching
   painful intercourse
   foul odor of discharge
2. Diagnosis—culture by health practitioner.
3. Treatment—oral antibiotics or other prescribed medications—oral Flagyl is the most common medication.
4. Treatment of Partner—Your partner must be treated at the same time, and you both must complete the full course of treatment to prevent reinfection.
5. Special Instructions—Sex is OK as long as you use condoms for the length of treatment.
6. Prevention—Avoid multiple partners.

Chlamydia (Chlamydia trachomatis)

1. Symptoms
   burning on urination
   vaginal discharge
   symptoms of PID (pelvic inflammatory disease)
2. Diagnosis—culture by health practitioner
3. Treatment—oral antibiotics.
4. Treatment of Partner—Your partner must be treated at the same time to avoid reinfection.
5. Special Instructions—With concurrent treatment sex is OK.
6. Prevention—Avoid multiple partners.
7. Potential Complications—An untreated infection may affect a woman's fertility.

Cystitis (Honeymoon cystitis)

1. Symptoms
   pain, burning urination
   frequent urination
   foul smelling cloudy urine
   lower abdominal pain
   blood in urine
   painful intercourse
2. Diagnosis—urinalysis by health practitioner.
3. Treatment—oral antibiotics and often Pyridium, a urinary anesthetic, to decrease pain and bladder spasms.
4. Treatment of Partner—only when needed.
5. Special Instructions
   drink 8–10 glasses of water per day for length of treatment use condoms
   Follow up urinalysis 3–4 weeks after treatment
6. Prevention
   urinate often
   wear cotton underpants—nylon underwear and hose hold in moisture which leads to increased bacterial growth
   good personal hygiene—wash genitals once a day and dry thoroughly
   drink cranberry juice—increases acidity of the urine and less infections
   urinate after sex
7. Potential Complications—bladder infections can recur.

Gonorrhea (The clap, drip, Neisseria gonorrhea)

1. Symptoms
   female—usually none, some have puslike vaginal discharge, vaginal soreness, lower abdominal pain, painful urination
   male—cloudy, puslike discharge from the penis, burning on urination, about 20% of men have no symptoms
2. Diagnosis—Bacterial smear and culture of male urethea or female vagina by health practitioner (throat culture if oral-genital sex)
3. Treatment—Penicillin or other antibiotics.
4. Treatment of Partner—Essential. Any sexual partners must receive treatment.
5. Special Instructions
   refrain from oral-genital sex
   use condoms or avoid intercourse until treatment is complete and follow-up evaluation by health practitioner.

6. Prevention
   avoid multiple partners
   spermicides provide some protection
   use condoms
7. Potential Complications—If untreated can cause inflammation, pain and sterility in male and female. Can cause infant blindness during delivery if infant passes through infected birth canal.
8. It is estimated there are 3,000,000 persons affected yearly.

Herpes Genitalis (also see special section)

1. Symptoms
   blisterlike sores on vulva, cervix, penis
   painful intercourse
   itching of vulva, penis
   painful urination
2. Diagnosis—pap smear of lesions and culture by health practitioner.
3. Treatment—no effective known treatment, local analgesics.
4. Treatment of Partner—no known treatment.
5. Special Instructions
   report herpes to physician if pregnant
   wear loose underwear
   avoid intercourse or use condoms if sores present
6. Prevention
   annual Pap smear
   good personal hygiene
   avoid oral-genital intercourse when sores present
7. Potential Complications
   about ⅓ experience recurrences
   herpes may be spread to newborn during birth causing serious problems
8. It is estimated there are 3–5 million persons affected yearly.

Monilia (Candida Albicans, Yeast infections)

1. Symptoms
   thick, cottage cheese vaginal discharge
   itching, burning sensation and redness of vulva
   painful intercourse
2. Diagnosis—microscopic evaluation, gram stain or culture by health practitioner.
3. Treatment—antifungal vaginal suppositories or creams (Mycostatin/Nystatin) are prescribed for usually 7 days. These are messy so you may want to wear a minipad or shield. Complete your treatment even if you get your period.

4. Treatment of Partner—only when needed—yeast is rarely transmitted sexually.
5. Special Instructions
wear cotton underwear
treatment may be needed for 2 cycles
pregnancy, birth control pills and diabetic conditions increase the risk by creating conditions in the vagina favoring the growth of yeast.
antibiotics can decrease vaginal bacteria and a yeast infection can result. Don't use tampons because they absorb all the medication.
if you do have sex, have your partner use a condom until your infection is over.
6. Prevention
avoid douching because it can destroy normal bacteria in the vagina
7. Potential Complications
recurrence

Pelvic Inflammatory Disease (PID, salpingitis or inflammation of fallopian tubes, endometritis or inflammation of the lining of the uterus)
1. Symptoms
abdominal/back/pelvic/leg pain
fever, chills, vomiting
painful urination
painful intercourse
post-coital bleeding
excessive menstrual bleeding
2. Diagnosis—gram stain, culture, exam and history by health practitioner.
3. Treatment—oral antibiotics as prescribed.
4. Treatment of Partner—only when needed.
5. Special Instructions
use condoms during treatment
bedrest is essential until pain subsides
avoid milk products if taking Tetracipline
watch for minilial flareups
6. Prevention
avoid multiple partners
use condoms
avoid IUDs (intrauterine devices)
7. Potential Complications
sterility
chronic pain and infections

Pubic Lice (Crabs, Phthirus pubis) tiny creatures not larger than a pinhead and under magnification look like crabs

1. Symptoms
   itching
   lice in pubic hair
2. Diagnosis—lice/eggs in pubic hair.
3. Treatment—Kewell shampoo—leave on 4 minutes then rinse (crabs are not affected by normal soap). May need to repeat treatment. Also RID is effective—should not be used by person allergic to ragweed. Follow directions carefully.
4. Treatment of Partner—only if infected.
5. Special Instructions
   remove all visible signs of infection
   wash infected clothing, bed linens, or sleeping bags and dry in dryer set on high heat. Crabs can survive 24 hours apart from host
   avoid intercourse
6. Prevention
   good hygiene
   do not sleep in other's beds, wear their clothes or use their towels
7. Potential Complications—none.
8. It is estimated that 1–2 million people are infected each year.

Syphilis (Loues, Treponema pallidum infection)

1. Symptoms
   Primary—3 weeks post-exposure
         chancre (painless sore) on penis/vagina/rectum/anus/cervix/mouth/throat
   Secondary—6 weeks post-primary
         rash on feet and hands
         loss of appetite
         fever and sore throat
         nausea
         painful joints
         headaches
   Tertiary—10–20 years—see complications
2. Diagnosis—dark field exam of fluid of chancre and VDRL (blood test) by health practitioner. This blood test is routinely done upon hospital admission, obtaining a marriage license, giving blood, joining the military and becoming pregnant.
3. Treatment—penicillin shot (stages 1 and 2)
4. Treatment of Partner—essential

5. Special Instructions
    use condoms for 1 month
6. Prevention
    avoid multiple partners
7. Potential Complications
    if untreated it can cause brain damage, heart disease, spinal cord damage and blindness
    an infected pregnant woman may pass syphilis on to her unborn child giving the infant congenital syphilis
8. It is estimated that approximately 400,000 persons are affected yearly.

Trichomoniasis (Trich, caused by a one-celled parasite)

1. Symptoms
    frothy, thin greenish vaginal discharge
    vulvar itching/pain
    frequent urination
    may be asymptomatic
2. Diagnosis—wet mount, culture and Pap smear by health practitioner.
3. Treatment—oral Flagyl as prescribed—usually 7 days.
4. Treatment of Partner
    essential although men usually don't have symptoms
    both must complete the course of treatment or you may reinfect each other.
5. Special Instructions
    use condoms during treatment
    avoid alcohol with Flagyl
    repeat Pap test in 2–3 months if original was abnormal
6. Prevention
    avoid multiple partners
7. Potential Complications—none.

Venereal Warts (Condylomata acuminata)

1. Symptoms
    dry, wart-like growths on penis, vagina, vulva, cervix
    constant discharge
    itching
2. Diagnosis—exam and possibly blood test (VDRL to rule out syphilis) by health practitioner.
3. Treatment—Podophyllin ointment or liquid applied to warts every 3–4 hours.
4. Treatment of Partner—only when needed.

5. Special Instructions
   several treatments per week
   use condoms
6. Prevention
   avoid multiple partners
7. Potential Complications—none.

Special Discussion on Herpes

If one was asked to name the STD of the 80's he would probably say herpes. However, the herpes virus has plagued mankind for at least 2000 years, but it has been on the rise in this country since the 1960's. According to the Centers for Disease Control (CDC) in Atlanta, this increase may be due to "changing sexual attitudes, multiple sexual partners and oral-genital sex."

In 1982, both *Time* magazine and *Newsweek* had feature articles about herpes. "An estimated 20 million Americans now have genital herpes, with as many as half a million new cases expected this year, according to CDC." (*Time* August 2, 1982, p. 62).

A recent study of UCLA students revealed a significantly higher incidence of herpes for students than for the general population leading researchers to speculate that genital herpes may be the most significant STD among college students. (Symaya 1980, p. 20).

Five types of herpes have been identified:

1. Herpes Simplex Virus I (HSV I or Type I) is the familiar cold sore or fever blister on the lips. It can infect the eyes and cause a serious corneal infection which can cause blindness.
2. Herpes Simplex Virus II (HSV II, Type II or genital herpes) is blister-like lesions in the anal or genitalia region (penis or vagina).
3. Herpes Zoster Virus causes chickenpox and shingles.
4. Epstein Barr virus causes mononucleosis.
5. Cytomegala Virus.

Herpes I can be found below the waist and Herpes II can be found above the waist. Indeed, oral sex has been a potent force in spreading both strains. This discussion will focus on genital herpes.

Herpes has become the most feared STD. The reasons are quite simple: at this point it is a life-long disease with no cure and has a tendency to recur. The victims frequently suffer more from depression, guilt, fear and worry than from the physical problems. Some have said they go through stages similar to the stages of dying: shock, emotional numbness, isolation, loneliness, depression and impotence.

Herpes begins with a fluid filled sore usually on or near the genital organs, but it may occur anywhere on the body. It usually appears about 3–20 days after sex with an infected person. It may also be accompanied with fever and headaches. The initial outbreak is usually the most painful and tends to last the longest, usually one to three weeks. Even though the herpes sore on the surface has healed, the virus may hide in nerve cells until the body's defenses break down and allow them to escape. Herpes attacks can recur if there are other viral infections such as a cold, stress, inadequate nutrition, menstrual period, exposure to the sun, insufficient sleep or emotional upset. "If there is a recurrence, it is generally less severe; and only one third ever have a recurrence." (Strong 1982, p. 213).

Herpes is spread by intimate contact during the active stage. "Two UCLA researchers have reported that herpes viruses can live on towels for up to 72 hours and on toilet seats for at least four hours." (*Time* 1982, p. 66). Many other studies disagree with this so more research needs to be done. It has recently been speculated that the virus may be able to live on the decks around hot tubs.

Do's and Don'ts with Herpes

1. Wash the sores with soap and water. Sometimes bathing in warm water with Epsom salts or Burrow's solution is soothing.
2. Do not use antibacterial creams and ointments—they retain moisture and may lead to secondary infections. Avoid over-the-counter drugs to heal the infection.
3. Don't touch your eyes since you may infect yourself with ocular herpes.
4. Don't kiss babies—they lack resistance to the virus.
5. A hand blow dryer on low heat may help dry and speed healing.
6. Don't pick at the sores.
7. Don't wear tight or nylon underwear—they trap moisture. Cotton underwear is important because it allows ventilation and absorbs moisture.
8. Dry area completely but don't share towels, especially with children.
9. Take aspirin for pain.
10. See your health practitioner—a new drug, acyclovir (Zovirax) can be effective if used early.
11. Tell your partner in a non-threatening way explaining what it is.
12. Be aware of your symptoms of recurrence (often burning, swelling and discomfort in the same site) and refrain from sexual activity.
13. Have an annual pap test to check for precancerous signs in the cervix.

At this time there is no known treatment for herpes. In March, 1982 the FDA approved acyclovir (Zovirax) as a 5% ointment useful in decreasing pain, decreasing viral growth and shortening the duration of the first attack. The drug is not curative and does not prevent recurrence (Conn 1983, p. 869).

If a pregnant woman has an active herpes infection, at the time of delivery, the infant may contract the virus as it passes through the birth canal so a Caesarian section may be necessary. If a women has herpes and becomes pregnant, she should be sure to tell her physician.

How can the RA help herpes victims?

1. You can be knowledgeable about the disease since there are many myths and much misinformation.
2. You could organize a floor program on SDTs. You might want to invite a guest speaker or show a film. There is an excellent film, *Jennifer,* the story of a young woman who has just discovered she has herpes.
3. You can be sensitive to the emotional needs of the victims and their partners. There is an excellent pamphlet by Greenwood and Bernstein entitled, "Coping with Herpes: The Emotional Problems". It is available from The Washington Center for Cognitive—Behavioral Therapy, 5225 Connecticut Avenue, N.W., Washington, D.C. 20015.
4. You can encourage the herpes victim to seek care and advice from a sensitive health care practitioner.

CHAPTER 13
Cult Activities on College Campuses

In the past ten years, cult activities on college campuses have increased. It is estimated that almost three million young people between the ages of 18 and 24 are active in 2,000 religious cults in the United States today. The 1981 Gallup youth survey found that, between 1978 and 1981 alone, there was an 18.1% increase in religious cult membership among teenagers. On college campuses, it is estimated that approximately one in every twenty college students has turned to some form of nontraditional religious activity. As an RA, you have the greatest contact with new students. These students are the most vulnerable to becoming involved in destructive religious cults. The information provided in this chapter will assist you in understanding what a religious cult is, how its members go about recruiting students on campus, the effects that membership has on the abilities of an individual, and the things that you can look for in your residents that may give early warning signs of one of them experiencing problems in this area.

Defining Religious Cults

The distinctive features of a religious cult, as we will be discussing it in this chapter, involve a close allegiance to a charismatic leader, an inordinate preoccupation on the part of the group with the attainment of money, and the use of behavior modification practices and brainwashing techniques to convert members. Cults are distinguished from the more traditional forms of religious groups by their highly syncretic beliefs and practices coupled with some form of separation from society.

Newspaper articles and scholarly books have referred to groups such as the International Society of Krishna Consciousness (Hare Krishna), Sun Myung Moon Unification Church, The Divine Light Mission, Church of Scientology, and the Children of God as examples that fall into the category we are discussing, however, there are hundreds of smaller groups which employ many of the same practices.

Cult Recruiting on College Campuses

There is substantial evidence that college campuses are among the primary targets for cult recruiting. In a study of 237 members of Moon's Unification Church, Mark Gantler (1979), a professor of psychiatry at Albert Einstein School of Medicine, discovered that almost half (42%) of the members studied were attending college at least part-time at least six months prior to joining the group, and nearly one-third (31%) were full-time students. Only 25% of the members completed college after joining the Unification Church, although 58% had begun.

Recruiting techniques used on college campuses are many. Some organizations specifically target freshman and senior students because of their vulnerability as they experience uncertainty about their future in college, or the future after college. Recruiters have used counseling centers at universities to find students in personal crises, by either waiting in the waiting rooms, or outside the counseling centers to find students who are troubled. Through a technique known as "love-bombing," they entice these students into participation in their organization. Residence halls have always been a favorite place to recruit students, particularly on the weekends, when recruiters can wander the corridors and find students who are alone, instead of with friends. Not even libraries are safe from the intrusive proselytizing of cults. Recruiters search the library stacks to find students who are exploring questions that might provide opportunities for the cult recruiter to entice the person into taking the first step toward joining the cult organization. Other ways that have been used by cult organizations on campuses run the gamut from running ads in campus newspapers for students to do "Peace Corps" type work, to starting student organizations with lofty principles to entice students into joining the organization.

Under the guise of such things as vegetarian cooking classes, yoga classes, or organizations dedicated to some lofty principal, universities have recognized some of these groups as student organizations or have given these organizations permission to operate on campus. Using front groups to hide their actual identity, cults frequently lure students into organizations without students having full knowledge of the actual purposes of the organizations. Moon's Unification Church, as one example, is associated with over 140 different front groups. On college campuses, it is known variously as the Collegiate Associate for the Research of Principles (CARP), New Educational Developmental Systems, and the Students for an Ethical Society, to name but three. Many students are deceived into membership in one of these groups only to discover the identity of the group some months later. Richard Delgado, Professor of Law at UCLA, described the problem with the recruiting practices of cults before a special US Senate Committee in 1979, as follows: "The recruiter . . . uses deception and concealment to forestall truth. Gradually, the recruit gains knowledge of the cult, its identity, its demands. This information is parcelled out only as the cult perceives that he or she has lost the ability to assess it according to his or her usual frames of references. A convert thus never has full capacity and knowledge. One or the other is impaired by the cult design." (p. 60)

It is important to understand that cults, through their recruiting process, attack people psychologically and emotionally, not intellectually. Everyone is vulnerable to the deceptive proselytizing of cult groups.

The Conversion Process

The conversion process, sometimes referred to as mind control or brainwashing, is based on two fundamental principles; (1) if you can get a person to behave in the ways you want, you can get him to believe what you want, and (2) sudden, drastic changes in the environment leads to heightened suggestibility, and drastic changes in attitudes and beliefs. The best way to describe the conversion process is to consider it in three stages: unfreezing beliefs, conversion or snapping, and refreezing of new beliefs or indoctronation. The first stage is devoted to an unfreezing of the person's current belief system. This is where most of the mind-control or brainwashing techniques are employed. Organizations approach this differently, however, there are commonalities in the use of the techniques employed in the conversion of new members. Although the foundations of the techniques of "brainwashing" were first advanced in the Chinese thought-reform camps during the Korean Conflict, new technology, based on research on persuasion, propaganda, motivation, behavior modification, group dynamics, nonverbal communication, light, color, sound, texture, eye contact, and altered states of consciousness (Conway, 1979) used by the cults today are more effective and produce profound changes in the individual.

In the initial stages of conversion (the unfreezing of beliefs) the new recruit is usually isolated from all but cult members. This often takes place at a weekend retreat or workshop, but may also be seen when individual students are not left alone and are constantly in the company of cult group members. The new recruit is subjected to long, boring lectures, deprived of sleep, maintained on a diet low in protein and sometimes required to chant or meditate for long periods of time. The recruit may also be subjected to tremendous peer pressure, guilt manipulation, personal confessions, and personal intimacy which promotes a sense of family through hugging, kissing, touching and flattery. Deprived of the opportunity to validate beliefs outside of the cult, and maintained in a state of mental and physical exhaustion, the recruit becomes quickly absorbed in a world of new happenings and new experiences. Finally, the person's individuality and personal control slips away and the person enters a state not unlike a trance—a state of altered consciousness. As the person's attention is narrowed, he undergoes what has been described as a sudden personality change. Conway and Segalman (1978) describe it as "snapping." They define this moment as an "overpowering, holographic crisis of the brain." This period may temporarily energize or exhilarate the individual, but has a devastating effect upon individuals' ability to function as they did before. It is as if a wall has been constructed blocking the person's personality. With this accomplished, cult members begin the final stage of the conversion experience—indoctrinating the new recruit with its particular set of beliefs and practices.

For a period of time immediately following this snapping experience, the person is highly susceptible to absorbing new information. It is in this period that the person is programmed or indoctrinated with beliefs of the cult. New beliefs become locked into the new personality, and become the guide by which this person functions in the world. Beliefs such as parents are disciples of Satan, all people outside of the group are evil, thinking for one's self is bad, and the cult must be obeyed without question are programmed into the individual.

Robert Lifton (1961), a psychiatrist who studied the brainwashing process in thought-reform camps in China during the Korean Conflict, established eight principles used in mind control. These principles coupled with some of the new information on mind-control techniques are employed today in the conversion of new members. The eight psychological themes are as follows:

1. *Milieu control.* This is the ability of the cult to control the environment of the individual. They control not only the physical environment, but usually control communication by restricting the nature of the conversations. During workshops or retreats, cults control the person's life through the use of a detailed schedule which determines the nature and timing of each event throughout the day, even the most mundane in nature.

2. *Mystical manipulation.* This form of manipulation uses every possible device the cult has available, no matter how painful or bizarre. Its purpose is to provoke "specific patterns of behavior, and emotions in such a way that these will appear to have arisen spontaneously from the environment." (p. 422) The cult requires the recruit to trust it because it has a higher purpose. As the person gives more of his trust to the group, the group takes on increased importance. The person begins to feel that he cannot escape from the organization and begins to surrender to its will.

3. *The demand for purity.* In most religious cults, there are absolute goods and absolute evils. People are either good or they are evil. Those who are in cults are good, those who are not are evil. This bi-polar-

ization of absolutes provides the opportunity for the person to be good by joining the organization. The process used is to make the person feel guilty about all the evils associated with not being in the particular group.

4. *The cult of confession.* Cults generally demand that people show shame and confess their sins to the group. These personal confessions are explained as purification, but are used as a way of exploiting the individual and as a way of enhancing guilt that the individual must feel for being part of the evil world of the outside as opposed to the good world of the cult members.

5. *The sacred science.* No matter what cult group is discussed, each claims to have the "word"—the sacred science. There is something unique about their truth; something divine about their approach, something special separating them from the rest of the world. This "special insight" is viewed as the final answer, the correct path.

6. *Loading the language.* Language is a very powerful tool. It is the way that we understand and conceptualize. Cults have a system of making language value loaded. Common words are given special meaning by cults. This special ideological jargon soon becomes a way for the person to demonstrate his membership involvement and participation in the group. The person is rewarded for using it, and is looked on as an insider in the use of it.

7. *Doctrine over person.* The human experience of the past is always subordinate to the claims of the doctrine. No matter what one's practical knowledge and past experiences have been, it is not a substitute for the "truth," as explained by the dogma of the religious group. Thus, it is never possible to challenge the dogma or doctrine on the basis of human experience, no matter how foolish or how contrary it is to the person's past experiences.

8. *The dispensing of existence.* Because only those in the cult organization are good, it follows that those outside the cult are bad. It also follows that good is better than evil, and good should exist, and evil should not. It is often recognized in the group that only those people who are involved in the group will be saved, or have the right to exist. Those who are not part of the group do not have the right to exist, or will not be saved. Somewhere in the cult doctrine there is usually the allegation that these people will be dealt with by a divinity who rewards people who are in the organization and punishes those who are not.

Reasons for Joining

One might at this point ask why anyone would subject themselves to this kind of experience. Intellectually, cults would probably recruit very few people. However, the process of conversion attacks the person emotionally and psychologically, not intellectually. College students are particularly vulnerable to the deceptive proselytizing of these groups. The normal developmental issues encountered in the transition to adulthood leave students searching for identity, emotional support, and answers to complex questions of values and ethics. Cults, with their emphasis on community and a well-defined dogma are enticing alternatives to students confronted with developmental issues that would normally lead them to more complex reasoning and emotional maturity. Cults continue to grow stronger as faith in the normally competing social institutions of education, church, family, and government diminish.

Psychosocial developmental issues encountered during the late teens and early twenties increase the vulnerability of college students. In earlier chapters, we discussed the developmental theories of Chickering and Coons. Both of these theorists acknowledge conversion into a fundamentalist cult or religious movement as a path taken by some students to resolve the task of development toward adulthood. John Clark (1976), a professor of psychiatry at Harvard Medical School, states that about 42% of the cult members he studied in his clinical work joined cults during this period of normal development leading to adulthood.

Cognitive development in this late adolescent period is another developmental factor in the susceptibility to cults. William Perry (1970), the director of counseling at Harvard University, in his theory of the intellectual development of college students, reasons that students initially think dualistically. In this dualistic scheme absolute truths and falsehoods exist and are known to authorities. The authorities are usually professors but others may also serve in this role. Students seeking absolute truths can easily be drawn to a charismatic leader of a cult as an authority who offers clear, absolute truths and falsehoods. In other circumstances, unresolved cognitive conflicts may push the student on to more complex ways of relating to the world of ideas. The highly structured environment, limited personal freedom, and an impersonal atmosphere found in many cults, are environmental conditions that support this dualistic thinking.

Other reasons for the susceptibility of college students to cults may be that universities have grown so large and complex that a sense of belonging or community that once existed within the university has been replaced by a feeling of isolation by some students. Where the generation of college students of the late '60's and early '70's were drawn together by political issues and social causes, the generation of the late '70's and early '80's is drawn apart by competitivism and an uncertain economic future. Harvard theologian

Harvey Cox (1977) believes that it is this need for community or belonging that is the principal attraction of cults. If this is true, and students continue to become more isolated within the university, there is every reason to believe that the attraction of cults will grow stronger in the years ahead.

Harms of the Cult to the Individual and to Society

Persons who have undergone the conversion experience and who have been programmed as members of cults are sometimes distinguished by such characteristics as glassy-eyed stares, fixed smiles, and an almost programmed, zombie-like appearance. Often, the new convert's speech will lose vocabulary and will tend to take on a memorized style which demonstrates a loss of the ability to think abstractly. Generally speaking, these individuals will have difficulty reasoning. Their I.Q. points drop, and their ability to handle complicated situations and jobs is diminished. Other mental harms include a reduction in cognitive flexibility, lessening adaptability, a narrowing and blunting of affection, and a regression of behavior to child-like levels. Possible pathological symptoms include disassociation, delusion, and similar mental disorders (Delgado, 1977).

Physically, cult member often suffers from poor diet, lack of sleep, severe stress, and emotional and physical exhaustion. Problems associated with these things range from ulcers and scabes, to untreated injuries. Nutritional anemia, vitamin deficiencies, tumors and other diseases are not infrequently found among members of extremist religious groups.

The harms to society are significant. The fund-raising projects are seldom if ever for a worthy or philanthropic cause. They are usually directed at supporting the wealth of the organization, and involve everything from fraudulent street scams to quick money-change deals. One large cult group uses female members as prostitutes, and has recently begun promoting the prostitution of the young children associated with the organization.

Avoiding Cult Involvement

Many cults have specially trained recruiters whose sole purposes is to convince people to join their organization. These recruiters will use deception, manipulation, high-pressure sales techniques, and anything else to get a potential candidate to take the first step in becoming a member of the organization. They know that if they can get the new recruit to take the first step in an environment the cult controls, they are well on their way to recruiting a new member. As an RA, you need to be aware of some of the approaches commonly used by cult recruiters, both for your own information and to disseminate to your residents. The Citizens Freedom Foundation (1982), a nonprofit organization dedicated to educating the public about destructive cults, makes the following recommendation to people about cult recruiting:

1. Beware of people who are excessively or inappropriately friendly. There are no instant friendships.
2. Beware of groups that pressure you because "everyone else is doing it." No one knows what is right for you except you.
3. Beware of groups that recruit you through guilt. Guilt induced by others is rarely a productive emotion.
4. Beware of invitations to isolated weekend workshops having nebulous goals. There is no reason to be vague unless there is something to hide.

Symptoms of Cult Involvement

There are some signs or symptoms that you can observe in others that may indicate that the person is involved, or is in the process of being recruited by a religious cult. Some of the signs that you as an RA can observe are as follows:

1. Beware of a sudden and dramatic change in behavioral patterns of an individual. If the person stops going to class or spends inordinate amounts of time reading religious materials or begins behaviors that he has not previously exhibited.
2. Beware of a breakdown in communications with parents, old friends, roommates, etc., and the person becoming more secretive and defensive.
3. Beware of a sudden rush of new friends, particularly nonstudents and an abandonment of old friends.
4. Beware of the person thinking society is evil, and the expressed need for personal purification.
5. Beware of absence for long weekends in which the person returns to the residence hall dramatically changed.
6. Beware of a lack of rational ideas and an inability to discuss concepts without parroting dogma and scripture of a particular cult.

Just through personal observation, you should be able to determine some of these dramatic changes in behaviors, attitudes, and practices in your residents. It is simply not normal for a student to be a "normally functioning college student" one week, and after one weekend at a workshop or retreat, to return to the residence hall and begin breaking a record collection because "rock music is evil," destroying pictures of friends, and sanctimoniously going about condemning people to hell.

Intervention

Intervening when a student has surrendered his personality and beliefs to the doctrine of a religious cult is difficult. If you observe some of the things discussed in this chapter in one of your residents, it is appropriate for you to discuss it with a senior staff member. The alternatives that senior staff will need to consider rest in part with university policies and in part with the laws of your state. It is advisable for them to work with the student's parents, with a psychologist, and with people knowledgeable about cults.

Deprogramming is an effective method of helping the individual regain his personality. It is an intense process, which focuses upon helping people begin thinking for themselves again. One of the characteristics of a person who is programmed by a cult is that they have lost the freedom to think and act independently. Deprogramming helps people sever the dictates of the religious cult, and invites them to begin thinking and making decisions for themselves. The earlier this deprogramming takes place, the greater the likelihood that the deprogramming will be successful. The longer a person remains in the cult group and functions at the will of the organization, the more difficult it will be for that person to regain control over his life.

Students need to understand that it is normal to occasionally feel alone, overwhelmed by decisions that need to be made, or as if things are falling apart. These are normal emotions and feelings that are often experienced. Cult organizations do not have the answers to these questions. They only cloud the person's mind so that it becomes impossible for the person to feel, to live properly, and to fulfill lifelong goals and ambitions.

Some states are now granting guardianship to parents of children trapped in cults. Once parents have legal custody, they may consider some form of psychotherapy or deprogramming. As an RA, you can be sensitive to the needs of your residents, and to some of the behavioral signs associated with cult involvement. The earlier you are able to discover it, the greater the opportunity the student will have to fulfill his potential.

There is no question that destructive cults rob young people of the very thing that educational institutions are designed to teach. Where education expands the mind and enhances personal development, membership in destructive religious cults closes off the mind and retards this development. Approaching this problem is not easy. It requires sensitivity, understanding, and the ability to help students understand options. Strong support systems exist, and where students feel involved, welcome, and have a sense of belonging, there is less likelihood that students will be seeking fulfillment of these needs through involvement in religious cults.

SECTION 5

Educational Outreach

CHAPTER 14
Programming

Programming may not be as easy as the professional staff in the office of residence life may tell you it is, but it is not nearly as difficult as some of your fellow RA's make it out to be. It does take time. It does take planning, and, it is not always successful. The hardest thing about programming in the residence halls is getting your residents involved. The thought of sitting through another lecture or being expected to learn one more thing after spending a long day attending classes and studying, is often too much to expect. There are days when all a student might want to do is vegetate in front of a television and escape. As the semester proceeds, stress increases, and it becomes increasingly difficult to stimulate interest in educational programs.

You might ask, why bother? It would save time for everyone if you weren't expected to do programming. And, in some ways you might be right. It would save you the trouble of helping others learn the skills of planning and organizing, and it would surely save effort for the speakers, who might be asked to a program. But, it is always easier to run a dorm as a hotel than as a residence hall. One of the important differences between the two approaches is that residence halls are designed to contribute to the educational experience of the student. If college residence halls were in the business just to provide shelter, they would not need RA's and could probably contract with a hotel chain to do a better job of management.

Programming is one of the major vehicles available to you to make the experience of living in a residence hall part of the educational experience of college.

Education in college should be viewed as a total experience and not just as the twelve to eighteen hours each week a student may spend in class. As a total experience, all aspects of the environment must contribute to the students' education. Woodrow Wilson expressed it this way: "So long as instruction and life do not merge in our colleges, so long as what the undergraduates do and what they are taught occupy two separate, air-tight compartments in their consciousness, so long will the college be ineffectual" (Wilson 1913).

In the residence hall, the formal manner by which instruction and life are merged is through various leisure-time programs which blend the common interests of individuals into shared experiences leading to new opportunities for self-discovery. Programming is teaching. It is the forum that you, as an educator, use to organize, with your residents, activities that make a positive contribution to the learning environment and the students' education. Programming is the tool that is used to change the impersonal atmosphere of a residence hall into an integral part of the educational environment. Without programming, residence halls are little more than shelter and the RA little more than a caretaker.

As students in the residence halls share programs, they are drawn closer together and open new mediums of communication. The interface of these common educational experiences creates a fertile atmosphere for discovery, creativity, and self-exploration. Programs can inform, give people the tools to develop, and bind people to one another in a sense of community.

The parameters of programming have been defined as narrowly as the interaction between two people and as broadly as the assembly of a theater audience. We shall define it as follows: programming is any organized activity designed to make a positive contribution to a student's education.

The Goals of Programming

There are four basic programming goals in residence halls. They are:

1. To develop a community.
2. To educate.
3. To involve students in their own learning.
4. To provide an outlet for the release of emotions.

The development of community in a residence hall is enhanced when people have mutual respect for one another, respect one another's rights, trust one another, and have a commitment to the group as a whole. Programming that creates interaction among students on educational topics related to their common interests helps build understanding and acceptance within the group. As the group becomes mutually supportive and understanding of one another through personal experiences, a respect for the other person's positions and rights are gained.

Programming also serves the goal of educating. Through programming, people can learn new hobbies, develop new leisure-time activities, and explore new interests. A program on mountain-climbing may foster a sense of community and togetherness and at the same time provide information to students interested in exploring this aspect of their potential. Skill-development programs for personal growth in areas such as assertiveness training, time-management, and value-clarification also serve to educate the students. Parties, social exchanges, and dinners teach social and interpersonal skills that contribute to the students' general education and may aid in the release of emotions.

Students who participate in residence hall government or arrange programs are involving themselves in their own learning. People who spend time in a group discussion on values, or developing a workable study schedule are also involving themselves in their own learning. Programming brings about the opportunities for this involvement.

Programming also assists students in the release of emotions. Intramural athletics, aerobic dancing, any form of physical competition, canoe trips, overnight camping trips, and survival-training programs are examples of programs that would aid in achieving this particular goal. Participation in these programs help students release aggressions, tensions, stress, anxiety, and similar emotions. The fun and excitement of the activity helps students escape from the pressures of college and provides a legitimate time for students to revive themselves.

Types of Programs

Most programmers divide programming into six general categories:

1. *Educational programs* are generally information-oriented. Speakers, documentary movies, and group discussions centering on a particular current affairs topic are often categorized in this area of educational programming.
2. *Recreational programs* are entertainment-oriented. Such programs as movies, teaching hobbies/crafts, field trips, canoe trips, hiking, mountain climbing, parachuting, and other similar types of activities are generally in this category.
3. *Cultural programs* include concerts of various types, mime artists, art shows, and similar activities.
4. *Athletic programming* includes intramural sports, inter-residence hall athletics, and other athletic competitions.
5. *Developmental programming* is considered skill development. It concentrates on such things as assertiveness training, time-management, workshops on overcoming self-defeating behavior and career- and life-planning workshops. These programs help people develop important personal skills that will assist them in their growth toward maturity. Participation in group counseling, some form of encounter group, or biofeedback training are all developmental.

6. *Social programs* are those activities that join people together to teach social skills, to have fun, and to release tension, anxiety, and frustrations. Parties, dinners, and most gatherings for the purpose of socializing are activities that would be classified under social programs.

How to Program

Programs that are presented early in the fall term help establish the expectation for more programs. Students quickly come to accept programs as part of the natural order of life in residence halls. However, you should remember that the expectation or habit of attending programs and participating in activities is inhibited by presenting programs during midterms or toward the end of the semester. Many RAs who have programming requirements wait until the last minute to plan their programs: obviously, their motivation is more to meet job requirements than to contribute to the educational development of residents. If you have ever attended one of these programs, you will recognize it immediately: speakers on information or educational-oriented topics brought in at the last part of the year. When this is the first attempt at programming, it is doomed to fail.

If a good foundation for programming is laid, students will anticipate attending programs. Programming will become a normal part of the environment and the routine of college life.

There are two ways to arrange programs—the spontaneous way and the organized way. The spontaneous approach is not the same as a last-minute program. Spontaneity is important in programming and must be recognized as a legitimate programming effort. The spontaneous program capitalizes on the creative uses of available resources. A spontaneous program may happen when you discover that in two days a well-known speaker will be on campus. You might try to arrange for that person to eat a meal in the residence hall with your residents or to have the person stop by for an informal reception and discussion. Another spontaneous program might relate to a campus power failure. You might respond by inviting somebody from the university physical plant to come the next day to discuss what took place and how the university gets its energy, how much it spends on utilities, etc.

The organized approach, however, is the one that is most often successful and provides the greatest latitude of programming. It is simply not feasible to attempt to plan a canoe trip a hundred miles from your campus in forty-eight hours without some prior planning or much help.

Ten Steps to the Perfect Program

The ten steps given in this section are the organized way to do programming. This is the way the majority of your programs should be accomplished.

It pulls in different resources and allows you to move clearly to your objective of a successful program.

Step 1. Needs-Assessment

All too often people attempt to arrange programs without assessing the needs of the group. Needs-assessment can be handled in several different ways. Many educational programming teams in residence halls begin the year by administering an interest survey, which lists a number of possible programs and asks people to evaluate how they feel about having such programs in the residence hall. You can generate your own list of ideas for an interest survey. On pages 246–247 is a sample of an interest survey that you could use and adapt to your own particular campus:

Interest surveys can be particularly helpful in gaining an understanding of the common interests of your residents. They can give you an idea of the scope of programming and also the way in which to direct your programming; that is, they give a general evaluation of the available options. They do not, however, permit people to create their own programming ideas. People will respond on surveys according to the options you provide. If you use surveys, try assessing programming needs through the survey at the beginning of the year, and then, intermittently throughout the year, review the surveys with groups of your residents. This will help you discover new program ideas in the ensuing discussions.

Brainstorming at a floor meeting is another good way to generate ideas for programs. Brainstorming is a very simple technique that requires a person to ask some basic questions and facilitate the flow of conversation and ideas. The key to using this technique in a small group is to allow a free flow of ideas, no matter how bizarre, without any limitations on their feasibility. It is really an idea-generating time. You may use the following brainstorming formats:

1. A small group of people is called together and the general topic of programming is introduced.
2. The facilitator chooses a second person to assist him in writing down ideas.
3. The group is instructed to imagine any possible program in which they or others might be interested.
4. Generally a time limit is placed upon the length of this brainstorming activity. The facilitator, however, may wish to extend the time limit or alter the time limit depending upon the interests and ideas being generated by the group.
5. The facilitator asks the basic question, "What programs, activities, or interests would you like to see us undertake this year?"

Program	Not Interested	Mildly Interested	Interested	Very Interested	Could Help Teach
Recreational Programs					
1. Photography					
2. Jogging					
3. Hiking/backpacking					
Self-Improvement Programs					
1. Weightlifting					
2. Assertiveness Training					
3. Resume Writing					
4. Yoga					
Educational Programs					
1. Income Tax Workshop					
2. Speed Reading					
3. Study Skills					
4. Consumer Protection					
5. Bicycle Repair					
6. Astrology					
Social Programs					
1. Talent Show					
2. Bluegrass Festival					
3. Coffeehouse					
4. International Dinner					
5. Fifties Dance					
6. Picnic					
7. Wine-Tasting Party					

Program	Not Interested	Mildly Interested	Interested	Very Interested	Could Help Teach
Public Service Programs					
1. Christmas Caroling					
2. Dance Marathon					
3. Hospital Volunteer					
4. Nursing Home Volunteer					
5. Big Brother Program					
Athletic/Recreational Programs					
1. Softball					
2. Basketball					
3. Football					
4. Volleyball					
5. Ping-pong					
6. Bicycling					
Involvement in Hall Activities					
1. Would like to be involved in hall government					
2. Would like to be involved with hall newspaper					
3. Would like to be involved in Intramural Activities Council					
4. Would like to be involved in special programming committees					

6. The facilitator instructs his assistant to write down all the ideas that are generated. This is usually done best on a newsprint pad at the front of the room or on a large sheet of butcher paper.
7. The facilitator may offer a few ideas of his own but should encourage the group to generate most of the ideas. It helps if the facilitator reinforces people who offer ideas with comments like "That's a good idea, let's get that one down," or "Great idea!"
8. When the group has run out of ideas, the facilitator brings the brainstorming session to a close.
9. The group is then asked to rank those programs in which they would like most to participate.
10. Feasibility of the programs may be discussed at this time, relative to the rank order.
11. The top three or four programs are discussed and selected consistent with the group needs.

Another version of this brainstorming approach is to take a number of items (*i.e.,* a fountain pen, a ball, a book, and other objects) and place them in a box or paper bag. Ask the group to divide into smaller groups, then ask each small group to suggest programs they could arrange with each one of the objects in the box or bag. The small groups then share their programming ideas with the larger group. This can be conducted as a competitive contest among the small groups. These ideas can eventually be built into a series of programs.

Both brainstorming and interest surveys are formal techniques for determining programming needs within the hall. Informal contacts and discussions with students can also help determine needs. In your discussions with the residents of your living unit, certain needs may become apparent. For example, if a number of students mention some apprehensions and difficulties about meeting class assignment deadlines and are frustrated in their studies, perhaps they are expressing a need for a study-skills program; you may then wish to approach individuals in the living unit with such an idea to see if there is any interest. Or, you may be sitting in on a late night bull session during which the group begins to discuss their values related to sexuality. This might provide you with the opportunity to invite a speaker to discuss human sexuality and to answer some of the questions raised in the bull session.

Step 2: Objective-Setting

An objective can be defined as a statement that describes the process by which a goal should be attained; describing both the performance and the key conditions under which the performance is expected to occur (Mager 1972). Objectives are useful in clearly delineating exactly what you intend to do.

They are particularly helpful in communicating to others what you are attempting to achieve and why. You can use the following five-step plan to state what is commonly referred to as a performance objective:

1. Identify who is to engage in a particular behavior (who will be affected).
2. Describe the behavior that is to be done in behavioral terms (what will be done).
3. Describe conditions under which behavior is expected to occur (how performance is to be manifested).
4. Specify standards of acceptable performance (how well should behavior be performed).
5. Specify criteria on which performance of behavior will be judged (how will behavior be judged).

Examples of performance objectives are as follows:

1. One hundred percent of the students in my unit will have participated in at least one floor and one hall program before the end of the winter term, as measured by an informal poll of the residents on the floor during a floor meeting the week before finals week in the winter term.
2. On June 4, there will be a program on human sexuality in the floor lounge at which at least 25 percent of the residents of my floor will participate and will rate it as "interesting or very interesting" on an evaluation form that I will distribute at the end of the program.

Objectives are important because they state clearly for you and others exactly who is to be affected, what specifically will be done, how it will be done, and how you will know that it has been accomplished.

Step 3: Involve Others

One of the most important elements of learning takes place through direct involvement in programs. It is the most efficient way in which to arrange programs, as well as the most educational way to accomplish them. As an RA, you are in a position of responsibility requiring organizational and coordinating skills. However, you should not feel compelled to do all of the work in designing and implementing programs yourself, because the programs then become *your* programs. Instead, most programs should be collective efforts. People are more likely to participate in programs to which they have contributed. If people design a program together, they become ego-involved in its success. On the other hand, if the program is your program, you must elicit the loyalty and faith of others in order to accomplish it.

This is a basic difference between a team-management approach and an autocratic style. The democratic, or team-management, approach is the advisable way to work with students in programming. Though the other way may have limited success, it will by no means accomplish the goal of helping people involve themselves in their own education. Nor will it be the best way to achieve the programs that you want. So, you should try to share the responsibilities with your residents.

Try these three ways to involve others:

1. *Delegate.* Delegation is essential to successful programming. When a person delegates responsibility, he also delegates authority. Place the responsibility clearly on the person and let him know that the rest of the group will be depending upon him. Always select a specific person to assume responsibility. This is preferable to asking for volunteers, because when you do that, you are communicating that the responsibility is not very important and that anyone could do the job. Compare that message with the one communicated by "John, we need your assistance with the sound system because of your knowledge of electronics." What you communicate to a student with a statement like this is that John has a special talent of which the group has a need. This not only reinforces John by confirming your faith in him, but also makes John feel special.

2. *Coordinate.* The responsibility of a person organizing a program is to coordinate the program. This means attention to detail and continual follow-up with people to whom you have delegated responsibility. Though you may have asked others to assist with the program, for the time being the success of the program is still your responsibility. Undoubtedly, you will be thinking that it is easier to do some of these things yourself, and it probably would be; however, one of the goals of programming is to involve others in their own learning. Programming is a process, and students learn from that process. So, for now, coordinate the skills of others keeping in mind that your ultimate goal is eventually to move to the next step.

3. *Abdicate.* Abdicate your involvement as quickly as possible. Try to put someone else in charge of designing, organizing, and coordinating the program. Become truly an advisor. Advise your residents on how they can accomplish what they need to do, but do not do it for them. The one exception to this rule will perhaps occur at the beginning of the year, when it is necessary to role-model good organizational and programming skills to give your residents the opportunity to learn from you. One of your personal goals should be to turn over as much of the programming responsibility to one or a group of students in

your living unit. Ideally, these students should be the ones thinking of the ideas, arranging the programs, evaluating the programs, and gaining any of the reenforcement or glory from the success of those programs.

4. *Motivate.* Encourage, support, and reward those in the group who are helping with a program. Mention, in front of others the accomplishments of these students, and tell them how much you appreciate their contribution.

Step 4: Preprogram Planning

You have, by this stage, assessed the needs of the group, determined your specific objectives, and involved others in the formation of the ideas and the organization of the program. You and your residents are now ready to plan the program's general format. Essentially, what you will be examining is the feasibility of your proposed program. In this stage of the planning, you will need to find answers to the following questions:

1. Are facilities available?
2. What resources will we need to accomplish this program?
3. What tentative dates would be possible for this program? Are there any conflicts?
4. What monetary support is necessary for the success of this program?
5. What special equipment or facility (sound equipment, etc.) is needed for the completion of this program?
6. Who on the programming staff should be contacted to get approval for the program or to get additional information?
7. Does this program comply with university policies regulating residence hall activities?
8. Who will attend the program (coed group, people from other living units, etc.)?

Draw up a tentative plan. Does the plan meet the needs of the group? If it does not, revise the objective or revise the plan. You are now ready to move on to the next step—actually planning the program.

Step 5: Plan Program

Every good program needs a good title, a title that will motivate, excite, and encourage people to attend. If the audience that you have defined in the preprogram plan is the residents of your living unit, your title may be different from what it might be if the program were intended for the entire residence hall. If your audience will consist of the residents of your living unit, you may wish to choose a title like "The Art of Keeping the Group in the South Wing

Quiet" or "Study Skills for the Stereo Buff." If the audience is to be the entire residence hall, you may wish to title the program something like "Academic Success Through the Art of Studying."

Good programmers keep accurate records. If you are writing to companies for promotional items or contacting speakers, it is necessary that you keep good records of these contacts. Try setting up a file for each program that you are planning. Although getting too meticulous about paperwork can inhibit programming and make it overly complicated, it is better to be slightly too organized than not organized enough to complete the program. You will find that good organization will save you time.

Below is a general checklist for you to follow in helping design a program.

1. Determine program title.
2. Set specific date.
3. Set specific location.
4. Delegate responsibilities.
5. Reserve facilities, equipment, speaker(s).
6. Determine budget (if applicable).
7. Do publicity.
8. Set time for program.
9. Review policies related to program (if applicable).
10. Review program with hall director.
11. Set deadlines for each project and delegated assignment.
12. Confirm dates, time, place, topic, telephone numbers, money in writing.

Step 6: Publicity

If you have done everything correctly up to this point, you probably have the design of a reasonably good program, but the program will not achieve your objective unless people actually attend. No matter how much de-emphasis is put on evaluating programs solely on the basis of attendance, attendance *is* important. If you spend $100 on a program that only one student attends, this is not a good allocation of money—even if the student really enjoyed the program. Poor attendance can be attributed to (1) poor needs-assessment, (2) poor planning and organization, or (3) poor publicity.

Publicity is a key element in the success of a program. Good publicity that motivates and encourages people to attend will help bring people in contact with what your program has to offer. Poor publicity will turn people off and will limit the success of your program. Doing the publicity is not easy; it is hard work, and it takes a lot of time. This is why delegating responsibilities is a key. Publicity is one of the items that people most often do not like to do. If you find somebody who is interested, especially an artist, cherish that person dearly. He can mean the success or failure of many of your programs.

Fancy and elaborate publicity is not generally necessary in a residence hall. It is more important to be creative in the way the program is advertised. Some publicity ideas that have been used successfully are:

1. A note about a program placed in a bottle hung in the shower.
2. Logos or buttons worn by residents carrying the time, date, and place of the program.
3. Telethon within the residence hall.
4. Notes on the cafeteria line.
5. Flyers in the floor restrooms, on the back of urinals, and on the mirrors.

Do not forget the importance of a positive attitude and word-of-mouth. A group of people who communicate excitedly about having a program can often be the most effective publicity. People want to go to programs that other people are attending. If a group of your friends are attending a program, you are much more inclined to go whether or not you are interested in the specific topic. You can help communicate this idea when you talk positively and excitedly about the program. Ask specific people in your living unit to attend the program. When you go to a program, gather several other people to go with you. Ask several of the residents in the living unit to do the same. If you have five or six people who agree to bring four friends each, you now have a group of twenty-five to thirty people. That could be a reasonably good showing and will allow more people to be introduced to the program.

Step 7: Final Checklist

Simply check what you have done. Go through every step and make sure that you have accomplished what you need to accomplish. The checklist should be a review of your program plan. This is the time for you to check with everyone who has been delegated something to do to confirm that he has done it or will do it.

Step 8: The Day of the Program

On the day of the program, check your speaker or program material to see that everything is ready. Make sure that the facilities are clean, neat, and usable. If there are to be refreshments, call to confirm that they will be delivered or that somebody will pick them up. Have special publicity prepared for the day of the program and the day before the program. People usually notice new items on the bulletin board, so this is a good publicity technique to encourage attendance.

Be at the site of the program at least one-half hour before the program is to start. This will enable you to work out any unexpected problems or to answer any last-minute questions. Make sure that somebody will be meeting the speaker or will have the material necessary for the program.

Step 9: At the Program

If the program has a speaker, somebody needs to introduce him. This could be you, but preferably it should be someone else who has worked with the program. Make sure that the speaker is introduced to any university representatives who may be at the program, and make sure that the speaker has the opportunity to meet as many students as possible prior to the beginning of the program.

Before the program, think of some questions that you believe will help stimulate discussion. You may wish to provide a few members of the audience with questions ahead of time. People ask questions when they see others doing it. You can start the discussion by asking some general questions and having your friends do the same.

Remember, nothing succeeds like success. A successful program, well executed, will mean better attendance, more support, more involvement, and better attainment of your program goals for future programs. Poor programs produce opposite results. If a program is boring, too long, or does not meet the needs of the students, people will not be likely to come to the next program.

Step 10: After the Program

Once a program has concluded, evaluate what has happened. You can do this in several ways. The survey is probably the most common, although people often do not like to fill out surveys at the end of a program. Surveys are useful in that they give you a collective reaction. However, they are somewhat formal, and they may not be appropriate for all programs.

Another form of evaluation is an informal discussion that occurs later that evening or directly after the program. Make a point of asking people what they thought of the program—what they liked, what they did not like. Ask how they think the program could have been improved and whether they would recommend it to other people. Whether or not you hand out formal evaluations to a number of residents or talk informally with a group, you should make some summary comments on every program that is presented. After all, you cannot determine whether your objective has been accomplished until you evaluate it.

It is important to reinforce those students who helped with the program. This is best done publicly. Call them by name and say something like, "John found the speaker for this topic, and I think he has done a very good job. Let's give him a round of applause." Publicly congratulate and praise people who helped. This, after all, is the only payment that they will probably receive. Recognition and reinforcement are two key ways of communicating your thanks for their help. There is nothing worse than leaving a program that you have put much of your time into without some expression of thanks. If they did not do well, reinforce what they did do well and make some suggestions on what could have been done better.

Thank-you notes to speakers are always appropriate. Never invite a speaker to your living unit without sending a formal thank-you letter. If it was a large program presented to the entire residence hall, it may be appropriate to send a formal thank-you letter to the speaker with a copy to his supervisor. You should check this idea with your hall director to determine which times he thinks it is appropriate.

Do not count on many rewards for yourself. Though you may feel a sense of accomplishment for what took place, people may not congratulate you. Your rewards will come later, in knowing that you have presented a successful program and that people are interested and motivated to go to your programs. Other RAs in the building, as well as your hall director, will recognize the work and effort you contributed to accomplish this successful program.

How to Plan an Unsuccessful Program

If you really want to do a poor program, one that is almost guaranteed to fail, here is what you should do:

1. Guess at what you think others want to do.
2. Don't plan anything. Don't have any goals.
3. Wait until the last minute to prepare the program.
4. Don't involve anyone else—after all, you can do it better yourself.
5. Tell as few people as possible, and make sure you wait until they have made other plans.
6. When you do tell people about the program, tell them how wonderful you were to have planned such a great program. Make sure to take all the credit and don't involve anyone else. People will especially like this.
7. Don't meet your guest speaker, but let him try to track you down in the best way he can. This will give him an opportunity to show resourcefulness. When introducing a speaker, make sure you give a long introduction pointing out how important *you* are. Add unrelated details and give many unrelated facts about yourself.
8. Don't evaluate. Don't thank anyone. I am sure you won't want to see the evaluation, and you will get all the thanks you deserve.

Programming Tips

Listed below are some tips that you can utilize to make programming easier. Chances are that your hall director or other people on your residence life staff also have a number of special tips that will help you:

1. *Approval.* Get approval from superiors for all programs.
2. *Transportation.* Do not use your automobile to transport people to a program unless your insurance covers such transportation or unless there is a special clause covering transportation related to your position as an RA.
3. *Financial Transactions.* Do not use your personal account for any financial transactions.
4. *Publicity.* Publicity should be heaviest the day before a program and on the day of the program.
5. *Speaker.* A speaker should be informed beforehand of the conditions under which he will speak and whether there is a possibility that the group may be small.
6. *Location of the Program.* Central lounge locations where there is a heavy flow of traffic will attract a number of people. These locations are generally good for programs designed to accommodate the entire residence hall.
7. *Room Set-up.* Do not trap students in the program by putting the speaker in front of the door. Keep a free flow of traffic for people to enter and exit easily if they choose.
8. *Length of Program.* Talk with the speaker or programming committee and determine an approximate length for the program. People's interest spans vary, but generally an hour to a maximum of two hours is considered a good length for programs; however, the topic and interest of the participants should ideally determine length. Make sure before the program starts that you know how long it is to last. This will make a difference to the person conducting the program. If a speaker knows he is responsible for a thirty-minute lecture with thirty minutes of questions, that takes one type of preparation. If he is expected to present a longer program, this may mean that he can incorporate other activities into the program.
9. *Time.* The best programming time varies from campus to campus. Generally speaking, Sunday to Thursday evenings prove to be the best time for programs. Most schools find that immediately after dinner—between the hours of 5 P.M. and 7 P.M.—is a good time for programs. Part of this depends on assessing the habits and interests of the people in your living unit. Groups that are already formed and have a particular interest, such as a club or hobby group, will set their own times.

10. *Theme Programs*. Theme programs or a series of programs on the same topic can be effective. These should be held, when possible, at the same time, place, and location each week. Movie series programs are often popular, though very expensive.

11. *Refreshments*. If refreshments are to be provided, this should be mentioned in the advertisements. Some people may come to have refreshments and listen to the speaker. Every program need not have refreshments. Work with the residence hall or campus food service to determine the quantity needed. Be aware of what packaged items can be returned to the food service for credit and which items cannot be returned. Compare the prices offered through the food service with the price of similar packaged goods at the grocery. Cookies, for example, may be less expensive from the grocery than from the food service.

Conclusion

The only limits to programming are those set by your institution or by your own creativity. Individual living units within residence halls have joined together to plan such programs as ski trips, field trips off campus, organization and promotion of a commercial carnival on campus, and speakers on almost any conceivable topic. Programming should be seen as an opportunity for your residents to share a common experience.

Although some educational programming may take some funds, these usually can be obtained from the residence hall council or from your housing administration. Many programs can be done for little or no expense. Some of the most creative programs take the least amount of money. Programs that permit people to interact, to learn organizational or leadership skills are always worthwhile.

CHAPTER 15
Community Development

Defining Community in the Residence Halls

Perhaps one of the greatest tragedies of the latter half of the twentieth century has been the breakdown of the community and the rise of individualism. Community is both a sense of attachment to a group and a set of values that are commonly shared within a group. As one writer has stated, "the quest for a feeling of community has centered around three romantic or utopian hopes:—that life be more caring, that people have more concern, affection, and love for each other, and that the immunition in social life be reduced;—that life be more intimate, more like family that we idealize but rarely achieve, and that closeness replace the unconnectedness that so many people experience in their normal lives;—that life have greater depth, that people mature to each other, and that this shared depth and meaning replace the superficiality and shallowness that are still characteristic of most social relations" (Gibb 1978, p. 212). Hillery (1955), in considering some ninety-four different definitions of community, discovered that there were many similarities among them. Upon these similarities he developed a definition of community as "a group of individuals engaged in social interaction, possessing common interests and goals, who show concern for and are sensitive to the needs of other members, and are primarily interested in furthering the group's goals over all others" (p. 118).

For students in residence halls, community may be found in a sense of belonging with the other members of the group and in a set of shared common experiences that bind them together and make them a mutually identifiable group. For the student, the attachment to the other people in the living unit forms an all-important sense of belonging. In many ways, it is like a substitute family.

Why is this important for you as an RA? Very simply, the behavioral setting and the influence of peers within that setting are connected. The behavior of students in the living unit is shaped by interaction with the other students who comprise their group. Both the formal structure of the facilities and the informal structure of the peer subculture have an influence. If the peer subculture can be developed in such a way as to promote concepts consistent with a supportive community feeling, it follows that students will internalize these values, assist one another in the accomplishment of their goals, and in general learn to function as members of a mutually supportive and sharing community. The far-reaching effects of having grown in such an environment, both in terms of one's self-image and the residual effects through community involvement in later adult years, are evident.

Specifically, a community transmits common goals and values. It fosters the ability to achieve deeper, more intimate relationships with people, frees interpersonal relationships, and increases self-acceptance and acceptance of others. It aids in shaping and developing a sense of personal integrity and ethics, shapes attitudes and values, and modifies human behavior in a positive direction.

The community also acts as a reference point for the individual. It is an identifiable group to which the person may point and claim allegiance. It provides specific social ties for the individual, encourages the development of adult social skills, and helps identify social contacts. One of its most important functions is as a mirror to assist the individual in developing a more accurate picture of himself. Peers are used as a way of gauging one's behavior relative to group standards. A supportive community not only reflects positive values, but can assist an individual in gaining a better perspective of his own behavior. Of more intrinsic value, the availability of a community in which the student trusts others, aids the student in times of crisis, need, and emotional stress.

Elements of a Community

Perhaps the real questions we need to answer are what is necessary to establish a community, and how can you, as the RA, help foster a supportive community that will aid students in the accomplishment of their goals? The establishment of a community includes the following elements:

1. Social contact. There must be a degree of physical proximity to allow people to have appropriate social contact with one another.
2. Shared values and common purpose. There must be an identifiable set of shared goals and values toward which the group commonly ascribes and which it is seeking to fulfill.
3. Primary group. The individual members must view the community as constituting their primary group of friends and acquaintances.
4. Power/Authority. The members must recognize that the group has the power or authority to act in some way.
5. Commitment to cooperative survival. Members of the community must make a commitment to the community through a sense of energy output or self-sacrifice.

6. Personal transcendence. Community members must recognize that the group is more important than any individual in it, and by virtue of this belief they must surrender some degree of individuality for the sake of the group.

7. Communion. This is the sense of member identification, an acting out of a sense of self within the group.

8. Process. The group must have a sense of informal or formal process by which it operates. This may be a parliamentary type of meeting style, or it may be some much more informal style of interaction. However, a process must exist, at least in the minds of the members.

9. Survival need. The community must be based on a sense of mutual dependence, and there must be some reason for this mutual dependence—that is, a sense that survival can be achieved only through cooperation.

10. Solidarity/Solitude. Community members must be able to distinguish the boundaries of the group. Solitude or some degree of isolation helps in defining the physical boundaries of the group.

11. Faith/Abandonment. In order for a community to survive at its most humanistic level, individuals must enter the community with faith in the ability of the community and with some degree of abandonment of their own personal desires in favor of those of the community.

12. Time. Community is dependent upon individuals having enough time to contribute to the community, to meet, to interact, and to share common experiences.

13. Standards. A community is supported when it has the authority to define the laws, standards, or rules by which it will operate. In other words, the community defines a standard of behavior.

Before going any further, it is necessary that you understand that the literature student personnel speaks of different types of communities within the residence hall context. One is a formal structured community, which often involves a special cooperative housing program, the support of the residence life staff, and a set of structured experiences that promote the "sense of community." These communities may take the form of living-and-learning center programs in which students may do many of the same things together by design of the program. Generally, these programs are characterized by a contract the student signs, faculty involvement, a set of goals to be accomplished during the committed experience, evaluation of the progress of the community, work as part of the students' contribution to the community, and similar activities designed to elicit a communal environment.

This is certainly one way of approaching the development of a community environment, and a very successful way in many institutions. However, it is also possible to establish a "sense of community" in a unit within a residence hall and—depending upon the size of the building—perhaps in a residential building as well.

How to Establish a Community

At this point you know what a community is, what it tries to achieve, and some of the factors necessary for a community to exist. Now we will explore how you, as a resident assistant, can establish a community. How can you, as an RA, stimulate a sense of community within the group? The first thing that you need is an appropriate physical setting that allows people to be in close proximity to one another. Residence halls are ideal for this purpose, although large residence halls are less ideal than smaller living units. Generally speaking, groups of about ten to twenty individuals offer the best hope of establishing a community involvement in a living unit; however, larger groups can be structured to develop community by breaking down the groups into subgroups.

The physical structure of the living unit plays a major role in helping establish the community. If your living unit is somewhat isolated from other living units, through physical barriers such as walls, doors, etc., or if the building that you occupy is small enough and isolated from other buildings, these physical things help define the boundaries or territory of the community.

The group needs to define its territory in some fashion. Many residence life programs permit students to "mark their territory", defining it as their own by decorating foyers, hallways, and lounges.

The second component in the establishment of a community is a set of mutually shared experiences. This is where programming and general group activities such as intramural sports play an important role. The more opportunities the students have to interact in the same experience and with the same goals, the greater the chance of community to exist. Intramural sports serve this function very well. If together we participate on a football team in competition with a group outside of our residence hall, we enjoy a mutually shared experience with a common goal—winning the game. This experience helps build a sense of team accomplishment and requires that individuals commit to one another, share skills with one another, and depend upon one another for the accomplishment of their mutual goal. Building something together is another way of helping to establish a mutually shared experience that will promote a sense of community. Whether this experience is sewing a quilt, building some cabinets in the lounge, or painting murals on the walls of the corridor, it contributes to helping identify the territory and allowing students to have a mutually shared experience with a common goal.

Communication and trust are intermingled to form the next element necessary for the development of a community. By *communication* we mean not just superficial talking to one another, although this is obviously the first step, but also an exchange of values and a sharing of personal emotions and intimate experiences of the kind that you share only with people whom you trust. Communication and trust are dependent upon one another. These bonds can be enhanced by structured human relations experiences, such as may be found in the interpersonal training and self-awareness workshops that may be conducted by your campus counseling center, and by informal discussions about values and beliefs that may occur in late-night discussions in a person's room. As the RA, you can act as a facilitator for the development of these discussions and can assist in further exploring the reasoning behind a person's values.

Through this communication and trust-building, a student should come to establish a sense that the group offers support for his/her individual accomplishments. This interpersonal support becomes self-perpetuating by both enhancing the community and maintaining the importance of the community to the individual and collectively. People must be encouraged to share with one another at a level of personal intimacy and to feel that what they share on a personal level will not be used to their disadvantage at some later time.

The community seems to crystalize when the group is faced with a task to accomplish, is threatened in some way, or experiences a crisis. When these things exist, the group can readily identify a goal, a reason to work together, a reason for mutual support. Through the crisis or conflict, the group comes to recognize a common purpose in sharing and mutual dependance. Whether this crisis is contrived or is real, the end result is the same. A sense of external threat helps to stimulate a sense of community.

It is unlikely that your residence hall will ever be threatened with attack from outside or that you will need to band together for mutual protection or support. There are other ways of developing a sense of community, however. One way is through the establishment of a common goal at a general meeting of all your residents. An identifiable common goal, something the group really wants to accomplish—whether it is winning a football trophy or remodeling the floor lounge—is a good way to inspire the commitment necessary for the development of a feeling of community. People must have some reason to band together. This reason must be recognized as important by the group as a whole and must be considered attainable.

Whatever the group identifies as its goal or common purpose, this purpose must be reaffirmed through a sense of communion within the group. The communion is a way of maintaining the inner group identity and reaffirms the recognition of the community by the individual. Just seeing the entire living unit assembled is a visible sign of one's position within the community. But the members of the community need to be made to feel involved in the community's accomplishments, its failures as well as its rewards. Every person must be solicited for his involvement. This contact serves to maintain the group.

In a more tangible way, it may take the form of social interactions, recognized group accomplishment, rewards given to individual members, mutual recognition of individual members by the group, and shared authority within the community group. Whether these group-maintenance activities are parties, football games, attending concerts together, building something, decorating something, changing a policy or a program, or developing something new, they are important because they encourage the group to recognize and accept such activities as part of their identification with the group.

Conclusion

The French Revolution was predicated upon the basic premises of liberty, equality, and fraternity. The United States has done much in the past few years to help ensure liberty and has come a long way in trying to establish a policy of equality. Fraternity, or a sense of group community, has not been achieved, primarily because there are fewer opportunities for people to learn the skills or sharing with one another and to place allegiance to the group above commitment to self. As one looks at political leaders in this country, it is easy to identify a lack of leadership and a lack of support from members of the constituency. Apathy on campuses across the nation is no less than apathy in the voting booth. Somehow, this situation needs to change. Community membership is not something that simply exists; it is a commitment that one must learn and have experienced. If one can achieve and accept the goals of the community and learn the skills to work within the community, benefiting from the intimate support that it offers to the individual in the accomplishment of individual and personal goals, this will surely benefit our existence as collective groups of people living together in towns, cities, and states. The survival of a democratic society may rest upon the attainment of this final level of commitment to the individual to the greater good of the whole.

SECTION 6

RA Survival Skills

CHAPTER 16
Time Management

Time management is self management. It is a system by which you determine your priorities and plan the allocation of units of time to accomplish what you believe is important. How well you learn to use the 24 hours that make up each day, the 168 hours of each week, and the 720 hours of each month is time management. People who organize and plan their time in light of their objectives will usually make better use of their time.

Learning to manage your time is learning to manage yourself. It involves planning, self-discipline, learning to use and maintain a schedule, knowing your own habits, and learning to set priorities. The average college student who is taking a full academic course load and sleeping approximately 8 hours a night still has at least 80 hours of uncommitted or plannable time each week. How effectively the student uses this time for study, social activities, and recreation may have a major effect upon the success of his or her college experience.

Making a schedule helps you get started. It is a way to prevent yourself from avoiding those subjects or duties you dislike. More important, it is a way to discover more time for the things you enjoy and to help control the time that is imposed on you by other people. By planning your schedule, you can eliminate last-minute cramming for exams and still have recreational time for yourself. Planning can make studying more enjoyable and will open new blocks of time that you can devote to other interests and better relationships with students in your living unit.

The most common mistake people make in planning their schedules is to overplan. Many people believe that they must schedule every minute of every day. Schedules need to be realistic. Every person needs time each day for some type of recreation and relaxation. Your psychological health is a key element in your ability to concentrate and in your motivation to study. The remedy for study problems is generally not more studying but more efficient and better use of the time used for studying—in other words, *quality* studying time as opposed to *quantity* studying time.

As you enter this time management system, remember that schedules are products of your own invention. They should be used to assist you in allocating your time and using it effectively. Do not be a martyr to your schedule. Let your life-style determine your schedule, rather than allowing your schedule to determine your lifestyle.

Time can be catagorized into three general types. The first type of time is the time over which you have little or no control. This time we shall call *predictable time*. Such things as classes, organizational meetings, a team practice, an RA staff meeting, eating in the cafeteria, and sleeping are predictable times. If you know that the cafeteria is open between 4:30 P.M. and 6:00 P.M., you will in all likelihood be eating during some portion of that block of time. The same applies to sleeping. You can predict that you will probably spend between six and eight hours each day sleeping. Depending upon your life-style, you can predict that this will occur sometime between 10 P.M. and 8 A.M. each day. Predictable time is time that is predictable for you, that your schedule dictates as committed time over which you have limited control. The only decision you exercise over this type of time is whether or not you choose to attend a particular class, to eat, to sleep, and so on.

Items such as studying, recreation, social activities, and most hobbies are plannable. These activities fall into the second time area, which we will call *discretionary time*. Discretionary time is time that is uncommitted. It is time that should be planned in a manner consistent with your life-style toward the accomplishment of the priorities in your life.

The third type of time is *other-imposed time*. It is unpredictable time. Activities included in other-imposed time include emergencies, individual student crises, telephone calls, people coming to visit, and job- or school-related assignments.

Time management is a system of (1) learning to assign priorities to the tasks you wish to accomplish, (2) maximizing discretionary time by minimizing predictable time and other-imposed time, (3) planning the use of discretionary time, and (4) learning to be more efficient. The key to being an efficient time manager is learning to maximize discretionary time.

Predictable Time

Predictable time is time set aside to accomplish a specific task. It is time over which you exercise the least amount of control. Though you may choose whether or not you wish to perform the particular task or attend a particular meeting, you have no real control over *when* you will do it. Students who are involved in many campus activities soon find that the number of meetings they must attend and the number of classes they must attend substantially increase their predictable time. When a manager in industry has a disproportionate amount of predictable time, the business experts usually say that he is letting his job run him, as opposed to him running the job. This can also apply to the RA position and to being a student.

For example, assume that we have a student who is enrolled for 15 semester hours requiring approximately 15 hours per week of class attendance. Most students sleep approximately 8 hours a night, spend at least 1½ hours a day eating, at least 1½ hours a day for personal hygiene, and a minimum of 1 hour a day for traveling to and from classes. This amounts to 93 hours per week of predictable time. In addition, let's say this student has a daily exercise program of jogging that accounts for approximately 1 hour per day. This moves our student's predictable time up to 100 hours a week. This means that the student has only 68 hours of discretionary time each week. The majority of the student's time is already devoted or is predictable.

When we discuss scheduling, we are really talking about how one goes about using these remaining 68 hours or less. Remember, this is for the bare minimum of predictable time a student would have: RAs usually have much less. Most residence hall programs require that the RA take "duty" at least once a week, and many require that the RA work at the information desk a specified number of hours per week. These two items may account for another 10 hours of predictable, job-related time each week. And let us not forget about the regular weekly RA staff meeting. These vary, but they generally take 1 or 2 hours, and sometimes longer. Already we find that the RA has approximately another 12 hours of committed time per week as the week begins. This does not include time that may be predictable within any one given week, such as intramural events that the RA has helped to organize, or a program that the RA will hold that week, or a special committee or organization with which the RA is working.

On the average, RAs devote at least another 2 to 3 hours per week to miscellaneous meetings and programs that are somewhat associated with the RA's job. With this additional 3 hours, we find our total of predictable hours for the RA is 115, leaving only 53 hours of available or discretionary time.

Take out a piece of paper and list how much predictable time *you* have during a given week. Remember to include in that list the items that are predictable for *you*. If you spend an hour every night watching Johnny Carson, you can count on that as being predictable time. If you have a regular exercise routine, such as jogging, you can count on that time as predictable time. If you belong to a fraternity or sorority and attend a regular chapter meeting every Monday night, you can count on that as predictable time. Add up the number of hours that you have as predictable time for yourself and subtract it from 168 (the total number of hours in a given week). The remaining time is discretionary time. You should find that you have between 50 and 60 hours of discretionary time per week. If you have more discretionary time than this, you are doing better than most. If you have less than 50 hours of discretionary time, chances are that you have a very tight schedule and may have possibly overcommitted yourself.

Discretionary Time

The 50 to 60 hours you have left per week is plannable time. You may start to plan this discretionary time by following five steps to time management, scheduling, and planning.

Step 1: Personal Assessment

The very first step in determining a schedule for yourself is to know yourself. People function differently. Some people are very active in the early morning and can accomplish much at that time. Others find that their peak intellectual time is later in the day. Make some assessments about yourself. To do this, try answering the following questions:

1. At what time of day do you feel you can concentrate best (early morning, midmorning, after lunch, late afternoon, early evening, late evening)?
2. Do you like to go to bed early and get up early or go to bed late and get up late?
3. When do you most feel like exercising (morning, evening, afternoon)?
4. When are most of the people in your living unit available, during the day or evening (before dinner, after dinner, late evening)?
5. When is your living unit most quiet (and thus more suitable for study) and when is your living unit noisiest (and thus most suitable for socializing)?
6. When do you most often like to socialize?
7. When are you most likely to engage in social activities such as dating (Friday night, Saturday night, or Friday and Saturday nights)?
8. The most frequent reason I give for not accomplishing certain tasks such as studying is. . . .
9. I am the type of person who, when asked by a friend to go some place with him/her while I am studying, will usually. . . .
10. When I have free time, I most often spend it in the following ways. . . .
11. The most frequent interruption I get that interferes with my studying is. . . .

This information will be used in planning your schedule. Set it aside for now. It will be used later.

Step 2: Goal Assessment

The purpose of time management is the accomplishment of goals. These goals can be grouped into two general categories. There are those goals that relate to career, vocational, and professional aspirations, and those goals that relate to personal life aspirations. Though one could argue that the two are really the same thing, for the purpose of this discussion they will be considered as separate categories.

Take a few minutes to answer the following questions.

1. What are your long-term personal goals?
2. What are your long-term professional goals?
3. What are the objectives must accomplish to achieve each of the long-term goals?

Time management maximizes the utilization of time to accomplish goals. It does no good to learn how to use time more effectively for things that you should not be doing in the first place—that is, things that do not contribute to the accomplishment of a specific goal.

If what you are doing, the task you are performing, does not relate to the accomplishment of one of your personal or professional goals, then you may be able to put that time to better use. The one exception to this rule is time imposed on you by your employer. This time is necessary to maintain your RA position and to accomplish the goals that your hall director or the Office of Residence Life have for you. After all, as an RA you are learning skills that will aid you in the accomplishment of personal or professional goals. This position may also be assising you in financing your education, which is, no doubt, one of your objectives. Thus, to the extent that the tasks that you are accomplishing are directly related to the fulfillment of your job expectations and/or related to other personally identifiable goals, the accomplishment of these tasks should rate a high priority.

Step 3: Getting Organized

Now that you have looked at yourself, made some personal assessments, determined what your goals are and what you want to accomplish, it is time to get organized. The first step in getting organized is to purchase or make some type of scheduling notebook. This may seem like a rather simple task, but you would be surprised how many people do not use this necessary instrument. Many people who do have them have the wrong type. A good scheduling notebook should have times listed for the times you do things. If you arise at 7 A.M. and work until 11 P.M., then your scheduling notebook should include those hours as schedulable time. You can buy several good scheduling notebooks that come close to meeting this timespan. An appointment notebook, similar to the type found in many doctor's offices, is generally good. There is space allocated for the use of every fifteen minutes during the day. When you open the scheduling notebook, you should be able to plan the entire week. This basic scheduling tool is an important part of time management. It will be used for keeping important lists. Now that you have your basic tools, you are ready for the next step.

Step 4: The To-Do List

Consider all the things that you wish to accomplish, and make a list of them. Put the list on one sheet of paper, preferably in the notebook that you bought for that purpose. List long-term projects and big projects. They will be covered separately in a special way. Use only one sheet of paper for this list. Do not put every item on a separate sheet of paper. You will find that this soon becomes very cumbersome and that shuffling papers will distract you.

This list is called a "to-do list." You should make a to-do list every day, listing on it every task that you wish to accomplish during that day. You should try and make this to-do list at the same time every day, in order to assure that the list will get done and will allow you some time each day (predictable time) to plan the day ahead. Though you will need to plan more than just from one day to the next, a day-to-day planning list is important to refresh your memory and set priorities for each day.

Now that you have your list, assign priorities to the items on it, using the following three criteria:

1. Tasks that are directly related to the accomplishment of the most important task you have set for yourself should rate an *A*. Other items that would rate an *A* are those directly related to the accomplishment of a goal about which there is some urgency.
2. Items that are related to a less important goal or that do not have immediate urgency can rate a *B*.
3. All other items receive a *C*.

Work on *As* first until they are completed. When you finish the *As*, begin working on *B* items. If you finish all the *As* and all the *Bs*, then do the *Cs*. Do *C* items *only* when everything else is finished.

Suppose you have the following things to accomplish during the day:

1. Read a chapter in history.
2. Write a short essay for English class tomorrow.
3. Buy some posters for your room.
4. Do your laundry.
5. Return a telephone call from a friend.
6. Read the *Wall Street Journal* for your economics class.
7. Find ten new resources for your term paper in economics.
8. Talk with your hall director about an upcoming program.

Having listed these eight tasks, you now must identify the ones you consider most important. Depending upon your individual priorities, probably number 2 (write an essay for English class tomorrow) would rate an immediate *A*. But equally important could or should be reading the chapter in history and looking up the ten resource items for the term paper in economics. Calling a friend, buying posters, and doing laundry would probably rank as *Cs*, and the rest of the items would be rated as *B*.

The most important thing that this system of ranking does is help you decide *what* you want to accomplish and *when* you want to accomplish it.

Step 5: Scheduling Time

Now that you know what it is that you wish to accomplish, you must determine the schedule in which it should be accomplished. This is where you use the appointment calendar and questions you answered in Step 1. If you have not purchased an appointment calendar, you can make one very easily by taking a sheet of paper and drawing an hourly schedule for the week.

On the schedule, do the following:

1. Using a pencil, write in all of your predictables with regularly scheduled hours for the week or as far in advance as you wish to plan (*i.e.,* classes, team practices, student organization meetings, church, RA staff meetings, etc.).
2. Block out time for sleep. Be realistic. You need eight hours a night to rest properly. If your class schedule or life-style is such that you sleep until noon each day, that is fine. Start your schedule there.
3. Write in times when you usually eat. If you skip breakfast but have a late-night snack, then don't schedule breakfast but do schedule the snack.
4. Select some recreational time each day. For most college students, 4 P.M. to 7 P.M. tends to be a good time to plan some type of recreation. It is recommended that, if possible, this be some type of physical exercise. This will not only help keep you healthy but will occupy your mind and give you an opportunity to escape some of the pressures of the day.
5. Using your to-do list, starting with the *As*, schedule the things you would like to accomplish for the day. If you just have a list of things to study, all of which are of relatively equal value, here are some study scheduling hints that may help you:
   a. Plan roughly two hours of study time for each hour of class time. This will vary with the difficulty of the course, the demands of the course, the demands of the individual professor, and your skill in the subject area.

    b. Adapt the length of time you spend studying to the type of material being studied. For most subjects, studying in twenty to thirty minute blocks, with five- to ten-minute breaks, for periods of approximately one hour per subject works well. This, however, is only an approximation. Drill work involving rote memorization differs in length of time from reading a novel.

    c. Eliminate dead hours from your schedule. If you have an hour between classes, do not waste it. Schedule that hour to review your lecture notes from the previous class or to prepare for the next class.

    d. One hour of studying during the day can be worth as much as one and a half hours of studying time at night. Use daylight hours for studying.

Other-Imposed Time

There are three types of other-imposed time: (1) necessary, (2) unnecessary, and (3) unavoidable.

Necessary Other-Imposed Time

Necessary other-imposed time involves legitimate crises or important issues that need your attention. Because you are an RA, you will have many of these contacts. A student who is undergoing some type of important emotional crisis has a right to interrupt you to discuss his problem. A fire drill, a fight in the residence hall, a student who is experiencing a major problem, or a program that you must attend is other-imposed time that is necessary for job function. Many times you will find that you are in a situation in which only you have the information or authority to make a needed decision. This also is necessary other-imposed time. The last form of other-imposed time is employer-imposed time related to legitimate job functions.

If the residence hall director must call a staff meeting on a particular day or needs your assistance, this is related to a legitimate job function and, therefore, falls into the category of necessary other-imposed time. These are things for which you must learn to adjust your schedule. You can minimize them only to the extent that you can ask that some of them be handled at a later time.

Unnecessary Other-Imposed Time

Unnecessary other-imposed time is a serious problem for most RAs. Items that fall into this category are telephone calls from people who wish only to chat, visitors you had not planned for, regular meetings in which very little or nothing is accomplished, trash mail, poor communication that needs further clarification from your superiors, disorganized meetings, campus red tape, unavailability of people you need to contact, questionnaires, and writing reports that nobody ever reads. You can minimize unnecessary other-imposed time in creative ways. Try some of the techniques that others have found successful. They take some self-discipline, but they may help increase your discretionary time.

1. Take the phone off the hook while you are studying.
2. Avoid visitors by studying in places other than your room or by putting a sign on your door informing people that you are studying.
3. Go to meetings on time and demand that they start at the time scheduled. If the meeting was to start at 1:30, demand that it start at 1:30 and not at 1:45 as is probably customary. If that does not work, just plan to be there at 1:45.
4. When you receive trash mail, stack it in your room and read it when you get a chance or throw it out immediately without bothering to open it.
5. On communication that is unclear, write on the communication that you do not understand it, and ask the sender to explain.
6. Bureaucratic red tape is a problem for everyone. You can find out who on your campus does what and send people to the appropriate sources to begin with. Or if it is an internal matter within the residence programs, the best course of action is to use the person under whom you work. Ask your supervisor to help work out the problem.

Unavoidable Other-Imposed Time

Unavoidable other-imposed time is time wasted over which you have no control. Everyone finds himself wasting time for one reason or another. One such unavoidable other-imposed waste of time is traffic jams. There is no excuse for them, yet they occur and there is little that can be done about them. Waiting for an appointment in a doctor's office or a dentist's office is another kind of unavoidable other-imposed time. Being stopped in the hallway by a faculty member or stopped by a friend to talk is unavoidable other-imposed time. The important thing is to minimize these and not let them destroy your schedule.

Conclusion

Time is your most precious commodity. You must learn to use it efficiently. Time wasted is time lost forever. However, you can utilize time and gain maximum benefits from it by setting goals, organizing yourself, assigning priorities to your daily tasks, and scheduling your time. You will find that the better organized you become in working with your time, the more time you will discover that you have.

CHAPTER 17
Study Skills

The last chapter covered one of the critical elements of developing good study skills—that of time management and scheduling. The solution to most study problems is not spending more time studying, but learning how to study better in the time allotted. There are some simple techniques that you should know about studying. These will help you in your academic pursuits.

Poor study skills produce anxiety and frustration. The need to achieve high grades is a reality. Students feel this pressure both in meeting their own personal goals, and the expectations of parents. Often students' misbehavior in the living unit is a release of stress that has accumulated due to anxiety over not studying enough or not achieving academically for the amount of time invested in studying. It is a major stress producer for students.

Students seldom take the time to learn how to study. This chapter is devoted to this subject. It is divided into four basic areas. The first of these areas deals with preparation for study. It will address the study environment, how to get started in studying, procrastination, scheduling, and realistic attitudes about studying. The second section examines the skills necessary in acquiring the information. This includes text book reading, classroom behavior, notebooks and similar issues relating to how you acquire information. The third section deals with the process of learning the information. And the final section of this chapter is devoted to test taking and examinations. Overall, we can look at studying as getting ready to study, hearing or reading information, learning the information, and giving the information back to the professor through a test, examination, or term paper.

Preparing Yourself to Study

The whole area of preparing yourself to study is often overlooked by students. Most people need to get "psyched up" in order to concentrate on learning information. Preparing oneself to study follows an old adage "plan your work and work your plan." The first element of planning your work is learning to use a study schedule. The previous chapter on time management addresses how to create a workable schedule to allot maximum time for studying and other activities. If you have not already developed a study schedule, you should do so by reading the chapter on time management.

Creating Your Study Environment

Residence halls are reported as the location most often used by students as the primary place to study. Libraries are generally ranked as the second location. Because residence halls are an important place to study, it is important that this environment be conducive to study. It is interesting to observe the myriad of distractions that many residence halls present. As you walk down the corridor of a residence hall, you can often observe students attempting to study with their doors open and playing their stereos. Their desks are lined with pictures of girlfriends/boyfriends, their automobile, or other mementos and different items may be dangling from strings overhead. In the corridor, a group of people may be congregated talking, while in the room next door a group of people may be cheering over a Monday night football game. This hardly presents a conducive study environment. It is true that students can learn to adapt to a noisy and distracting environment; however studying in this environment requires greater concentration. If the noise is background noise, having little or no associative value, the distracting quality is diminished. A good example of this is a student who is studying and listening to the radio at the same time. If the background music is music with which the student has little association, chances are that it will present only a mild distraction. If, on the other hand, a song is played with which the student identifies, her thoughts will be inclined to drift toward the song. Many students claim they can study better when their stereo is playing. This may be true for some students. There has been some research indicating that background music of a nonassociative value tends to help some males focus their concentration. For females this was not true. Most music distracted females from their concentration in studying. It could be that in some situations, playing music of little associative value may help muffle or drowned other distracting noises in the environment. Part of this preference and the degree to which it may influence one's ability to concentrate may have to do more with whether or not a person's primary way of perceiving the world is visual or audiological. People who perceive the world audiologically as a primary means of sensing, may be more influenced by extraneous sound in the environment. Whatever your situation may be, the general principle for most people is that less noise is preferable when attempting to concentrate.

There are other kinds of distractions. Pictures, memorabilia, and other items with which students often clutter their desks can also be distracting. A student looking up catches a glance of a picture pinned to the bulletin board in front of her desk and spends a few minutes recalling some past experiences. This break in concentration can be as distracting as an auditory disturbance.

In arranging your room for studying, you should attempt to place your study table or desk against a wall. Do not pin, paste, or post anything against this wall that may distract you. Do not place your desk in front of a window; the activity on the outside could be a distraction. Pay special attention to removing anything that will compete with your concentration. Proper lighting in this area is important. Glaring fluorescent or overly bright lights can be distracting, and are more tiring to the eyes. If your desk has a plastic laminated top, light may reflect off the glossy surface into your eyes. This is easily solved by placing a cover or blotter over the top of the desk.

One key to using a study environment successfully is to develop positive study habits in that environment. If possible, try to use your study area only for study. Try not to play cards, sit and make telephone calls, or do anything else unrelated to studying in this area. This will establish a positive, reinforcing atmosphere for study in this location. Soon the area will become associated with concentration and study; eventually it will reduce the time necessary for you to prepare for concentration. The fewer distractions and the more prepared your environment is for study, the quicker you will be able to start studying. You will be able to spend less time studying since the time you spend will be of greater quality.

The principles for helping to establish a positive study environment are as follows:

1. Use your study area only for studying.
2. Have all materials available and within easy reach.
3. Keep the area free from all distractions.
4. Study at the same time and in the same location whenever possible.
5. Spend your study time in this area wisely. If you cannot concentrate, do not spend time there.
6. Keep the room moderately cool rather than moderately warm.
7. Assume a posture conducive to work and not one suggestive of relaxation. Lying on the bed with your feet propped against the wall, is not conducive to concentration.
8. Study when you are most alert and best able to concentrate. For most people, this is during the day. It is generally held that one hour of study time during the day is worth at least an hour and one-half at night when you are less able to concentrate, have more distractions, and are more tired.

Keeping Well

People who are healthy, study better. If you are tired, anxious, and irritable, it is difficult to concentrate and therefore difficult to study. Drugs, alcohol, caffeine, and foods high in sugar tend to detract from your ability to study. Sugary foods and alcohol make you drowsy. You should approach studying in college as you would approach a job. Unless your body is functioning well, it will be difficult to study.

Many students have a regular exercise routine. Exercise reduces stress, which is a major inhibitor to effective studying. Relaxation techniques such as meditation, biofeedback techniques and a host of other relaxation procedures may also be of assistance to individuals in reducing stress. If you are well in mind, body, and spirit, you have a better chance of performing at your optimum level.

Practical Realities of Studying

Before engaging in serious study, you must recognize some realities about the process. You will not automatically learn material by reading it. You may have to read some chapters in a textbook several times to understand it. In writing an essay or term paper, you will need to make more than one draft. The first draft is a general expression of ideas. It is in subsequent drafts that you refine this information in a way that can be presented best to others.

Waiting until the last minute to undertake term papers or study for tests increases one's anxiety. Starting early allows you greater freedom to plan your time, review your work, and to fine tune your knowledge or improve a term paper. Try finishing an essay or paper at least two weeks before the deadline date—whenever possible. Let the paper sit for several days, and then reread it. You will find areas that you may want to improve.

The more you are pressured in study situations, the more stress you experience and the less you are able to produce. Some people claim they work best under pressure. This is usually not true. What is true is that some people are able to motivate themselves only when they are under great pressure. This does not mean they do their best work; only that when left with no alternative but to do the work, they finally do the work.

Remember that studying a particular topic is a gradual process. It involves learning bits of information and stringing it together over the period of the course. Studying a little each day, doing your reading as required throughout the course, and reviewing the material as you go, is the process of studying. Putting everything off until the last minute, and hoping to "cram" all the information the night before an examination is the last act of a desperate student. It seldom offers the reward that the student is seeking.

Getting Started

Plan the work you want to study within the time you have available. Set a goal for yourself for each study period. If your goal is to read one chapter in that scheduled period, then read the chapter and move on to something else. Perhaps all you want to do is scan the chapter, or scan the chapter and take notes. What every you choose, make a conscious choice to do it. Plan it ahead of time.

If sometimes, you just don't feel like studying, try easing yourself into the process by doing something mechanical such as surveying the chapter headings, or rewriting or rearranging some of your notes. As you move through these tasks spend time concentrating, examining, and questioning the material. This should begin to increase your concentration.

One of the things that deters people from studying is the tendency to look at major projects as being overwhelming. Thinking about the material that one must compile, analyze, and write in a term paper is so overwhelming for some people that they constantly put it off. If everyone approached their work in this way, very little would get accomplished. The best way to approach large projects, such as term papers or large books, is to break them up into small segments. If you think about writing a term paper 40 or 50 pages long as writing 10 segments of five pages, it won't seem nearly so difficult. If you need to read a book that has 50 chapters, you really only need to read two chapters a day for 25 days.

I spoke with a student recently who was about to take the LSAT examination. She said she was very apprehensive about taking the exam. The thought of sitting down to take the four-hour examination frightened her, until she stopped to think that what she was really taking was eight smaller tests lasting 20 to 30 minutes each. If you think of each segment of studying or writing a paper as a single segment and reward yourself after each segment, long projects and large books will seem easier.

Procrastination

Procrastination is another word for avoidance or displacement. The energies that you should devote to studying are sometimes channeled into other areas. The more a person delays studying, the more anxious she becomes. Procrastination may serve another function. Some people procrastinate because they subconsciously prefer not to succeed. Others are not willing to surrender the freedoms or the time that is required for studying.

People procrastinate by replacing something that they don't want to do, with an alternative. This way they avoid the thing that they don't want to do. If a person procrastinates to the extent that she can no longer function in school or places herself in situations which create great anxiety, then she probably needs to discuss this procrastination with a trained counselor.

It is probably true that everyone procrastinates to some extent, and that a little procrastination is acceptable. However, when somebody avoids and delays a project that needs to get done to the extent that it causes great emotional stress, there is a reason for such behavior. As said earlier, this is an issue worth exploring with a counselor. You may be able to help students who are experiencing this problem by having them talk about the reasons that they are procrastinating. You can offer them some encouragement, and perhaps review some of their study techniques. It is possible that if their studying has been very unrewarding, this may be part of the reason for their procrastination. One is more likely to be willing to undertake academic projects in areas that they have succeeded than in areas where they have failed.

Basic Skills in Acquiring Information

A person acquires information in one of three ways—reading, listening to lectures, or experimentation/application.

Textbook Reading

Textbooks are outlined to permit students to obtain an overview of the material. The outline for each chapter is determined by the headings and subheadings throughout the book. When looking at a chapter in a textbook, the first thing that you should do is become familiar with what that chapter will cover. There are a number of methods for the initial reading in a textbook. One successful method employs a five-step process. First, survey the chapter to determine what the chapter will cover. Second, while surveying the chapter ask yourself some questions about the material to be covered. Third, read the chapter, looking for answers to the questions you have previously asked. Fourth, review the outline of the chapter again, and fifth, recite your answers to the questions and other pertinent information that you have discovered.

This is one method for reading a textbook. There are others that work just as well. Reading to answer questions and thinking about how certain material applies to specific situations will help you make the material meaningful. If you can associate the material in the textbook with an experience, or in some way make it meaningful to you, it will facilitate your memory of the material. Underlining or highlighting sections of the textbook will aid in retention of the material. Highlight only the most important material. It does little good to highlight large segments of material. A similar technique is to write comments or questions in the margins of the book. This reinforces what you've read and helps you summarize. It will be particularly helpful to you when reviewing the material later.

Many students believe that they must read a textbook as quickly as they read a novel. Textbooks are not meant to be read with great speed. They are meant to be read, thought about, studied, and reviewed. It is often necessary to reread sections of a text in order to get the full meaning.

Classroom Behavior and the Lecture

The purpose of the lecture is to provide you with information that is not covered in the textbook, or to explain textbook material in greater detail. In many courses the lecture is the focus of the course and the textbook or other supplementary reading is used to augment the information covered in the lecture. Whatever the case, attending a lecture involves the process of active listening. Active listening does not just mean taking a voluminous series of notes. It does mean listening carefully to what is said, understanding the relationships provided by the lecturer, taking meaningful notes in an outline form that will aid in remembering the material covered in the lecture, and ask relevant questions. Many students believe that they must take down every word that the lecturer says in order to take good notes. This is simply not true. Notes of this detail become awkward and cumbersome. Often a student is so involved in transcribing words that the important concepts are missed.

Good note taking should consist of formulating an outline in sufficient detail to stimulate your memory of the information covered in the lecture. It is often helpful to include examples the lecturer gives. Lecturers provide examples, and tell stories about experiences to aid students in drawing relationships between the information they are giving and its application. If one can associate the information with the example, it is usually easier to remember the information.

In taking notes, it is generally preferable to use single sheets of paper that may be placed in a loose leaf notebook. This will allow you to add things, rewrite or modify your notes. Use only one side of the paper. Save the back side to add material later or to clarify examples that have been given.

Basically your notes should reflect an outline. You should use abbreviations where possible, include examples the professor gives, and make sure that you include statements that the lecturer has emphasized or stressed. Focus first on concepts and then on details. After the lecture it is sometimes helpful to recopy the notes. Although this takes additional time, it helps in review of the information and in the accuracy of the notes.

Most students who record lectures will in all likelihood not get as much from the lecture as a person who is actively listening and taking notes. Having to relisten to lectures becomes cumbersome and time consuming. It's like having to do all the work again. It also is difficult to refer back to information unless one wishes to spend time spinning through tapes and relistening. Using a tape recorder is only helpful if the material is very complex, and you use it immediately following the lecture to supplement your notes. Remember, your notes do not need to be in such great detail that you catch every word. Your notes should be an outline of concepts, ideas, and important facts covered by the lecture.

College professors who lecture, have the responsibility to teach. This means that as a student, you paid for the right to ask questions, and to talk with them during their office hours. They should be available to help explain material that you do not understand, or have graduate assistants who can do the same. Know the course instructor and do not be afraid to consult with her when you have questions. Generally, you will find that faculty members are available for these conversations and are more than willing to explain material that you do not understand.

Experimentation and Application

The third way we learn is through experimenting, or applying information. Labs associated with chemistry, physics, and similar fields are examples of learning through experience. Art, music, and the area of rhetoric and public address are other areas in which we acquire information by experimentation and application.

One of the things you often hear students say is that they find much of their academic work to be impractical because they are not able to see how this information will benefit them in later years. Information is easier to learn if you can see how it is to be applied. Doing research for an intercollegiate debate is a good example. Debaters usually do voluminous amounts of research on the given topic. For all practical purposes, they become experts in that topic. They research both sides of the question, so that they can argue on either side in a tournament. Debaters who seriously invest themselves in the activity are usually voracious researchers. They read to gather information, while constantly thinking how that information might be put to use in a debate, or in formulating their presentation of the issue. They have learned to read for specific information. This increases retention because they know how it will be put to use. In using the information in a debate, the speakers come to know the information better. They not only understand its application, but have experimented with the information. Experimentation and application are important ways to acquire information.

The Studying Process

Studying is a process of reading, organizing or outlining, reciting, and reviewing. Studying should be done on a regular basis and not just for exams.

In reading through chapters of the textbook, you should focus on the outline presented, noting particularly the notes that you have made in the margin and things that you have highlighted. The idea in reviewing the textbook is to get concepts and the major facts presented. It is sometimes helpful to make an outline of the chapter with accompanying facts and details that you need to remember.

Reviewing your notes is done in a similar fashion. First, read through the notes and then condense this material into a shorter outline. Review the notes, and perhaps condense the outline again until it is such that you can remember it or understand it without having to look at it.

Review your text, outline, and the notes again and try to recite what is covered. Try to visualize the outline of the text and the outline of the notes that you have made. Think about how one supports or relates to the other. Focus particularly on examples that will help trigger the information you need.

Memorizing is generally required in cases where you will be given objective examinations, or where you need to have access to certain dates or formulas. Generally speaking, sciences tend to require more memory work than humanities. Music requires memory work for pianists and vocalists, but not for most other musicians. Memorize only the material you need to memorize. For most courses professors are primarily interested in your understanding of the concepts and information presented. It may be necessary for you to demonstrate this by remembering certain facts about a particular battle, or certain theoretical approaches that are attributed to a particular psychologist. However, it is generally more important to be able to discuss the psychologists' theories and what they mean, or describe and explain the causes and what happened during a battle than to present dates, facts, and figures. Generalizations in this area are hard to make. It depends so much on what individual faculty members are expecting. The best way to find out what faculty members think is important and what type of information they will require of you, is to ask. Most will answer candidly.

For memory work, first write the important facts that you wish to memorize on a sheet of paper, or on a series of 4″ × 6″ cards. Break large sections of information that you need to memorize down into smaller sections. Start by memorizing smaller sections and link these smaller sections together until you can memorize the larger piece of information. Visualizing the material often helps either by visualizing what actually happened, or by visualizing the actual words on the page. If you can associate facts that you need to remember with examples, your ability to remember those facts should be increased. One technique people use to remember other people's names, for example, is to associate the person's name with a physical feature of that individual. So if the person's name is Eileen, you may think of Eileen as a person who wears a certain type of eye glasses.

Memorization is done by reviewing and reciting. Some techniques that generally help are to review and recite the information before going to bed at night. At night you may dream about some of this information. First thing in the morning, try to recite the information. Review and recite again. Do this over a two or three day period, and the information will become yours. Some researchers say that the information must be recited verbatim at least seven times before you can retain the information. The more times you use the information, review and recite it, the more you will remember the information and for a longer period of time.

Test Taking

College professors do not always ask the questions you would like to have them ask. You do not always have an opportunity to show them everything that you know about a given topic. Instead they tend to test students to determine the varying degrees of information they have about a topic. In every test there should be some questions which you cannot answer, or find very difficult to answer. Testing does not test how much knowledge you have about a subject, it tests what information you have about the questions asked in a given format, and your ability to take the type of test being administered.

To prepare to take a test, you first must know what type of test you will be asked to take. There are basically three types of tests that are administered. They are objective, multiple choice, and essay type. Some tests are a combination of the three. A professor will usually tell you before hand what type of test is to be administered. If he/she does not, ask.

Taking Objective Type Exams

An objective exam is one that calls for total recall. It is the most difficult type of exam to take. Fill in the blank type questions and short answer questions are forms of objective tests. You either know the information being sought, or you do not. If you do not know the information, write what you think is the right answer unless the professor indicates that she will deduct points from your total score for incorrect answers. Go through the exam and answer those questions you know, then go back and answer the questions that you are less sure of, leaving the most difficult questions until last.

As with all examination questions, read thoroughly to make sure you understand exactly what the question is asking.

Multiple Choice Questions

Multiple choice, or multiple guess questions come in many forms. The most obvious is where you are given a question and four or five alternatives. Versions of this include being given a question in which more than one of the alternatives may be correct and you are asked to pick the best answer. Sometimes it will be worded in such a way that your choices include the first two possibilities but not the third and the third possibility but not the fourth. It is important to read multiple choice questions very carefully. The directions to them vary. Know particularly whether or not there is more than one right answer to each question.

First, look through the questions and answer those of which you are sure. Next, go back through and examine each question. Eliminate the obviously incorrect alternatives. You should be able to narrow the options to two or three, thus giving you a better chance of determining the correct answer. Among these two or three, look for global statements such as "always," "in every case," "never," and "absolutely." You can usually eliminate one of these alternatives. It is rare that an authority would make such a global statement.

Finally if you still cannot decide which is the correct answer, and the professor is not deducting from your total score for answering incorrectly, take your best guess. You could have a percentage chance of being right.

True and false questions are a form of multiple choice. If you don't know the correct answer in a true-false test, take your best guess (unless the professor counts off for wrong answers). Never leave a yes or no question unanswered. You always have a 50-50 chance of choosing the correct answer.

Taking Essay Type Exams

Essay exams call for you to organize your thoughts and present them in a coherent way that speaks directly to the question asked. This is your opportunity to express in your own words, your understanding of the question raised. Remember to watch your time on essay exams. Do not spend all of your time writing an elaborate answer to one question, only to find that you do not have enough time to answer the remaining questions on the test. Start by outlining in the margin of your paper or in your head what you want to say. Each essay question is looking for certain facts the professor wants. Think what those key elements must be, and organize your essay around them. If there are three parts to a theory that the professor has asked you to explain, start your essay by saying there are three parts to the theory and the first part is, the second part is, the third part is. The purpose of an essay is for you to explain what you know, not for you to create a great literary masterpiece. This does not mean that you should be haphazard and careless with your grammar and spelling. Quite the opposite is true. If you express yourself clearly, using correct English, it will add to the credibility of your response.

Include only the information necessary in the essay. Don't waste your time and the instructor's time by adding extraneous material padding the essays. If you feel you must pad the answers, do so in moderation. Remember that college professors are experienced students, and experienced readers of essays. It is surprisingly simple to differentiate between students who have an understanding of the topic on a essay question, and those students who are simply padding questions with extraneous information.

If you absolutely have no idea how to answer a particular essay question, and again the professor will not deduct for wrong answers, write something. Even if it is extraneous material, the professor may, out of pity, give you one or two points for an attempt.

Test Anxiety

Some students get so anxious about a test, that they block (unable to remember information they have studied). You might call this a type of stage fright. A student can feel nervous, have a headache, feel dizzy, and develop a fear reaction. In other words, they panic. There is more than one way to combat test anxiety. The one thing that always helps, is to have confidence in your ability to do well on the examination. If you have studied, and know the information, this will help provide you with the confidence to do well. Success on other tests, also tends to help build the confidence in test taking. The more confident the person feels about the information they have covered, the more confident they should be about taking the examination.

Even though some students are confident they have studied enough, they nevertheless panic when beginning the examination. Relaxing before the examination is one way to help reduce anxiety. Another way is to take several deep breaths before taking the examination, and look through the examination to find the easiest questions first. Sometimes by answering a few easy questions in the examination, the student builds enough confidence to go on and answer some of the more difficult ones. Students should have a realistic perspective on any examination. Few examinations are a make or break situation for a student. If you experience some test anxiety, you need to think about positive test experiences that you have had. Admit to yourself that you are not going to be able to answer all the questions right. Remember that a test examines the depth of one's information, and it is normal for people to miss answers to some questions. If you cram just before a test, this will no doubt heighten your anxiety. Sometimes looking at your notes just before entering the exam only heightens your anxiety.

One of the techniques used by some counseling offices to reduce test anxiety is a technique in biofeedback relaxation. They have the student explain each segment of going to take an examination, starting with the student getting up in the morning all the way through the student actually sitting down to take the examination. As a student relates each segment of his/her behavior prior to the exam, they physically have the student relax. This process takes place in a safe and secure environment. The student learns to associate the relaxation response with the experiences leading up to the test. This process is usually coupled with some therapy which focuses upon issues of self-esteem, and the issue of fear of failure.

If you or some of your residents experience serious test anxiety to the extent where you cannot function during the exam, you should talk with a university counselor about the problem. Some anxiety before a test is normal. It is not normal, however, to be so anxious and disturbed that you cannot remember or produce the information that you know you have learned. One final word about taking examinations. Most exams are given in a specified amount of time, usually one class period. You need to be conscious of how much time you are allotting to questions and the value of those questions. In a 60 minute class period, it is not a good use of time to spend 30 minutes responding to a ten point essay, leaving the remaining 30 minutes of the class period to answer the remaining 90 points on the exam. A few professors will let students write as much as they wish with no time constraints. Find out before hand how long you will be given to take the exam. If it will be one class period, use your time wisely, apportioning appropriate time to the value assigned to individual questions. If no specific value is assigned to each question, inquire as to whether or not they will receive equal weight.

Cramming

Cramming for a test is better than not studying at all, but it is not a substitute for studying the material over a period of time and learning it throughout the course of the semester. If you are in a position where you must cram, set aside a block of time and begin by condensing the material you have into an outline from which you can work. Try to get some help from another person in the class in determining what areas she believes are particularly important in the course. Review the outline and the information that person believes will be on the exam, and disregard trying to read the entire textbook again, or trying to copiously review someone else's notes.

If you must cram do so systematically and from outlines that summarize the material covered. Use the outline to explore specific areas you believe are likely to be on the examination. Don't try to review everything in the course, it will overwhelm you and will squander your limited study time.

Academic Honesty and Dishonesty

A surprising number of students choose to cheat on examinations or plagiarize term papers. This reprehensible conduct seriously jeopardizes the academic integrity of the institution and raises the question as to whether or not that student should be permitted to continue at the institution. One of the reasons the university exists is for the purpose of helping students master information. If a student chooses to represent to the faculty that she has mastered information that she has truly not mastered, it calls into question the purpose that person has in attending the institution. There is no excuse for academic dishonesty. Despite the pressures to get good grades, or whatever personal problems may exist, it does not excuse the lack of integrity and breach of trust demonstrated by academic dishonesty.

Some students will experience personal problems that prevent them from studying. The solution is not for them to press on with their course work, but to explain the situation to the appropriate college authorities and seek their advice and help in resolving the problem. Most schools will allow students to take incompletes when they have a legitimate reason. Students should be aware when they can withdraw from courses, and when that is not longer possible.

In cases of serious mental, emotional, or physical health problems, the college counseling or health center will usually be able to assist the student in securing an extension for the course, or perhaps a retroactive withdrawal. Whatever the institutional policies, there are usually alternatives. There are always alternatives if a student acts soon enough. Help students on your floor understand what their options are. The stigma of being expelled or suspended from a college or university is much greater than receiving a failing mark in a course.

Spend some time talking with the residents of your living unit about the issue of academic honesty. Help them understand that "everybody" does not cheat, and that academic dishonesty will not get them through college. Make sure they understand the university's position on academic dishonesty. They are issues of honor, integrity, and scholarship.

A college education trains not only the mind, but also the character of the individual. It is this issue, of the student's character, that is challenged when she chooses to act dishonestly. If you know of academic dishonesty you should confront the students who are involved. It is appropriate for you to consult with your hall director on how your particular institution handles these situations, and what is expected of you in this situation.

CHAPTER 18
Stress Management

All of us are exposed to stress in our lives. We experience stress both physically and emotionally. It comes to us in a variety of ways: jobs, insecurities, other people's perceptions of us, our perception of ourselves, interpersonal relationships, and unfulfilled expectations among others. As an RA, you are exposed to the same stresses as other students in addition to the stress of balancing your academic goals with the responsibility of your job.

Stress is intense exertion, strain, and effort. It is brought about by the continual adjustments and demands we place upon ourselves as we react to given stimuli. The more we are called upon to adjust to changing situations, the more stress we acquire. As one's environment becomes more complex, demands significantly increase. We are called upon to make more and more changes—to respond to an increasing diversity of situations.

Psychologically, any time a person feels threatened, is anxious about a forthcoming event, or is injured, the body reacts. First the nervous system chemically transmits a signal to the pituitary gland which releases a hormone called ACTH. This in turn releases adrenalin from the adrenal glands into the body. These hormones prepare the body to respond more quickly to a threat. This physical reaction, designed for survival, has come to be known as the fight or flight response. Fear, whether real or imagined, sets off a reaction of tension in the body that causes nervous impulses to increase and the adrenalin to be rushed through the system. The adrenalin causes the heart rate and respiration to increase, and the body becomes prepared to deal with the threatening situation. Because we live in a civilized community, the need to fight or flee has been replaced with socially learned customs to deal with the same anxiety-producing situations.

Modern society, however, produces its own special set of stress situations our ancestors never had to confront. Driving in traffic, the fear of failure when taking an exam, and living in close proximity to a number of other people—such as in a residence hall—all produce stress. Physically, the signs of stress in an individual include uncontrolled anger over small things, higher blood pressure and blood sugar, an inability to concentrate, and a desire to retreat or escape from others. The best indicator of stress is your body. Not being able to sleep, constant worrying about something, and a general irascibility are usually signs of stress.

Young people today generally have more stress than the people of past generations. The technology of today and the less structured moral options present more choices to individuals. Twenty years ago drugs were not as readily available as they are today, and there was little social pressure to experiment. Sexual activity among young people who were not married occurred, but there was strong social pressure against this experimentation—much more so than today. The technology of television, increased crime, the mobility of our society, the breakup of the nuclear family through divorce, and the perception on the part of many that the economic future of the country is in doubt are new questions confronting today's college generation with greater intensity than in the past. The results of this stress can be seen in the disproportionately high suicide rates among adolescents, and the use of drugs and other substances to escape. Mental health problems and violence among young people are other indicators.

Stress becomes intensified when it lasts for a long period of time or a number of stress situations accumulate over time. It is also intensified if a person must deal with a number of stressful situations or the stress situations are coupled with other adjustment difficulties. Generally, all stress is intensified by the person's perceived importance of the stress producers. Thus, if a person needs to get a high grade in organic chemistry in order to get into medical school, chances are the final examination in the course, because of its perceived importance, will intensify the stress for the exam. The GREs, the LSAT, or the MEDCAT as national preprofessional standardized tests are other good examples of intensified stress producers because of perceived importance.

Coping with Stress

It is important to relieve stress as it accumulates. Make stress work for you by doing something you find personally satisfying after a stressful situation. Find a way to relax or direct those energies to an enjoyable task.

For individuals who are having difficulty recognizing signs of stress, biofeedback training can be of help. Many institutions offer a mini-course in biofeedback training which helps a person become aware of certain physiological signs associated with increased stress and anxiety. A form of biofeedback technique is often used in test anxiety reduction programs run by college counseling centers. Through this program, a student becomes aware of specific elements that produce fear and through a step-by-step progression learns to deal with elements of the fear producers. The biofeedback training usually includes some type of relaxation training, as well as training in recognizing physical signs of increased stress.

Some people have turned to forms of meditation as a way to handle the stress of modern society. Several meditation programs, including Transcendental Meditation, and Zen meditation, are examples of techniques available. These techniques can help a person reduce the cumulative effects of stress by teaching one how to relax for a few minutes each day. The relaxation responses that occur during meditation are the opposite of the flight or fight response. Stress is reduced as the person enters an altered state of consciousness which puts the body into a state of relaxation. Most of these techniques of meditation are simple and require only minimal training.

One of the best ways to deal with stress is to learn to prevent or avoid it. Perhaps the most common cause of stress is taking on more responsibility than you can handle. It is important to be able to balance work commitments with recreational commitments. The old adage "all work and no play makes Jack a dull boy" might better be stated as "all work and no play makes Jack uptight, tense, anxious, frustrated, and stressed."

Regular exercise is a good stress prevention technique. It provides the opportunity to physically express aggressive feelings and frustrations through such exercise activities as running, swimming, or biking. Being able to concentrate on a racquetball game, golf game, tennis match, or some other athletic endeavor for a short period of time provides the mind with an opportunity to escape, if only temporarily. As mentioned in the chapter on time management, recreational time should be scheduled just like other activities. Times spent in regular exercise and recreation is time well spent—not wasted. Time spent in recreational and athletic endeavors will contribute to your efficiency and your ability to deal with other tasks.

Sleeping plays an interesting role in dealing with stress. Sometimes people become upset to the extent that they feel they can no longer cope. One way of retreating from this stress is to escape by sleeping. Psychologists look to sleeping patterns as indications of a person's personal problems. People who try to escape stress in this manner may sleep from twelve to fifteen hours a day on a regular basis. Though occasionally everyone finds a need to put in an extra long day to accomplish things that need to be done, this should be the exception. Those who try to exist on four hours of sleep a night for prolonged periods of time, believing that this increases their efficiency, are probably reducing their efficiency by not getting adequate rest. One of the reasons that young children need more sleep than adults is that the complexity of learning new things and of dealing with their new environment requires that they remove themselves from these situations and synthesize the complexity of their environment in sleeping. It is also true, that college students probably need more sleep than middle aged adults because of the complexity of their new environment and the academic demands placed upon them.

Emotionally, one can do a lot to prevent stress and relieve it by learning to talk over problems. One of the best skills for coping with stress is learning to talk over your problems with someone else. Sitting down and sharing the problem and gaining someone else's perspective can alleviate part of the pressure we sometimes feel. The freedom to do this is important. Encourage others to talk over their stress producers with you and in turn share some of your stress producers with others. You will find that you not only gain insight into your problems, you will find that your problems are not unique.

Few of the stresses that we experience are of a life and death nature. It is important that we keep our problems in perspective, viewing the situation realistically. Although the thought of failing a course, losing a girlfriend, not completing a term paper, or not finding summer job seems at a particular moment to be the most important thing in the world, it is. Life will continue, and people's perceptions of you will not be dramatically altered. Once you have been able to confront the worst possible thing that could happen to you if that particular event took place, you should be better able to cope with the stress.

Learning to accept things that we cannot change is part of being realistic. If you have no control over an event, it does little good to worry about it. If the decision making authority is beyond your control, then the stress you experience by worrying about it is hardly worth the effort.

On occasion, psychological stress, occurring persistently, may be a sign of a physical problem. Consult a physician if you have this concern. If no medical problems are found to be the cause, discuss your stress with a physician or a counselor at the college. It is unwise to prescribe self-medication for stress producers. Self-prescribed medications seldom make the problem go away.

When stress gets to the point you cannot cope with it, you should discuss your stress with a counselor. Most colleges and universities have a counseling center staffed by trained counselors to assist students with just these types of problems. You will find the people in the centers are highly qualified, concerned, and experienced in dealing with the stress that college students experience.

Perhaps one of the greatest stress producers for students is the belief that whatever they do must be done perfectly. The adage of "if it is worth doing, it is worth doing right" has probably done more to increase the stress and anxiety of Americans than any other phrase. Perfectionists acquire stress because they believe that everything must be done perfectly, and as a result they accomplish very little. They are too worried about all their work being perfect. In truth, some things are not worth doing perfectly—others are not worth doing at all. If you are ironing a shirt you plan to wear under a sweater, it may not be worthwhile to be overly meticulous about how the sleeves and the body of the shirt are being ironed. If you are writing a letter to a close friend, it probably does not matter if you cross out a word or erase something.

College is a very hectic time in a person's life. It is even more so because of your responsibilities as an RA. You must not only contend with the day to day pressures of academic work, but also with the stress brought on by the intensity of personal relations that are strained by your job responsibilities and that are magnified by living with those that you are trained to assist. Everyone needs quiet time each day—time in which you know that you will not be interrupted. This might be an hour set aside just for you to do whatever you want. If it is only for fifteen minutes at the end of the day, it may help you relieve some of the stress, deal with your job, and other people's problems more objectively.

The Overstress Index

Psychologists have found that a person undergoing a series of major stresses in a short period of time can become what is referred to as overstressed. Some of the major stress producers include such things as a major job promotion, marriage, divorce, and a death in the family. An accumulation of too many of these major stress producers in a short period of time can overstress a person. It is not unusual to see new freshmen coming to college and facing a series of major stress producers. All change produces some stress. Freshmen confronted with moving away from home, adapting to a new living facility, a new roommate, and a new social system are under considerable stress. Some of the acting out behavior in the first few weeks of school is no doubt a reaction to this overstress. Some of the homesickness that you may see on the part of some of your residents may be a result of overstress. Finally, some of the people that develop deep depression, suicidal tendencies, and similar problems may be exhibiting signs of overstress.

Conclusion

Stress affects everyone. The key to dealing with stress is to recognize when you are under stress and learn what situations produce stress for you. If you can learn to cope with and prevent stress in yourself, you can more efficiently accomplish the goals you have set for yourself. This process will help you become more aware of yourself, your skills, your strengths, and your weaknesses. As you learn these things about yourself, you will become better prepared to deal with change now and in the future.

Bibliography

Alberti, A. E. and Emmons, M. L. *Your Perfect Right*. 2nd ed. San Luis Obispo, CA: Impact, 1974.

Albrow, M. C. "The Influence of Accommodation Upon 64 Reading University Students—An *ex post facto* Experimental Study." *The British Journal of Sociology,* 1966.

"Alcohol Resource Information Manual." East Lansing, MI: Residence Hall Program Office, Michigan State University, 1976.

Altret, E. "Housing Selection, Need Satisfaction, and Dropout from College." *Psychological Reports,* 1966.

Archer, J. and Lopata, A. "Marijuana Revisited." *Personnel and Guidance Journal.* 59, (1), January, 1979..

Archer, J. and Lopata, A. "Marijuana—A Summary of Current Research on Psychological Efforts." A report prepared for the Delaware Advisory Commission on Marijuana, 1978.

Astin, A. *Four Critical Years*. San Francisco, CA: Jossey-Bass Publishers, Inc., 1977.

Astin, A. "The Impact of Dormitory Living on Students." *Educational Record,* Summer 1973.

Balser, B. and Masterson, J. "Suicide in Adolescence." *American Journal of Psychiatry,* 1959.

Beal, P., and Williams, D. "An Experiment with Mixed-class Housing Assignments at the University of Oregon." Student Housing Research, ACUHO Research and Information Committee, February, 1968.

Bednor, R., and S. Weinberg. "Ingredients of Successful Treatment Programs for Underachievers." *Journal of Counseling Psychology* 17 (January, 1970): 17.

Benensohn, H. "Suicide Attempts Increase." *Guidepost.* July 22, 1976.

Bernstein, B. *Class, Codes, and Control,* London: Routledge and Kegan Paul, 1971.

Betts, N., and Newman, G. "Defining the Issue: Sexual Harassment in College and University Life." *Contemporary Education.* Vol. 54, Fall 1982, 48–52.

Bial, B. "Roommate Impact Upon Academic Performance." Unpublished (manuscript), Harcum Junior College, 1971.

Binstock, J. *The Futurist.* April, 1974.

Birth Control Handbook. Montreal: Montreal Health Press, Inc., 12th ed., 1975.

Blimling, G., and Hample, D. "Structuring the Peer Environment in Residence Halls to Increase Academic Programming in Average Ability Students." *Journal of College Student Personnel,* July 1979, 20, 4.

Bormann, E., Howell, W., Nichols, R. and Shapiro, G., *Interpersonal Communication in the Modern Organization,* Englewood Cliffs, N.J.: Prentice Hall Inc. 1969.

Boston Women's Health Book Collective. *Our Bodies, Ourselves—A Book by and for Women.* New York: Simon and Schuster, 2nd ed., 1976.

Brecker, E. and Editors of Consumer Reports. *Licit and Illicit Drugs,* Boston, MA: Little, Brown and Company, 1972.

Briggs, R., Tosi D., and Morley, R. "Study Habit Modification and Its Effect on Academic Performance: A Behavioral Approach." *The Journal of Educational Research* 64 (April, 1971): 341–50.

Cantor, P. "The Adolescent Attempter." *Life Threatening Behavior.* 1972.

Chickering, A. *Education and Identity.* San Francisco: Jossey-Bass Publishers, 1969.

Chickering, A. *Commuting Versus Resident Students.* San Francisco: Jossey-Bass, 1974.

Chickering, A. *Education and Identity: Implications for Residence Hall Living.* Empire State College in Student Development and Education in College Residence Halls, DeCoster and Mable (eds) Washington, D.C., American College Personnel Association, 1974.

C.H.U.C.K., "Committee Halting Useless College Killings." P.O. Box 188, Sayville, NY, 11782 (Newsletter, 1979).

Citizen Freedom Foundation, Destructive Cults: Mind Control and Psychological Coercion, (brochure) 1983.

Clark, J., "Cults". *Journal of the American Medical Association,* 1979a, 242(3), 179–281.

Coelho, G., Hamburg, D., and Murphy, E. "Coping Strategies in a New Environment." In *The College Student and His Culture: An Analysis,* Yamamoto (ed), Boston: Houghton Mifflin and Company, 1968. Reprinted from the *Archives of General Psychiatry,* November 1963, Vol. 9, pp. 433–443. Copyright 1963, by American Medical Association.

Coleman, J. *Abnormal Psychology and Modern Life.* Glenview, IL: Scott, Foresman and Co., 1972.

Combs, B., Hales, D., and Williams, B. *An Invitation to Health—Your Personal Responsibility.* Menlo Park: Benjamin/Cummings Publishing Co., 1980.

Conn, H. *Current Therapy 1983.* Philadelphia: W. B. Saunders Co., 1983.

Controlled Substances: Uses and Effects. Washington, D.C., U.S. Department of Justice, Drug Enforcement Administration, 1979.

Conway, F., and Siegelman, J. "Snapping: America's Epidemic of Sudden Personality Change". Philadelphia: J. B. Lippincott, 1978.

Conway, F., "Testimony before a Special U.S. Senate Committee entitled. 'Information Meeting on the Cult Phenomenon in the United States.' (Transcript of proceedings), February 5, 1979.

Cooke, C., and Sworkin, S. *The Ms. Guide to a Woman's Health.* Garden City: Anchor Books, 1979.

Coons, F. "The Developmental Risks of the College Student." In *Student Development and Education in College Residence Halls.* DeCoster and Mable (eds), Washington, D.C.: American College Personnel Association, 1974.

Cowley, W. "Student personnel services in retrospect and prospect." *School and Society,* 85:20, January, 1957.

Cowley, W. "The History of Student Residential Housing." *School and Society.* December 1, 1934, Vol. 40, No. 1040, pp. 705–712, (continued) December 8, 1934, Vol. 40, No. 1041, pp. 758–764.

Cox, H., "Eastern Cults and Western Culture: Why Young Americans are Buying Oriental Religions. *Psychology Today,* July 1977, 11(2), 36–41.

Creaser, J. "Evaluation of a college study habits course using scores on a Q-sort test as the criterion." *Journal of Educational Research.* 56 (January, 1963): 272–74.

Cunningham, M., and Berryman, C. "Conflict: How to Deal with It Effectively." Lecture presented at the First Annual Bowling Green All-Greek Leadership Conference, March 6, 1976.

Danskin, D., and Bennett, C. "Study techniques for those superior students." *Personnel and Guidance Journal* 31 (December, 1952): 181–86.

DeCoster, D. "Some effects of coordinating classroom and residence hall assignments for college freshmen: A pilot project." Paper presented at a meeting of the American Personnel and Guidance Association, Las Vegas, March 1969.

DeCoster, D. "Some effects of different classroom conditions upon interpersonal relationships, personal adjustment, and achievement for college freshmen." *Dissertation Abstracts,* 1970.

DeHaes, N., and Schuerman, J. "Results of an Evaluation Study of Three Drug Education Methods." *International Journal of Health Education,* 1975, Vol. 18.

Delgado, R., "Religious Totalism: Gentle and Ungentle Persuasion Under the First Amendment." *Southern California Law Review,* November 1977, 51(1), 1–98.

Delgado, R., "Testimony before a Special U.S. Senate Committee entitled 'Information Meeting on the Cult Phenomenon in the United States,' (Transcripts of proceedings), February 5, 1979.

Department of Health, Education and Welfare, *Second Special Report to the U.S. Congress on Alcohol and Health,* June, 1974 (DHEW Publication No. HSM–72–9099).

Dublin, L. *Suicide: A Sociological and Statistical Study.* New York, The Roland Press, 1963.

Duncan, C., and Stoner, K. "The Academic Achievement of Residents Living in a Scholar Residence Hall." *The Journal of College and University Student Housing,* Winter 1976/77, 6, 2.

Duncan, C., *et al.* "How the Poorer Student Studies: A Research Report." *Journal of Educational Research* 45 (December, 1951): 287–89.

Eklund, C., et al. "The Effects of Proximity, Willingness to Engage in Social Interaction, and Sorority Membership on the Initial Formation of Friendship Patterns Among Previously Unacquainted College Freshman." Paper presented at Southeastern Psychological Association, Atlanta, GA, 1972.

Elton, C., and Bate, W. "The Effects of Housing Policy on Grade-point Average." *Journal of College Student Personnel,* 1966.

Engel, G. *Bulletin of the Menninger Clinic.* 1968, 32.

Engs, R. "Drinking Patterns and Drinking Problems of College Students." *Journal of Student Alcohol.* Vol. 30, 1977.

Engs, R. "Let's Look before We Leap: The Cognitive and Behavioral Evaluation of a University Alcohol Education Program." *Journal of Alcohol and Drug Education.* 1977.

Entwisle. "Evaluations of Study Skills Courses: A Review." *The Journal of Educational Research* 53 (March, 1960): 243–51.

Erikson, E. *Childhood and Society.* 2nd ed. New York: Norton, 1963.

Erikson, E. "Identity and the Life Cycle." In *Psychosocial Issues,* Klein (ed), New York: International Universities Press, 1959.

Feinberg, M., *et al.* "Results of a Mandatory Study Course for Entering Freshmen." *Journal of Developmental Reading* 2 (Winter, 1962): 95–100.

Feldman, K., and Newcomb, T., (eds.) *The Impact of College on Students.* San Francisco, CA: Jossey-Bass, 1969, 2 vols.

Fensterheim, H., and Baer, J. *Don't Say Yes When You Want to Say No,* New York: David McKay Co., 1975.

Fielder, J., Neil, M., and Olson, B. "Alcohol Manual for Resident Assistants at Michigan State University." East Lansing, MI: Residence Hall Program Office, 1976.

Freeman, E. "Abortion: Subjective Attitudes and Feelings." *Family Planning Perspectives 10.* May/June, 1978, 150–155.

Fretz, B., and Schmidt, L. "Comparison of Improvers and Nonimprovers in an Educational Skills Course." *Journal of Counseling Psychology* 14 (March, 1967), 175–76.

Friedman, W., and Coons, F.: Unpublished data. Indiana University Student Health Center, 1967. Cited by F. Coons in "The Developmental Tasks of the College Student." In D. DeCoster and P. Mable (eds), *Student Development and Education in College Residence Halls,* Washington, D.C., American College Personnel Association, 1974.

Galanter, M., Rabkin, R., Rabkin, J., and Deutsch, A., "The 'Moonies': A Psychological Study of Conversion and Membership in a Contemporary Religious Sect. *American Journal of Psychiatry,* February, 1979, 136(2) 165–170.

Gallup Youth Survey, New York: Associated Press, 1978, 1981.

Gibb, J. *Trust: A New View of Personal and Organizational Development.* Los Angeles: The Guild of Tutors Press, 1978.

Gott vs. Berea College, 161 S.W. 204, Court of Appeals of Kentucky, 1913.

Greenleaf, E., et. al. (eds.). *Undergraduate Students as Members of Residence Hall Staff.* Washington, D.C.: National Association of Women Deans Administrators and Counselors, 1967.

Hall, R., and Willerman, B. "The Educational Influence of Dormitory Roommates." *Sociometry,* 1963.

Halpern, S. *Rape: Helping the Victim.* Oradell, N.J.: Medical Economics Co., 1978.

Harris, L. and Associates, Inc. "Public Awareness of the National Institute on Alcohol Abuse and Alcoholism Advertising Campaign on Public Attitudes toward Drinking and Alcohol Abuse." Study No. 2355. *National Institute of Alcohol Abuse and Alcoholism.* In *Alcohol and Health.* June, 1974. Second Special Report to the U.S. Congress, U.S. Department of Health, Education, and Welfare, Public Health Service.

Hatcher, R., et. al., *Contraceptive Technology 1982–83.* New York: Irvington Publishers, 1982.

Havighurst, R. *Human Development and Education.* New York: Longman's, 1953.

Heaps, R., Rickabaugh, K., and Finley, R. "Counseling Evaluation Inventory Ratings of Counselors and Academic Recovery through Structured Group Counseling." *Research Report No. 23, University of Utah Counseling Center:* 1977.

Heath, D. *Growing up in College.* San Francisco: Jossey-Bass, 1968.

Hecklinger, F. "How to Deal with the Drug Problem on Campus." *NASPA Journal.* 9, (1), July, 1971.

Henshaw, S., et. al., *Abortion 1977–1979: Need and Services in the United States, Each State and Metropolitan Area.* New York: Alan Guttmacher Institute, 1981.

Heron, P. "Behavior Modification . . . or Tea and Sympathy?" *The Journal of the Council of Associations of University Student Personnel Services* 5 (Spring, 1970): 13.

"Herpes: How Common? How Dangerous? Can It Be Cured?" *U.S. News.* August 2, 1982, Vol. 93, p. 61.

Herpes Pamphlet from Patient Information Library. Daly City, CA: Krames Communication, 1983.

"Herpes: The VD of the 80's." *Newsweek*. April 12, 1982, Vol. 99, pp. 75–76.

Hillery, G. "Definition of Community: Areas of Agreement." *Rural Sociology,* 1955.

Hyde, J. *Understanding Human Sexuality*. New York: McGraw-Hill Book Co., 1979.

Jessor, R., and Jessor, S. "Adolescent Development and the Onset of Drinking." *Journal of Studies on Alcohol*. Vol. 36, No. 1, 1975.

Keller, M. "Alcoholism: Nature and Extent of the Problem." In *Understanding Alcoholism*. Annual proceedings of the American Academy of Political and Social Science, 315:1, 1958.

Kendler, H. *Basic Psychology*. 2nd ed. New York: Appleton-Century-Crofts, 1963.

Kennedy, E. *On Becoming a Counselor: A Basic Guide for Non-Professional Counselors*. New York, NY: The Seaburg Press, 1977.

Kiev, A. "The Nonconformist Adolescent." *Excerpta Medica*. 1975, 1.

Kiev, A. *A Strategy for Success,* New York, Macmillan Publishing Co., Inc., 1977.

King, M. "Suicide among Young Seem at Epidemic Heights." *New York Daily News,* March 3, 1978.

Kinsey, A., Pomeroy, W., Martin, C., and Gebhard, P. *Sexual Behavior in the Human Female*. Philadelphia, PA: Saunders, 1953.

Klagsbrun, F. *Too Young to Die*. Boston: Houghton Mifflin, 1976.

Kraft, D. "Alcohol Related Problems Seen at the Student Health Services." *Journal of the American College Health Association*. Vol. 27, February, 1979.

Kraft, S., Teen Suicide: "Contagious Social Problem", A. P. Writer, *Baton Rouge Sunday Advocate,* August 1983, p. 4H.

Kubistant, T. Bulimarexia, *Journal of College Student Personnel,* 1982, 23, 333–339.

Kurtz, R., and Jones, J. "Confrontations: Types, Conditions, and Outcomes." *The 1973 Annual Handbook for Group Facilitators*. LaJolla, CA: University Associates, 1973.

Lakein, A. *How to Get Control of Your Time and Your Life*. New York: Signet Book, The New American Library Inc., 1974.

Lange, A., and Jakubowski, P. *"Responsible Assertive Behavior:* Cognitive Behavioral Procedures for Trainers," Champaign, IL: Research Press Co., 1976.

Lauersen, N., and Whitney, S. *It's Your Body—a Woman's Guide to Gynecology*. New York: Grosset & Dunlap, 1977.

Lee, E. "Suicide and Youth." *The Personnel and Guidance Journal,* 1978, 57, 4.

Lehmann, I. "Changes from Freshman to Senior Years." In *The College Student and His Culture: An Analysis,* Yamamoto (ed). Boston: Houghton Mifflin Company, 1968. From Irvin J. Lehmann, "Changes in Critical Thinking, Attitudes, and Values from Freshman to Senior Years." *Journal of Educational Psychology,* Volume 54, 1963, pages 305–315. Copyrighted 1963 by the American Psychological Association, and reproduced by permission.

Levine, A., *When Dreames and Heros Die,* San Francisco: Jossey-Bass Pub., 1980.

Levinson, D. *The Seasons of a Man's Life*. New York: Alfred A. Knopf, Inc., 1978.

Leonard, E., *Origins of Personnel Services in American Higher Education,* Minneapolis: University of Minnesota Press, 1956.

Lifton, J., *Thought Reform and the Psychology of Totalism,* New York: W. W. Norton and Company Inc., 1961.

Lingman, R. *Drugs from A to Z: A Dictionary*. New York: McGraw Hill Book Co., 1974.

Mackenzie, R. *The Time Trap*. New York: McGraw Hill Book Co., 1972.

Making Choices—Evaluating the Health Risks and Benefits of Birth Control Methods. New York: A Publication of The Alan Guttmacher Institute, 1983.

Marijuana and Health: Seventh Annual Report to the U.S. Congress from the Secretary of Health Education and Welfare, 1977. National Institute on Drug Abuse, U.S. Government Printing Office (#017–024–00890–7), 1977.

"Marijuana—What are the Risks?" *The Harvard School Health Letter,* June, 1980, V; (8).

Martin, R. "Friendship Choices and Resident Hall Proximity among Freshmen." *Psychological Reports,* Vol. 34, 1974.

Maslow, A. Motivation and Personality. New York: Harper and Row, 1954.

Maslow, A. *Toward a Psychology of Being.* Princeton, NJ: Van Nostrand, 1962.

Menne, J., and Sinnett, E. "Proximity and Social Interaction in Residence Halls." *Journal of College Student Personnel,* 1971.

Miller, G., and Steinbert, M., *Between People: A New Analysis of Interpersonal Communication,* Chicago: Science Research Associates Inc., 1975.

Miller, G., and Zoradi, S. "Roommate Conflict Resolution." *Journal of College Student Personnel.* May, 1977, Vol 18, No. 3.

Miller, T., and Prince, J. *The Future of Student Affairs.* San Francisco, CA: Jossey-Bass Publishers, 1976.

Morishima, J. "Effects on Student Achievement of Residence Hall Groupings Based on Academic Majors." In *Research on Academic Input: Proceedings of the Sixth Annual Forum of the Association for Institutional Research.* Bagley (ed), Cortland, NY: Office of Institutional Planning, State University of New York at Cortland, 1966.

Murphy, P., et. al., "Sexually Liberated College Student—Fact or Fancy." *Journal of American College Health Association.* October 1981, Vol. 30, pp. 87–89.

Murray, M. "The Effects of Roommates on the Scholastic Achievement of College Students." *Dissertation Abstracts,* 1961.

Mussen, P., Conger, J., and Kagan, J.: *Child Development and Personality.* 3rd ed. New York: Harper and Row Publishers, 1969.

National Center for Health Statistics, *1983 Reports.,* 1983.

National on Campus Reports. September, 1978.

National Survey on Drug Abuse, 1977. Rockville, MD: National Institute on Drug Abuse, 1978.

Newcomb, T. "Exploiting Student Resources." In *Research on College Students,* Sprague (ed). Boulder, CO: The Western Interstate Commission for Higher Education, 1960.

Newcomb, T. "Student Peer-group Influence." In *The American College,* Sanford (ed). New York: Wiley, 1962.

Newcomb, T., and Wilson, E. *College Peer Groups.* Chicago: Aldine Publishing, 1966.

NIAAA–DHEW (National Institute of Alcohol Abuse and Alcoholism). *Facts about Alcohol and Alcoholism.* DHEW Publications, 1974.

NIAAA–DHEW. *Alcohol & Alcoholism: Problems, Programs and Progress.* DHEW Publications, 1972.

NIAAA–DHEW. *The Whole College Catalog about Drinking.* DHEW Publications, 1976.

Nuwer, H. "Dead Souls of Hell Week." *Human Behavior.* October, 1978.

Ogden, G. "The Effect of Modified Class Scheduling on Student Alienation." Manuscript, University of Massachusetts, 1969.

Olson, L. "Students' Reactions to Living-learning Residence Halls." *Journal of College Student Personnel,* 1964.

Oncken, W., Jr. "Managing Management Time." A video course presented for the Saga Food Corporation, 1977.

Osofsky, J., and Osofsky, H. "The Psychological Reaction of Patients to Legalized Abortion." *American Journal of Orthopsychiatry.* vol. 42, No. 1 January, 1972.

Park, F. "Sex-role Adjustment and Drinking Disposition of Women College Students." *Journal of Studies on Alcohol.* 1975.

Pawlak, V. *A Conscientious Guide to Drug Abuse.* Do It Now Foundation, 1975.

Pemberton, C. "An Evaluation of the 1967–68 Living-learning Experiment at the University of Delaware." *University Impact Study.* Newark, DE: University of Delaware, November 1968.

Perry, W., Jr. *Forms of Intellectual and Ethical Development in the College Years.* New York: Holt, Rinehart, and Winston, Inc., 1970.

Piaget, J. *The Origins of Intelligence in Children.* trans. McCook. New York: International University Press, 1956.

Powell, J., Plyler, S., Dickson, B., and McClellan, S. *The Personnel Assistant in College Residence Halls.* Boston: Houghton Mifflin Company, 1969.

Pretzel, P. *Understanding and Counseling the Suicidal Person,* Nashville, TN: Abingdon Press, 1972.

Priest, R. and Sawyer, J. "Proximity and Peership: Bases of Balance in Interpersonal Attraction." *American Journal of Sociology,* 1967.

Prince, J., Miller, T., and Winston, R., Jr. *Student Development Task Inventory: Guidelines* (Revised). Athens, GA: Student Development Association, 1977.

Punk, W. *How to Study in College.* 2nd ed. Boston: Houghton, Mifflin Co., 1974.

Questions and Answers about Drug Abuse. Prudential Health Series, The Prudential Insurance Company of America, 1971.

Rachal, J., Williams, J., Brehm, M., Cavanaugh, B., Moore, R., and Eckerman, W. *A National Study of Adolescent Drinking Behavior, Attitudes & Correlates.* Research Triangle Park, NC: Research Triangle Institute, 1975.

Rathus, S. "Principles and Practices of Assertive Training, an Eclectic Overview." *The Counseling Psychologist.* 1975.

Read, D. *Healthy Sexuality.* New York: Macmillan Publishing Co., 1979.

Rindskopf, K. "A Perilous Paradox: The Contraceptive Behavior of College Students." *Journal of American College Health Association,* December, 1981, pp. 113–118.

Rockey, M. "Living and Learning at Central Washington State College." Paper presented at NDEA institute for college student personnel worker, Michigan State University, 1969.

Ross, W., "Today's Contraceptives: What's New? What's Best?" *Reader's Digest.* November 1983, pp. 217–226.

Rossi, P. "Effects of Peers on Socialization of College Students," National Opinion Center, University of Chicago. A paper presented at the Research Conference on Social Science Methods and Student Residence, University of Michigan, Ann Arbor, MI, November 28–29, 1964.

Rudolph, F. *The American College and University: A History.* New York: Vintage Books, 1962.

Sautter, J. "Understanding Your Residents: A Residence Hall Paraprofessional Counselor's Handbook." Lafayette, IN: John A. Sautter, 1974.

Schifferes, J., and Synovitz, R. *Healthier Living.* New York: John Wiley & Sons, 4th ed., 1979.

Schuh, J., ed. *Programming and Activities in College and University Residence Halls.* Association of College and University Housing Officers, 1977.

Scott, S. "Impact of Residence Hall Living on College Students." *Journal of College Student Personnel,* May, 1975, 6, 3.

Shelton, J., and Mathis, H. "Assertiveness as a Predictor of Resident Assistant Effectiveness." *Journal of Student Personnel,* 1976, 17(5).

Sherman, J. "The Student's Study Skill Needs." *Improving College and University Teaching* 19 (Summer, 1971): 214–16.

Shneidman, F. *On the Nature of Suicide.* San Francisco: Jossey-Bass Publishers, Inc., 1969.

Shochet, B. "Recognizing the Suicidal Patient." *Modern Medicine,* 1970, 38.

Smallwood, F., and Klas, L. "A Comparison of the Academic, Personal, and Social Effects of Four Different Types of University Residential Environments." *Journal of College and University Student Housing,* 1973.

Smeltzner, C. "Method for Determining What College Students Consider Their Own Difficulties." *School and Society* 32 (November 22, 1930): 709–10.

Smith, M. *When I Say No, I Feel Guilty.* New York: Dial Press, 1975.

Snead, R., and Caple, R. "Some Effects of the Environmental Press in University Housing." *Journal of College Student Personnel,* 1971.

Snodgrass, G., and Wright, L., "Alcohol and Polydrug Use Among College Undergraduates. NASPA Journal, 21(2), Fall 1983.

Sommer, R. "Study Conditions in Student Residences." *Journal of College Student Personnel,* 1969.

Spanier, G. *Human Sexuality in a Changing Society.* New York: Burgess Publishing Company, 1979.

Stanton, T. *How to Study.* 5th ed. Montgomery, Ala.

Stengel, E. *Suicide and Attempted Suicide.* Baltimore, MD: Penguin, 1964.

Straus, R., and Bacon, S. *Drinking in College.* New Haven, CT: Yale University Press, 1953.

Strong, B., and Reynolds, R. *Understanding Our Sexuality.* St. Paul: West Publishing Co., 1982.

Symaya, C., et. al. "Genital Infections with Herpes Simplex Virus in a University Student Population." *Sexually Transmitted Diseases.* January/March, 1980, pp. 16–20.

Taylor, R., and Hanson, G. "Environmental Impact on Achievement and Study Habits." *The Journal of College Student Personnel,* 1971, 12 (November).

"Teaching Responsible Drinking—A Comprehensive Alcohol Education Program." University of Wisconsin-Stevens Point, 1976/77.

Tebrock, H. *Drug Abuse and Misuse.* General Telephone and Electronics Corporation.

"The New Scarlet Letter . . . Herpes." *Time.* August 2, 1982, Vol. 120, pp. 62–66.

Upcraft, L., and Higginson, L., Eds. "Implementing a Student Development Model in Residence Halls." (Paper presented at ACPA Convention, Atlanta, Georgia, 1975).

Vreeland, R. "The Effects of Houses on Students' Attitudes and Values." In The Growth and Development of College Students, Whitley and Sprandel, (eds) *Student Personnel Series, American College Personnel Association,* 1970.

Weiner, I. "Depression in Adolescence." In *The Nature and Treatment of Depression,* Fisch and Draglie (eds). New York: John Wiley, 1975.

Whittaker, D. "Student Sub-cultures Reviewed and Revisited." *NASPA Journal,* 1969.

Williams, D. "Teen Age Suicide." *Newsweek,* August 28, 1978.

Wilsnack, S., and Wilsnack, R. "Sex Roles and Adolescent Drinking." In *Youth, Alcohol, and Social Policy,* Chafetz and Blane (eds), New York: Plenum Press, 1982.

Wilson, S., Strong, B., Robbins, M., and Johns, T. *Human Sexuality—A Text with Readings*. St. Paul, MN: West Publishing Co., 2nd ed., 1980.

Wilson, W. "The Spirit of Learning." In *Essays for College Men*. Edited by N. Fobister. New York: Henry Folt, 1913.

Wolpin, M. "On Assertion Training." *The Counseling Psychologist,* 1975, 5(4).

Zirkle, K., and Hudson, G. "The effects of residence hall staff members on maturity development for male students." *The Journal of College Student Personnel,* January, 1975, 16, 1.

Zucker, R. "Sex-role identity patterns and drinking behavior of adolescents." *Quarterly Journal of Studies on Alcohol.* Vol. 29, 1968.

Index